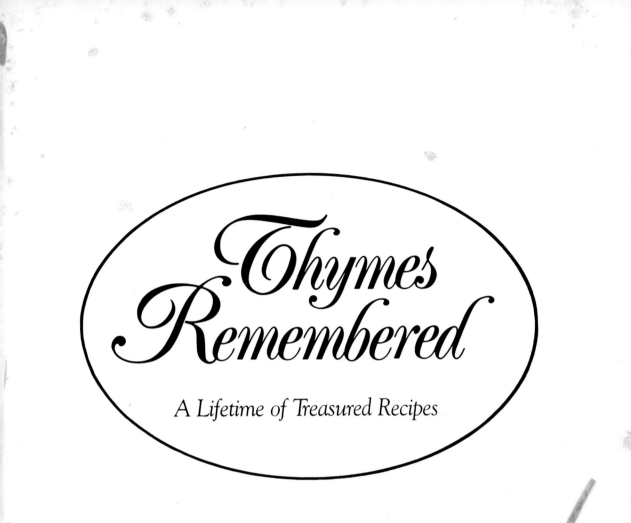

Thymes Remembered

A Lifetime of Treasured Recipes

The Junior League of Tallahassee, Inc.

Since its inception in 1949, the Junior League of Tallahassee has been committed to the goal of improving the quality of life in our community through effective voluntarism. Over the years, League members have given of their time, talent, and personal resources to provide Tallahassee with greater educational and artistic opportunities and give additional support to those citizens with special needs. We organize cultural programs, support our wildlife museum, develop science and other educational programs, assist our elderly and provide shelter for the homeless and abused.

Proceeds from the sale of *Thymes Remembered* will be returned to the community through the League's support of these and other volunteer projects.

Additional copies of *Thymes Remembered* may be obtained by calling or writing:

Thymes Remembered
The Junior League of Tallahassee, Inc.
259-B John Knox Road
Tallahassee, FL 32303
(904) 385-5305

Please enclose your return address with a check payable to *Thymes Remembered* in the amount of $16.95 per book plus $2.00 postage and handling. Florida residents add $1.02 sales tax per book.

Ray Stanyard, Photographer

Corporate Sponsors

Lafayette Vineyard LTD
Unijax, Inc.

First Edition, First Printing 15,000 copies, September 1988

ISBN 0-9620166-0-8
Library of Congress Card Catalog 88-81805

WIMMER BROTHERS
Memphis Dallas

Committee

Thymes Remembered evolved over three years from 1985 to 1988. Listed are those who served on the cookbook committee.

Sheila Melton . . . . . **Chairman**
Gini Hill . . . . . **Vice-Chairman**
Trude McCarty . . . . . **Editor**
Susan Renard . . . . . **Creative Writer**
Carol Cuneo . . . . . **Design Director**
Patty Ferrell . . . . . **Treasurer**
Beth Trotman . . . . . **Secretary**
Ellen Jablon . . . . . **Recipe Collection Coordinator**
Tricia Willis . . . . . **Testing Coordinator**
Fraser Smith . . . . . **Indexer**
Penny Dehler . . . . . **Writing Consultant**
Kit Guensch . . . . . **Cook's Tour Chairman**
Nella Schomburger . . . . . **Advisor**
Virginia Perkins . . . . . **Proofer**

Recipe Section Chairmen
Diane Cheek, Appetizers and Beverages
JoAnn Prescott, Breads, Eggs and Grains
Jonie Bettinger, Salads and Soups
Kay Williams, Vegetables and Fruits
Gayle Webb, Sandwiches
Ann Wilson, Meats and Game
Diane Stewart, Poultry
Carolyn Haley, Seafood
Carla Cowles, Desserts
Cindy Thompson, Assistant

Design Committee
Linda Knox, Chairman
Carol Cuneo
Vicki Munroe
Mary Solomon

Marketing Committee
Penny Dehler, Chairman
Kay Allen
Laura Rogers
Juliette Thompson
JoLen Wolf

Computer Operators
Marie Long
Jensi McDavid
Kaki Pope
Tricia Wood

Researchers
Aggie Bell
Chris Dobbins
Sissy Hofmeister

Public Relations Specialists
Leslie Allen
Prissy Kuersteiner
Judy Miller

Contents

Prelude

Linger for a moment over a timeless collection of special family occasions. Enjoy for a lifetime the exquisite atmosphere created when family, food and festivity are intertwined. Discover the flavor of the graceful lifestyle and casual elegance which is Tallahassee. **Thymes Remembered** is a portrait of the food and settings which convey an ambience reflective of our way of life.

Every locale has its notable distinctions. Since plantation days, the charm of Tallahassee's rolling hills, beautiful flowers and plentiful trees has beckoned many to make this city their home. The hallmark of Tallahassee is the nurturing atmosphere it provides families to flourish and create cherished memories so indicative of its style. Tallahasseeans consider their city a perfect place to call home.

In **Thymes Remembered** we share a classic collection of menus and recipes as they would be presented to family and guests on special occasions in the warm settings of Tallahassee homes. Won't you join us?

The Beginning

Times change, yet in our hearts all things remain the same. True joy comes from those gatherings of family and friends to mark special occasions, which represent the milestones of our lives, from courtship to twilight. We dine together and establish memories that last a lifetime. Whether traditional and formal, casual and spontaneous, an annual family feast, or a once-in-a-lifetime reception, the occasion has a special magical quality.

Our collection of wonderful moments begins at courtship, and with each season our memories become richer and more complex. We strive to create endearing moments of lasting impression as we approach the most important events of our lives — marriage, the birth of a child, a fortieth birthday, or a golden anniversary. Nothing is prepared with greater love than the birthday cake of our daughter's sweet sixteen party, the courses of our son's christening brunch, or his rehearsal dinner, which always comes a year too soon.

Seasonal changes provide us with an opportunity for continued renewal and celebration. Our early spring brings gorgeous flowering shrubs and blossoms, enabling us to highlight the festive mood of our parties and weddings. The impressive beauty remains until frost as we enjoy impatiens, periwinkles and picnics. We sample cheese and fruit, serenaded by the frolic of pets and children amidst a plethora of backyard flowers; or in summer, smack our lips from the flavor of spicy barbeque and juicy watermelon, or linger over supper on a Sunday evening savoring the last moments of togetherness.

Berries from a local patch, fruit from backyard trees or fresh vegetables and herbs from the garden remind us of the richness of the earth and provide us with colorful, delicious dishes. Fresh green lettuce, crispy cucumbers, plump peas, luscious sweet tomatoes, or melt-in-your-mouth corn are only a few steps away.

In the fall and winter, a memorable event is always created as friends and family are welcomed to our home with open arms, bountiful tables, and enthusiastic hospitality. You may find us enjoying this feeling of togetherness while cloistered near an open fire of smoking duck and venison, enjoying succulent Apalachicola oysters, and sipping a favorite wine. On another evening, we design a more elegant ambience with heirloom linens, silver and crystal, dining on pork crown roast and English fruit trifle. We share intimate dinners for two by candlelight and fire, or congregate with friends and family for time-honored traditions and holiday festivities. Time shared with family and friends adds the finishing touch to our memories.

Join us as we vicariously experience the special occasions of a couple who are beginning their life's journey together. Whether it is a blind date instigated by mutual friends, an unexpected meeting in an elevator, or a calculated encounter at a party, the introduction occurs. The flirtation commences, the adventure begins! From the beginning of history, dining together has been an essential part of courtship, providing us with a comfortable opportunity to become acquainted with someone special.

Vineyard Cocktails

Brie Board

Phyllo Flowers

Easy Elegant Grapes

Parmesan Twists

Smoked Venison Spread

Lafayette Plantation White

Remember This:

Plan for two to three ounces of wine per person when serving appetizer wines; a bottle of wine serves eight to twelve. If planning for a dinner party, allow six servings per bottle.

Drinking wine should be an enjoyable complement to the menu designed for a special occasion. Although you may choose to consult a wine connoisseur in making your selection, the ultimate test is whether a wine is pleasing to the palate.

Thymes Remembered

Our own Lafayette Vineyards, LTD, provides a picturesque setting for late afternoon parties.

Romance blossoms every second somewhere in the world, and yet it remains an elusive quality. It can happen as easily as placing two straws in a milkshake, wading barefoot in the ocean, humming a tune, or sitting on a bench in the moonlight. It can mean simplicity, extravagance, spontaneity, gallantry, quiet or bedlam. It means creating a mood where true love will grow.

A favorite choice for romance is a sumptuous dinner for two served near a roaring fire, or in some other cozy, private place. The surroundings are sure to kindle a spark or two, and your efforts will flatter and please that special someone. It's a chance to prove we are all incurable romantics at heart. We provide the menu — the rest is up to you.

It is an ancient question, but one which still inspires unparalleled joy, exhilaration and inspiration. From the beginning, this Valentine's evening carries a momentous air. The twosome feel elated as hearts and flowers are breathlessly exchanged. Sparkling eyes and lingering gazes signify what is yet to come. By candlelight, the pair dines on a meal attractively presented, wonderfully delicious. The conversation is engrossing, comfortable, sentimental. The elegant ambience is spell-binding...or is it the company? A pause arises and his question is courageously posed, "Will you be mine?" Without hesitation, she answers, "Yes."

Romantic Dinner for Two

Crab Mornay in Puff Pastry

Valley Châteaubriand

Better Brown Rice

Bleu Broccoli

Hearts of Palm Salad

Valentine Torte

Cafe Olé

Lafayette Blanc de Fleur

The Wedding

Weddings are definitely affairs of the heart. No other formal occasion equals that sweet, exquisite moment when two stand face to face and become husband and wife. Word of the upcoming ceremony quickly spreads to family and friends. Relatives of the bride and groom generously offer to provide flower arrangements from their own gardens and beautifully garnished food. Only truly special, time-tested delicacies are prepared for this occasion, and presentation is of utmost importance. Champagne and dancing contribute to the effervescent atmosphere.

Bridesmaids' Luncheon

Fruited Champagne Punch

Sweet and Salty Almonds

Elegant Turkey Salad

Almond Asparagus

Fresh Melons

Sour Cream Biscuits

Cream Cheese Pound Cake with Raspberry Sauce

She walks as if she's floating on air. Her gaze seems somewhat dreamy, her laughter slightly nervous and her mind definitely preoccupied with romantic notions. But don't think for a minute that the blushing bride doesn't treasure this moment as a highlight of her wedding festivities. Every detail of this occasion is tucked away in her memory to be affectionately recalled years later in quiet moments.

A bridesmaids' luncheon is the perfect setting for her to thank special friends who have so graciously consented to be a part of her wedding. Youthful reminiscences are the topic of the afternoon amidst feminine conversation and laughter. It's the ideal opportunity for friends to lovingly reassure the bride and calm her pre-marital jitters.

Thymes Remembered

Rehearsal Dinner

Champagne Cocktail

Grilled Bacon-Wrapped Shrimp

Mushroom Pâté

Beef Wellington

Salade aux Haricots Verts

Garlic Potatoes with Mushrooms

Spinach and Orange Salad

Angel Biscuits

Chocolate Soufflé à l'Orange

Remember This:

Throwing rice is symbolic of an ever-full pantry and an abundance of all good things.

The favorite month for weddings, June, is named for Juno, the Roman goddess of married women.

When wedding cake is shared by the bride and groom, it signifies their "sharing together" from this time forth. Originally, wedding cakes were a symbol of fertility. In Roman times, cake was broken over the bride's head at the end of the wedding ceremony to ensure a life of plenty. Guests then gathered the crumbs of the cake as good luck tokens.

Wedding Reception

Reception Punch

Beef Tenderloin with Béarnaise Mayonnaise

Seafood Élégante

Mushrooms in White Wine Sauce

Imperial Crab

Légumes Blanchis with Fresh Dill Dip

Elegant Cucumber Bites

Capital City Pâté

Cashew Wafers

Remember This:

Centuries ago, marriage records of royalty were chronicled in the beautiful handwriting of monks. Later, royalty issued formal invitations in this handwriting, referred to as "script." In the early seventeenth century, copper-plate engraving of script writing was first achieved, and the custom of sending engraved wedding invitations evolved.

Traditionally, the groom's gift of a gold wedding ring to his bride signifies that he trusts her with his property. The first engagement ring was given by Emperor Maximillian who presented a diamond ring to his bride as a token of his affection.

Thymes Remembered

Something old, something new...how about something delicious for two? Don't be surprised if the bride and groom find themselves departing from their wedding reception having hardly sampled a morsel of the delectable food there. They have been too busy greeting guests, graciously accepting congratulations and best wishes, and enjoying every minute of the festivities. Hours later they may wish they had a snack or two.

Fortunately, special friends or relatives have thought of everything. They send the bride and groom on their way with a basket packed full of an array of delicacies from the reception — perfect for a midnight snack or a champagne breakfast just for two.

Baby & Child

The time is drawing near. Month by month, the mother-to-be has prepared for her child's birth. In body and spirit, she follows the baby's growth, taking special care. What once was an ordinary room has now been completely transformed in pretty pastels adorned with bunnies, bears or clowns. A musical mobile swings over a brand new crib. Tiny clothes are scattered about and a rocking chair awaits its first lullaby.

Eager to provide support and show their affection, friends congregate to shower her with warm wishes, precious gifts and maybe a little unsolicited advice. The baby's possible name and gender are thoroughly discussed while enjoying the tasty food. Newborn stories, which only a mother could relate, are told; and friends tease the mother-to-be about the imminent sleepless nights and hectic days.

Baby Shower

Iced Crab Sandwiches

Toast Cups with Fruit and Cheese Spread

Almond Muffins

Pecan Tasties

Chocolate Dipped Strawberries

Melting Moments

The birth of a child begins a bright new chapter in our lives. Great celebration heralds and follows the child's arrival, and continues each year thereafter on the day of the baby's birth. Enthusiastically, we watch an entire new world of bright colors and natural wonders unfold as children share their excitement and discovery with us. We fashion parties and picnics, fun and games just to see their spirits soar and hear their happy laughter. These special times to come are imagined with happy anticipation as we await the baby's arrival.

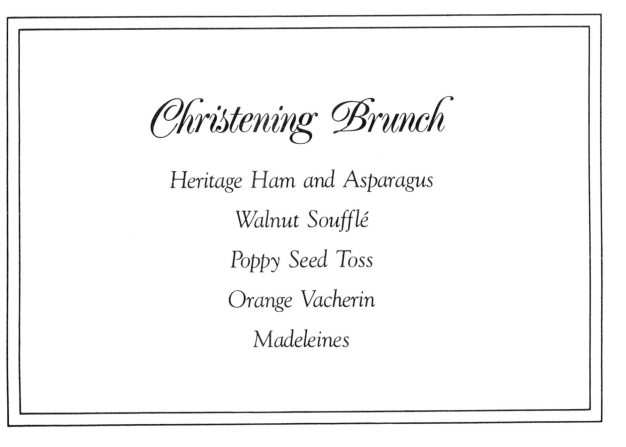

Christening Brunch

Heritage Ham and Asparagus

Walnut Soufflé

Poppy Seed Toss

Orange Vacherin

Madeleines

Remember This:

Predicting food quantities may prove difficult when your guests represent several family generations. Keep in mind that young children and elders usually eat less. Teens often eat more!

Brunch may be a hearty or light meal depending on the occasion. The appropriate time for serving brunch is between 10:30 AM and 1:00 PM.

Whether the guest of honor sheds a few tears, happily babbles, or drifts off to sweet slumber is of no consequence to the jovial mood of the christening brunch. Our baby, royally adorned with an heirloom gown, has just received a formal introduction to our world, bringing boundless cheer and loving admiration.

Linking the past to the future, our newborn signifies life's continual renewal. The baby is showered with attention and presented with grand pomp and circumstance. Gaiety abounds as childhood stories and words of advice are exchanged. Ancestral photographs are admired; a new name, the origins discussed in great detail, is added to the family tree; an antique spoon or cup is given to the proud parents; small children gently touch the baby hoping to elicit a smile. Everyone leaves with lifted spirits, reminded of the beauty of life's cycle and instilled with hope for our future.

Thymes Remembered

Springtime Lunch

Chilled Strawberry Soup

Rack of Lamb

Minted Carrots

Potatoes in Dill Cream Sauce

Broccoli, Orange and Walnut Salad

Coconut Cake with Lemon Filling

Lafayette Sunblush

Spring in Tallahassee is a time of unforgettable enchantment. Blooms seem to burst forth everywhere as if led by an exuberant conductor to play the crescendo of a beautiful symphony. An entire town pours outdoors, eager to share this amazing spectacle of nature with family and friends, and once again to celebrate life's seasonal renewal. Surrounded by brilliant white dogwoods, vibrant azaleas and the multi-hued splashes of delicate trees and shrubs, we happily put indoor revelry to rest for another year. Eagerly we march off to our playgrounds, parks and beaches waving light-hearted salutations to everyone in sight; or we relax on our verandas and patios, savoring the sights and aromas around us. Our children gleefully run about in the sunlight chasing butterflies as dusk approaches. Intermittently, they may edge back to hear a nature story or to check the progress of the ice cream churn.

By Easter, springtime regalement is at its pinnacle. After a flurry of holiday excitement, bonnets and baskets are assembled for the Easter egg hunt. With child-like wonder, we help little ones dash about searching for those brightly decorated eggs. Careful planning ensures that each child retrieves at least one. Afterwards, the grown-ups renew their energy, sharing in a much deserved appetizing lunch and swapping amusing anecdotes from the day's hunt.

Special Thymes & Friends

Clap your hands and get ready for good home cookin'! Sample some unrestrained, good-hearted fellowship and laughter with fine people as we go dining "family style." A family reunion is one occasion where the quality and quantity of food is equalled only by the fellowship shared. Whether we've come a great distance or just walked down the street, the minute we step across the doorway into our family's embrace, we know we've come home.

Prepare to suffer through friendly back-slapping, gushy kisses and genuine Glad-to-see-you-How've-you-been-doing greetings. Your children are looked over a time or two, followed by an exclamation of the only conclusion possible — they're a product of genetic perfection. A family reunion is the only place on earth where we are totally, unequivocally accepted, simply by virtue of our birthright.

Don't expect to find the exotic here. The food is reliable, like the people. Bountiful amounts of our favorite dishes are a true sign of our family's affection.

Family Reunion

Honey Glazed Ham • Pecan Fried Chicken • Corn Pudding

Country Green Beans • Herb Tomatoes • Southern Cornbread

Sour Cream Yellow Squash • Fig Jam

Coleslaw with Celery Seed Dressing

Plantation Pecan Pie • Grandmother's Pound Cake

Thymes Remembered

Thymes Remembered

We can only imagine what it was like to attend the first hunters' feast, occurring on that cool November day centuries ago. History informs us that the occasion brought together family, friends and people of different cultures to join in thanks for the blessings of earth and soul — mutual understanding, peace and harmony, abundant harvest and game. Gratefully, the inspiration for such a feast endures in today's world as well.

The woodlands surrounding Tallahassee are a source of great pride to our people — sportsmen and naturalists alike. The land is good to us, providing fertile ground for farming and a plentiful supply of game. Annually, on every weekend of hunting season, hunters hike outdoors to enjoy our temperate climate, demonstrate their sportsmanship and share in some camaraderie. Upon returning home, game is set aside to be shared with pride at later feasts with friends, or at an upcoming Thanksgiving dinner.

Warmly and boisterously, the invitations are issued. Guests are welcomed to home and hearth to feast on a delicious spread of home-cooked local game, complete with home-made breads and desserts. The flavorful aromas of simmering gumbo, roasting venison and frying quail remind us of our ancestral origins, the interdependence of man and nature, and our love for this place we call home.

Hunter's Feast

Duck and Sausage Gumbo

Marinated Duck Wrapped in Bacon

Burgundy Game Birds • Southern Fried Quail

Orange Venison • Almond Wild Rice

Steamed Broccoli with Creamy Mustard Sauce

Apricot Nectar Salad • Festive Fruit Sauce

Mini Pumpkin Muffins

Custard Lemon Bars

Cookies for Santa

Ambrosia Cookies

Gingerbread Men

Sugar Cookies

Christmas Morning

Fresh Orange Juice

Sausage Egg Casserole

Sticky Coffee Cake

Blueberry Muffins

Danish Puff

Mix the sugar and eggs, add the flour, and roll out the dough! A hungry Santa is on his way. Nothing brings more merriment and pleasure to our household than the gathering of our children in gleeful anticipation of a visit from the jolly old elf. Our delight is derived from experiencing the wonderment and excitement of Christmas viewed through the eyes of a child.

Gift giving is an integral part of the holiday season, yet the simplest, most profound gift of all is creating a meaningful holiday occasion our children will cherish for a lifetime.

Fill your kitchen with mommies, daddies and playmates mixing and baking Gingerbread Men, Sugar Cookies and Ambrosia Cookies. Mmm...It isn't easy for hands of any size to stay out of the batter!

Your kitchen is filled with the rich aroma of cookies baking and your children will have the satisfaction of creating a gift from the heart for that dear old white-bearded man, the most renowned gift-giver of all.

In the process, you may have originated a new family tradition, or simply orchestrated another wonderful afternoon for children and friends. For once, you look at a kitchen in total disarray and smile with a sense of satisfaction.

Thymes Remembered

Prime of Life

Age, it is reasoned, has its privileges. We may demand that our formality be humored with proper respect and, in the next breath expect that our spontaneous idiosyncrasies be tolerated. We entertain beautifully with exact ceremony or lavish our guests with a daring, creative flair.

Experience teaches us to be purposeful and sensible. Yet we long to grasp the joy of life's moments before it passes by. Such explains our comfort with the familiar, and our occasional exploits of wild abandon. A zest for life, love of people and invaluable hindsight help us pull it off!

Coming of age justifies celebration and commiseration. So, gather around the friend we thought would never grow up. Let's kick up our heels, whoop it up, and pull out all the stops in proper style and panache. After all, Father Time catches up with each of us sooner or later, and an incredible bash is guaranteed to make the guest of honor feel young at heart.

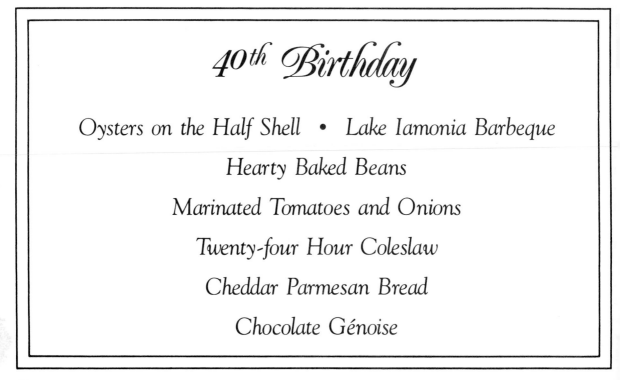

40th Birthday

Oysters on the Half Shell • Lake Iamonia Barbeque

Hearty Baked Beans

Marinated Tomatoes and Onions

Twenty-four Hour Coleslaw

Cheddar Parmesan Bread

Chocolate Génoise

Golden Anniversary

Pork Crown Roast with Celery Wild Rice Stuffing

Zucchini Mushroom Shells

Steamed Carrot Strips

Baked Pineapple

Lemon Vinaigrette Salad

Yeast Rolls

English Fruit Trifle

Remarkable feats deserve grand and memorable recognition. Remarkable people deserve a carefully planned and elegant tribute, a once-in-a-lifetime celebration which, for a few glorious hours, makes time stand still.

In a happy marriage, time seems to pass more quickly than the flicker of an eye. Even the rough spots are, in retrospect, merely ingredients that season a lifetime romance. Before we know it, our children are complaining of middle-age ills and our grandchildren are teenagers. Yet, in our hearts we feel as youthful as the day we answered "Yes" to that centuries old question, "Will you be mine?"

The years fall away as our family congregates to celebrate this enduring love. Old friends remind us of times gone by and the origins of lasting friendships. Wide-eyed grandchildren listen attentively to colorful reminiscences of a childhood and courtship of long ago.

For an evening, we recapture the magic of the life and love we've shared. In our honor, we stop the clock from running and preserve the memory of wonderful *Thymes Remembered.*

It is often said the greatest gift a host and hostess bestow on their guests is the sharing of their home and warm hospitality. Likewise, we invite you to step across our threshold and participate in special occasions significant to us, our family and friends. Tallahassee tradition inspires elegance and the exquisite ingredients which enable us to create memorable dining events. Great pleasure is derived in sharing our way of life.

May your application of the menus and recipes presented here result in superb culinary experiences for you and yours, bringing joy and festivity to your home.

Appetizers

Spicy Seafood Dip

15 servings

This elegant hors d'oeuvre may be prepared a day in advance and baked just before serving.

1 large green bell pepper, chopped
1 tablespoon olive oil
1 pound small shrimp, shelled and deveined
2 tablespoons butter
2 14-ounce cans artichoke hearts, drained and chopped fine
2 cups mayonnaise
½ cup thinly sliced green onions
½ cup drained and chopped roasted red peppers
1 cup freshly grated Parmesan cheese
2 tablespoons fresh lemon juice
4 teaspoons Worcestershire sauce
dash of Tabasco
3 pickled jalapeño peppers, seeded and minced
½ teaspoon salt or to taste
1 pound well picked crabmeat
⅓ cup sliced almonds, lightly toasted
Pita Triangles

- Preheat oven to 375 degrees.
- In a heavy frying pan cook green pepper in olive oil over moderate heat, stirring until peppers are soft; cool.
- Sauté shrimp in butter for 1½ minutes.
- In a large bowl, mix bell peppers, artichokes, mayonnaise, green onion, roasted peppers, Parmesan cheese, lemon juice, Worcestershire, jalapeño peppers, Tabasco and salt.
- Gently stir in seafood and correct seasoning.
- Transfer to a large buttered baking dish and sprinkle with almonds.
- Bake at 375 degrees for 25 to 30 minutes, or until top is golden and mixture is bubbly.
- Serve in a chafing dish with lightly buttered Pita Triangles.

Remember This:

When cutting jalapeño peppers, wear plastic gloves.

Beef Tenderloin With Béarnaise Mayonnaise

20 servings

Certain to be a crowd pleaser.

1 tenderloin, 5 to 6 pounds
4 tablespoons dried tarragon
⅓ cup tarragon vinegar
5 shallots, minced
⅓ cup dry white wine
3 large egg yolks
2½ tablespoons Dijon mustard
2 tablespoons plus 1 teaspoon fresh lemon juice
salt and freshly ground pepper to taste
1¼ cups vegetable oil
1 cup olive oil
up tomato paste

- Roast tenderloin to desired doneness; chill and slice.
- Place tarragon, shallots, vinegar and wine in a small saucepan.
- Bring to a boil over high heat.
- Reduce liquid to 1 tablespoon; set aside.
- Place yolks, mustard, lemon juice, salt and pepper in a food processor.
- Process with a steel blade for 12 seconds, adding oils in a thin steady stream to form a thick emulsion.
- Add tomato paste and shallot mixture.
- Process to blend and chill.
- Serve with beef tenderloin and a variety of rolls.

128 triangles

pita loaves
er, melted
salt
heese,
ional

- Preheat oven to 375 degrees.
- Cut each pita loaf into 8 wedges.
- Separate each wedge into 2 triangles.
- Place in a single layer close together on baking sheets, rough side up.
- Brush triangles lightly with butter and season with salt.
- If preparing triangles to serve with salads or soups, sprinkle with Parmesan cheese before baking.
- Bake for 10 to 12 minutes or until triangles are crisp and golden.
- Cool on cookie sheets.

Grilled Bacon-Wrapped Shrimp
8 servings

hickory, apple or cherry wood chips
½ cup soy sauce
1 tablespoon brown sugar
1 tablespoon dry sherry
1 large clove garlic, crushed
dash Worcestershire sauce
dash cayenne pepper
small piece fresh ginger root, peeled and crushed
1 pound large shrimp, shelled, deveined, leaving tail intact
8 slices lean bacon

- Cover wood chips with water and soak for 30 minutes.
- Combine all ingredients except shrimp and bacon.
- Cook over moderate heat to blend flavors and set aside for 1 hour.
- Cut bacon into one-thirds.
- Wrap a piece of bacon around each shrimp and skewer to secure.
- Pour marinade over shrimp and chill for 1 to 2 hours.
- Remove from marinade and grill over hot coals and wood chips for 6 to 10 minutes, turning once.
- Shrimp may be broiled in oven.
- Do not overcook.

Imperial Crab
10 servings

Beautiful served on a fan of blanched snowpeas.

1 envelope unflavored gelatin
1 pound lump crabmeat
¼ cup mayonnaise
1 teaspoon prepared mustard
1 teaspoon salt
3 tablespoons fresh lemon juice
1 tablespoon minced scallions
1 tablespoon minced fresh dill
1 cup heavy cream, whipped
toasted bread points
cherry tomatoes or radishes
sprigs of dill

- Soften gelatin in 2 tablespoons cold water.
- Melt gelatin in top of a double boiler and cool.
- Remove any shell fragments from crab.
- In a medium bowl, combine mayonnaise, mustard, salt, lemon juice, scallions and dill.
- Fold in whipped cream and crabmeat.
- Fill mold and refrigerate until firm or overnight.
- Unmold and serve with toasted bread points.
- Garnish with sliced cherry tomatoes or radishes and sprigs of dill.

Shrimp Sensational

6 first course servings

You will get rave reviews!

1 cup salted butter
1 cup vegetable oil
2 teaspoons finely minced garlic
4 bay leaves finely crushed
2 teaspoons rosemary, crushed
½ teaspoon basil
½ teaspoon oregano
½ teaspoon salt
½ tablespoon paprika
½ teaspoon cayenne pepper
¾ teaspoon freshly ground pepper
1 teaspoon fresh lemon juice
2 pounds shrimp in shells
French bread

- Melt butter over medium heat in a 4-quart heavy ovenproof saucepan; stir in oil.
- Add all remaining ingredients except shrimp and bread; cook, stirring constantly until the sauce boils.
- Reduce heat and simmer 8 minutes, stirring frequently.
- Remove saucepan from heat and allow to stand uncovered at room temperature for 30 minutes, stirring once or twice.
- Preheat over to 350 degrees.
- To cook shrimp, return sauce to medium heat.
- When well heated, about 3 minutes, stir once and add shrimp.
- Cook 5 to 7 minutes, just until the shrimp turn pink, stirring frequently with a wooden spoon.
- Remove from heat and bake for 10 minutes.
- To serve, ladle shrimp into heated serving bowls and cover each portion with ½ cup sauce.
- Stir sauce thoroughly each time mixture is ladled.
- Scoop out solids that have settled and spoon over shrimp.
- Serve immediately with French bread.

Oriental Shrimp
8 servings

2 pounds jumbo shrimp in shell with tails
1 cup dry sherry
1 cup light soy sauce
1 cup vegetable oil
2 cloves garlic, pressed
Butter Sauce:
1 cup unsalted butter
juice of 1 lemon
1 tablespoon Worcestershire sauce
1 tablespoon soy sauce
3 to 4 dashes Tabasco
½ teaspoon salt

- To devein shrimp, use kitchen shears to cut through shell along upper curve.
- Make cut just deep enough to remove vein and leave shell and tail intact.
- Rinse gently under cold water.
- To prepare marinade, mix sherry, soy sauce, oil and garlic.
- Pour into a shallow glass dish and add shrimp.
- Toss carefully and marinate for 4 to 6 hours or overnight.
- Remove shrimp from marinade.
- Prepare butter sauce by melting butter and adding lemon juice, Worcestershire, soy sauce, Tabasco and salt.
- Keep sauce warm and grill shrimp 4 inches from heat, 1 to 2 minutes per side or until shrimp turn pink.
- Can be broiled in oven until pink, turn and cook 2 more minutes.
- Serve immediately with warm butter sauce.

Crab Au Gruyère
10 to 12 servings

Extravagantly delicious!

2 pounds lump crabmeat
1 cup butter, melted
2 8-ounce packages cream cheese, softened
2 teaspoons Worcestershire sauce
4 dashes Tabasco
melba rounds or mild flavored crackers

- Remove any shell fragments from crabmeat.
- Combine butter and cream cheese.
- Add crabmeat, Worcestershire and Tabasco; stir to combine.
- Serve in a chafing dish with melba rounds or mild flavored crackers.

Shrimp And Artichoke Vinaigrette

20 appetizer or 6 first course servings

2 to 3 pounds medium shrimp, cooked, shelled and deveined
2 15-ounce cans artichoke hearts, drained and quartered
1 pound fresh mushrooms, halved
2 small yellow onions, sliced and separated into rings
1 3¼-ounce jar capers, drained
1 envelope Italian dressing mix
2 envelopes Cheese Garlic dressing mix

- Combine cooked shrimp, artichokes, mushrooms, onion rings and capers in a large bowl.
- Prepare salad dressing mixes according to package directions, substituting vinegar for the water required.
- Do not use any water in preparing dressing mixes.
- Pour dressing over shrimp mixture, cover with plastic wrap and refrigerate overnight.
- Drain and serve in a large glass bowl as an appetizer or in lettuce cups as a first course.

Shrimp Toast

8 servings

Also good with soup or salad.

½ pound fresh shrimp, shelled and deveined
8 water chestnuts
1 scallion, minced
1 egg, lightly beaten
1 teaspoon salt
1 teaspoon dry sherry
2 teaspoons cornstarch
6 slices thin white bread, 2 days old
3 cups oil

- Mince together shrimp, water chestnuts and scallion.
- Stir in egg and salt.
- Mix together sherry and cornstarch, stirring well to dissolve cornstarch.
- Add to shrimp mixture.
- Trim crusts from bread and cut each slice into 2 triangles.
- Spread one scant tablespoon shrimp mixture on each triangle.
- Heat oil to 375 degrees.
- Gently lower triangles into oil, shrimp side down.
- Turn after 1 minute.
- Drain on paper towels and serve.
- May be frozen and reheated at 350 degrees in a single layer on cookie sheets.

Oysters Rockefeller 4 servings

A fabulous way to showcase Apalachicola Bay oysters.

1 10-ounce bag fresh spinach
½ cup chopped parsley
1 cup unsalted butter
½ cup fresh French or Italian bread crumbs
2 tablespoons Worcestershire sauce
¼ teaspoon Tabasco
1 teaspoon anchovy paste or 2 fillets chopped fine
1 ounce Pernod liqueur
2 dozen fresh oysters in the shell
rock salt
freshly grated Parmesan cheese

- To prepare sauce, wash and stem spinach; drain well.
- Melt butter in a large skillet.
- Cook spinach and parsley until soft; add breadcrumbs, Worcestershire, Tabasco, anchovy paste and Pernod.
- Mix well and cook for 1 more minute to blend flavors.
- Place mixture in a food processor and process up to 30 seconds.
- Set aside or freeze.
- To prepare oysters, shuck and reserve the deepest shell.
- Do not wash oysters, but wash reserved shells.
- Pour a thick layer of rock salt in 4 aluminum pans.
- Place an oyster on each washed shell and lay in pans.
- Place exposed oysters under broiler for 1 minute, just long enough to curl the edges a little.
- Remove from oven and cover each oyster completely with sauce.
- Sprinkle with 1 teaspoon Parmesan cheese.
- Bake in a preheated 400 degree oven for 5 minutes or until completely heated.
- Run under broiler until lightly browned.
- Serve piping hot.

Seafood Elegante

20 servings

Perfect for a cocktail buffet, served with butter crackers or Toast Points.

- *1½ cups unsalted butter, divided*
- *1 tablespoon Madras curry powder, or to taste*
- *1 cup finely chopped yellow onion*
- *2 cups Granny Smith peeled and grated apples*
- *2½ teaspoons salt*
- *1 tablespoon sugar*
- *½ cup flour*
- *1 cup chicken stock*
- *2½ cups half and half*
- *3 pounds peeled and deveined small shrimp*
- *2 cups fresh claw crabmeat, well picked*
- *3 tablespoons fresh lemon juice*

- Melt ¾ cup butter in a heavy saucepan.
- Add curry and cook for 1 minute over medium heat.
- Add onion, apple, salt and sugar; cook until onions are soft.
- Add flour and cook for 2 to 3 minutes, stirring constantly.
- Slowly add stock and half and half, stirring constantly until mixture is thick.
- Remove from heat and set aside.
- In a heavy skillet melt remaining ¾ cup butter.
- Add shrimp and crab; cook until shrimp are just pink, stirring constantly.
- Do not overcook.
- Add seafood mixture and lemon juice to cream sauce; heat thoroughly.
- Serve in a chafing dish.
- May be prepared one to two days ahead or frozen.

Toast Points

- *butter*
- *very thin slices of white bread, with crusts trimmed*

- Roll bread flat.
- Lightly butter and cut into quarters.
- Bake at 250 degrees until crisp and lightly browned.
- Store in airtight containers for up to 3 days.

Capital City Pâté

50 to 60 appetizer servings

This pâté is worth the effort and may be prepared over several days.

2 pounds chicken livers, cleaned
12 imported bay leaves
6 cloves garlic, peeled
½ cup brandy
1 cup dry white wine
1¾ pounds mild bulk sausage
1 pound baked ham
10 slices firm French bread
½ cup heavy cream
grated zest of 2 oranges
1½ cups chopped natural pistachios, lightly toasted
salt and freshly ground black pepper to taste
1 pound sliced bacon
loaves of French bread
Hot Sweet Mustard

- Two days ahead, marinate chicken livers, garlic, brandy, wine and 3 bay leaves in a glass bowl; cover and refrigerate overnight.
- The next day, process chicken liver mixture to a purée in a food processor fitted with a steel blade.
- Transfer purée to a large bowl.
- Cook sausage in a large skillet over medium-high heat crumbling with a fork until meat is no longer pink.
- Be careful not to overcook sausage.
- Spoon off fat and process sausage until coarsely ground.
- Add sausage to liver mixture.
- Process ham until coarsely ground and add to liver-sausage mixture.
- Stir well to combine meat mixture.
- Process bread slices with heavy cream.
- Stir into meat mixture.
- Add orange zest, pistachio nuts, salt and pepper and mix well.
- To correct seasoning, sauté, cool and taste a small patty of meat mixture.
- Preheat oven to 350 degrees.
- Divide mixture into thirds.
- Place 3 bay leaves down the center of each of three 9x4-inch loaf pans.
- Arrange bacon slices crosswise in loaf pans to completely line pans.

Continued

Capital City Pâté (continued)

- Bacon slices may overlap and ends will hang over sides of pan.
- Pack meat mixture into pans and fold bacon ends over top of loaf.
- Tightly cover each pan with heavy aluminum foil.
- Set loaf pans in a larger baking pan and place in oven.
- Pour enough boiling water into outer pan to come halfway up the sides of the loaf pans.
- Bake 1½ hours.
- Remove loaf pans from water bath and cool for 30 minutes.
- To compress the meat, weight the pâtés by placing another loaf pan or board on top of pâtés.
- Place canned food in the pan or on boards and refrigerate.
- When thoroughly chilled, remove weights and unmold pâtés.
- Remove the fat around the loaf, leaving the bacon slices if desired.
- Wrap pâtés and refrigerate until ready to serve or freeze up to 2 months ahead.
- Allow pâté to warm slightly at room temperature, and serve with thick slices French bread and Hot Sweet Mustard.

Scallop Puffs 12 dozen

The delicate flavor of Gruyère compliments bay scallops.

3½ loaves Pepperidge Farm white sandwich bread
3 tablespoons unsalted butter
1 pound bay scallops, quartered
3 small cloves garlic, minced
2 teaspoons lemon zest, finely minced
3 tablespoons chopped fresh dill
2 cups shredded Gruyère
2¼ cups mayonnaise
dash of Tabasco
salt and freshly ground pepper to taste
Sweet Hungarian paprika

- Cut bread into 1-inch rounds and lightly toast.
- Melt butter in a medium skillet over medium-high heat.
- Add scallops, lemon zest and garlic.
- Stir constantly until scallops are just done, 2 to 3 minutes, being careful not to overcook.
- Add dill and cook 30 more seconds.
- Remove from heat and cool to room temperature.
- Preheat broiler.
- Stir to combine cheese, mayonnaise, Tabasco, salt, pepper and scallops.
- Scallop mixture will keep covered and refrigerated up to 4 days.
- Place toast rounds ½-inch apart on baking sheets.
- Top each round with a heaping teaspoon of scallop mixture, and sprinkle lightly with paprika.
- Broil 5 inches from heat for 2 to 3 minutes or until puffed and golden.
- Serve hot.
- Lemon slices and dill sprigs make a lovely garnish.

Panhandle Crab Dip

10 to 12 servings

Simply delicious!

8 ounces fresh crabmeat, well picked
11 ounces cream cheese, room temperature
1 tablespoon milk
1 tablespoon chopped onion
1 tablespoon horseradish
butter-flavored crackers

- Preheat oven to 350 degrees.
- Mix all ingredients except crackers together and place in a small baking dish.
- Cover and bake for 25 to 30 minutes.
- Uncover and bake for 5 to 10 minutes more, or until top is lightly browned.
- Serve hot or at room temperature with crackers.
- May be made ahead and frozen.

Mushroom Pâté

1½ cups

½ small onion
1 clove garlic
½ pound mushrooms
2 tablespoons butter
1 teaspoon oregano
1 tablespoon chopped fresh parsley
1 tablespoon chopped chives
¼ teaspoon salt
½ teaspoon freshly ground black pepper
10 ounces almonds, toasted
1 tablespoon sherry
1 tablespoon heavy cream
parsley and pimento
crackers or melba toast

- Mince onions, garlic and mushrooms together in a food processor.
- Sauté mixture in melted butter until liquid evaporates.
- Add herbs, salt, and pepper.
- Process almonds in a food processor fitted with a steel blade until paste forms.
- Add mushroom mixture, sherry and cream; process until fairly smooth.
- Pour into a small mold and refrigerate.
- Remove from mold and garnish with parsley and pimento.
- Serve with crackers or melba toast.

Smoked Venison Spread

10 servings

This is a tasty was to use smoked venison ham.

2 cups finely ground smoked venison
1 cup mayonnaise
2 teaspoons garlic salt
½ cup Durkee sauce
¼ cup dried minced onion
2 tablespoons cup Tiger sauce
juice of 1 lemon

- Combine all ingredients and stir until well mixed.
- Refrigerate spread several hours or overnight to combine flavors.
- Serve with crackers.

Wild Turkey Breast With Sauces

8 to 10 servings

½ large or 1 small turkey breast
2 cups milk
vegetable oil
1 to 1½ cups flour
1½ teaspoons seasoned salt
½ teaspoon freshly ground pepper
2 teaspoons Lawry's Pinch of Herbs
½ teaspoon garlic powder
parsley and orange twists

- Cut turkey breast into 1½-inch pieces.
- Soak turkey in milk for 30 minutes to 1 hour before frying.
- Heat enough oil in a deep fat fryer to fry turkey.
- Place flour and seasonings in a small paper bag and shake well to combine.
- Remove turkey from milk and drain slightly.
- Flour turkey in bag and fry in batches.
- Drain on paper towels.
- Transfer to serving dish garnished with parsley and orange twists.
- Serve with Hot Sweet Mustard Sauce or Festive Fruit Sauce, puréed.

Chicken Fingers With Currant Sauce

20 servings

6 whole chicken breasts, boned and skinned
1½ cups buttermilk
1 teaspoon grated lime rind
2 tablespoons lime juice
2 teaspoons Worcestershire sauce
1 teaspoon soy sauce
1 teaspoon paprika
1 teaspoon black pepper
1 clove garlic, pressed
⅓ cup sesame seeds
2 cups Italian bread crumbs
½ cup butter, melted
Currant Sauce:
2 teaspoons cornstarch
2 teaspoons prepared mustard
1 tablespoon lemon juice
12 ounces red currant jelly

- Cut chicken into 2½x½-inch strips.
- Combine next 8 ingredients.
- Add chicken and mix until well coated.
- Cover and refrigerate overnight.
- Preheat oven to 350 degrees.
- Drain chicken thoroughly.
- Combine bread crumbs and sesame seeds.
- Add chicken and toss to coat.
- Place chicken in 4 greased 13x9x2-inch baking dishes.
- Brush melted butter over chicken.
- Bake for 25 minutes, or until chicken is tender.
- To prepare currant sauce, combine cornstarch, prepared mustard and lemon juice in a small saucepan.
- Beat in jelly with a wire whisk.
- Cook over medium heat, stirring frequently until mixture boils for 2 minutes.
- Remove from heat and remove any foam that has formed.
- Pour into a small bowl and cool to room temperature so sauce will thicken.
- Double the recipe for more sauce, if desired.

Sesame Chicken Kabobs

10 servings

Served over rice, this makes a delicious main course.

- *2/3 cup white wine*
- *6 tablespoons mango chutney*
- *6 tablespoons olive oil*
- *1 tablespoon curry powder*
- *2 pounds boneless chicken breasts, skinned*
- *3 tablespoons sesame seeds*
- *wooden skewers, soaked in water for 5 minutes*

- Mix together wine, chutney, olive oil and curry powder; set aside.
- Cut chicken breasts into cubes.
- Pour mixture over chicken and marinate for at least 2 hours.
- Place chicken on wooden skewers and sprinkle with sesame seeds.
- Broil or grill for 3 to 5 minutes on each side.

Legendary Cheese Pie

24 appetizer or 9 brunch servings

- *10 large eggs*
- *1/2 cup flour*
- *1 teaspoon salt*
- *1/2 cup margarine, melted*
- *1 pound small curd cottage cheese*
- *1/2 pound Monterey Jack cheese, shredded*
- *1/2 pound sharp Cheddar cheese, shredded*
- *1/2 to 1 4-ounce can green chili peppers, drained and finely chopped*

- Preheat oven to 350 degrees.
- Beat eggs until light.
- Add flour, salt, melted margarine, cheeses and green chili peppers.
- Stir to blend all.
- Pour mixture into a greased 9x14-inch baking dish.
- Bake for 35 to 40 minutes.
- Cool slightly and cut into small squares.
- Reheat to serve.

Mushrooms In White Wine Sauce

25 to 30 servings

1/4 cup chopped fresh parsley
1/2 cup minced spring onion (use small amount of green)
4 tablespoons lightly salted butter
6 6-ounce cans button mushrooms, well drained
salt and freshly ground pepper to taste
1/4 cup white wine
1 16-ounce carton sour cream

- Sauté parsley and onions in butter.
- Add mushrooms, salt and pepper.
- Pour in wine and cook for 5 minutes.
- Add sour cream just before serving.
- Serve in a chafing dish with toothpicks.
- Stir occasionally.
- May be prepared ahead and warmed just before serving.

Vegetable Mushroom Caps

8 servings

2 pounds fresh medium to large mushrooms
1/2 cup butter
1/2 cup minced onion
1/2 cup minced celery
2 teaspoons Worcestershire sauce
1 tablespoon Italian parsley
salt and freshly ground pepper
Italian parsley sprigs for garnish

- Rinse mushrooms and pat dry.
- Remove and chop stems.
- Set mushroom caps aside.
- Melt 1/2 cup butter in a large skillet.
- Stir in mushroom stems, onion, celery, Worcestershire sauce, parsley, salt and pepper.
- Sauté until vegetables are tender.
- Brush mushroom caps with melted butter and spoon in vegetable mixture.
- Set aside unused caps.
- Place caps, stuffed side up, in skillet.
- Cover and simmer for 5 minutes.
- Remove mushroom caps from skillet and serve on a platter garnished with Italian parsley.
- Any unstuffed mushrooms may be carved for garnishes.

Pecan Stuffed Mushrooms

6 servings

A savory combination that may be served as a side dish.

12 to 14 large mushrooms
1 cup pecans, finely chopped
3 tablespoons minced fresh parsley
¼ cup unsalted butter, softened
1 clove garlic, crushed
¼ teaspoon dried thyme
½ teaspoon salt
dash of pepper
½ cup heavy cream

- Preheat oven to 350 degrees.
- Clean mushrooms, remove stems and set aside.
- Place caps in a shallow pan, hollow side up.
- Finely chop stems and mix with pecans, parsley, butter, garlic, thyme, salt and pepper.
- Stuff caps with mixture.
- Pour cream over all.
- Bake for 15 to 20 minutes.

Escargot Stuffed Mushroom

4 servings

For the ultimate first course!

24 medium mushrooms, cleaned and stems removed
½ pound unsalted butter, room temperature
2 cloves garlic, minced
2 tablespoons chopped fresh parsley
salt and freshly ground black pepper
pinch of freshly grated nutmeg
dash cayenne pepper
1 tablespoon fresh lemon juice
2 dozen canned escargot, washed and dried
crusty French bread
4 escargot dishes

- Place butter, garlic, parsley, salt, black pepper, nutmeg, cayenne pepper, and lemon juice in a mixing bowl.
- Mix until well combined.
- Mixture may be made ahead and frozen up to this point.
- Preheat broiler and move rack to top of oven.
- Place 6 mushrooms in each escargot dish with one escargot in each mushroom cap.
- Spoon approximately 1 tablespoon of butter mixture on top of each escargot.
- Place dishes on baking sheet and broil approximately 7 to 10 minutes, until brown and bubbly.
- Serve at once with hot, crusty French bread.

Mushrooms Strudel

64 miniature strudels

3 tablespoons butter
1 pound fresh mushrooms, sliced
¼ cup chopped onions
⅛ cup shallots
1 tablespoon dry sherry
1 teaspoon salt
8 ounces cream cheese, room temperature
1 cup fine bread crumbs
½ cup plain yogurt
½ cup sour cream
⅓ cup freshly chopped parsley
3 tablespoons chopped water chestnuts
2 large cloves garlic, minced
2 teaspoons lemon juice
½ teaspoon ground caraway seed
½ teaspoon freshly ground pepper
16 phyllo sheets
1 cup butter, melted
2 to 3 teaspoons poppy seeds

- Melt 3 tablespoons butter in a large skillet over medium heat.
- Add mushrooms, onion and shallots and sauté, stirring until the onion and shallots are transparent and the liquid has evaporated.
- Stir in sherry and salt; cook until sherry is almost absorbed.
- Remove from heat and drain well.
- Return mixture to heat.
- Add cream cheese and stir over low heat until blended.
- Stir in bread crumbs, yogurt, sour cream, parsley, water chestnuts, garlic, lemon juice, caraway seeds and pepper.
- Adjust seasonings.
- Preheat oven to 375 degrees and grease a baking sheet.
- One at a time, brush each of 8 phyllo sheets with butter and stack them.
- Spoon half of mushroom mixture in a strip down the longer edge of phyllo leaving a few inches of phyllo on each side of filling.
- Roll phyllo around mixture into a log, tucking in sides as you go.
- Repeat with other 8 slices of phyllo and remaining filling.
- Sprinkle with poppy seeds.
- Bake at 375 degrees for 25 minutes or until browned.
- Cool for 5 minutes and slice.
- May be prepared and baked 1 day ahead.

Mussels With Herb Sauce

40 to 50 mussels

3 pounds mussels
3 tablespoons olive oil
3 tablespoons butter
2 cloves garlic, minced
1 medium onion, chopped
¼ cup white wine
Herb Sauce:
1½ cups mayonnaise
½ cup sour cream
2 tablespoons minced green onions
¾ to 1 teaspoon curry powder
2 tablespoons finely minced parsley
1 tablespoon finely minced fresh dill
salt and freshly ground black pepper
dash of Tabasco

- Scrub mussels well in several changes of water to remove beards.
- In a heavy saucepan with tight fitting lid, combine olive oil and butter over medium heat.
- Sauté garlic and onion; add wine and bring mixture to a boil.
- Add mussels and cover tightly to steam, stirring occasionally.
- Mussels are ready when shells open, approximately 5 to 8 minutes.
- Discard any mussels that do not open.
- Remove mussels from saucepan and cool.
- Separate shells reserving one side for serving.
- To prepare sauce, combine all ingredients and blend thoroughly.
- Place a mussel on each reserved shell and cover with a dollop of herb sauce.
- Serve mussels on a large tray lined with seaweed or bean sprouts.
- Refrigerate sauce for several hours before serving.

Remember This:

If fresh mussels are not available, smoked canned mussels may be substituted.

Appetizers

Oysters Maska
4 servings

A delicious first course!

1½ pints fresh oysters
¼ cup lightly salted butter
¼ cup olive oil
⅔ cup Italian bread crumbs
½ teaspoon salt
½ teaspoon freshly ground pepper
⅛ teaspoon cayenne pepper
½ teaspoon tarragon
½ teaspoon oregano
2 tablespoons finely minced fresh parsley
2 teaspoons finely chopped green onion tops

- Preheat oven to 450 degrees.
- Drain oysters and set aside.
- In a heavy saucepan, melt butter over low heat.
- Mix in olive oil and heat for a few minutes longer.
- Add bread crumbs, salt, pepper, cayenne pepper, tarragon, oregano, parsley and onion.
- Stir to mix well and remove saucepan from heat.
- Place well-drained oysters in individual 4-inch ramekins or au gratin plates.
- Spoon equal portions of sauce over each.
- Bake until topping is well browned, approximately 18 minutes.

Herbed Toast
4 to 5 dozen

Excellent served with cheese and pâtés.

2 loaves day old French bread
½ cup good quality olive oil
1½ tablespoons fines herbes

- Preheat oven to 350 degrees.
- Cut bread into small, thin slices.
- Arrange bread in a single layer on cookie sheets.
- Lightly brush 1 side with oil.
- Sprinkle with herbs.
- Bake approximately 15 minutes, until crisp and light golden brown.
- Cool to room temperature and store in an airtight container.

Phyllo Flowers
24 to 30 servings

Astonishingly simple! Susan Turner, food editor and caterer, suggests you double this and freeze prior to baking.

2 cups ricotta cheese
½ cup shredded mozzarella cheese
2 eggs, slightly beaten
2 tablespoons chopped fresh parsley
¼ cup chopped fresh dill
freshly ground pepper to taste
8 sheets phyllo dough
1 to 1½ cups unsalted butter, melted

- Preheat oven to 375 degrees.
- Combine cheeses, eggs, parsley, dill and pepper; set aside.
- Layer four sheets of phyllo dough brushing each sheet generously with melted butter.
- Be certain to completely cover dough with butter.
- Keep remaining sheets covered with a damp kitchen towel.
- Cut dough into 2½-inch squares.
- Place each square in a mini-muffin tin.
- Gently press dough in muffin tin so it forms a cup with edges extending over top of rim.
- Repeat procedure with remaining phyllo sheets.
- Fill with about 2 tablespoons cheese mixture.
- Brush edges of dough with melted butter.
- Bake for 15 to 20 minutes or until dough is slightly browned and mixture puffed.
- Serve warm.

Sugared Nuts
2 cups

½ cup water
1 cup sugar
2 cups green peanuts, shelled
1 tablespoon vanilla extract

- Preheat oven to 350 degrees.
- Bring water and sugar to a boil.
- Add peanuts and vanilla.
- Stir constantly until liquid has evaporated.
- Turn immediately onto a foil-lined cookie sheet and bake for 15 minutes.
- Keeps well in a covered container.

Miniature Toast Cups

70 toast cups

A crowd pleaser!

1 loaf thinly sliced white bread
butter, softened

- With rolling pin, roll bread slices flat.
- Lightly butter one side of bread.
- Cut bread into 1¼-inch rounds.
- Do not cut into crust.
- Place in miniature muffin tins butter side up.
- Bake at 325 degrees 10 to 15 minutes or until lightly browned.
- Remove from tins and cool.
- Suggested fillings:
  Chicken Almond Spread; Mushroom Spread; Fruit And Cheese Spread; Spicy Seafood Dip; Veggie Spread; Panhandle Crab Dip; Smoked Venison Spread

Toasted Artichoke Rounds

8 to 10 servings

24 slices cocktail rye bread
1 14-ounce can artichoke hearts
1 cup mayonnaise
1 cup freshly grated Parmesan cheese
garlic salt to taste
dash of paprika

- Toast rye bread on one side.
- Drain and slice artichokes in half.
- Place one slice of artichoke on untoasted side of rye bread.
- Mix together mayonnaise, cheese, garlic salt and paprika.
- Spoon 1 tablespoon or more of mayonnaise-cheese mixture over artichoke and broil until bubbly.
- Serve immediately.

Cheese Asparagus Rolls

80 miniature rolls

Prepare in advance for easy entertaining.

20 slices Pepperidge Farm white bread, crust removed
3 ounces bleu cheese
8 ounces cream cheese, softened
1 egg, slightly beaten
1 10-ounce package frozen asparagus spears
1 cup butter, melted

- Roll bread slices thin.
- Blend bleu cheese, cream cheese, and egg.
- Spread cheese blend on each slice of bread.
- Cook frozen asparagus according to package directions.
- Drain well and pat dry with paper towels.
- Place one asparagus spear on each slice of bread.
- Wrap bread around asparagus.
- Dip in melted butter and place on a lightly greased cookie sheet; freeze.
- Remove from freezer when ready to bake.
- Slice into quarters and bake at 400 degrees for 15 minutes.
- Turn once during baking.
- Serve warm.

Chicken Almond Spread

Filling for 70 Miniature Toast Cups

1 cup finely chopped cooked chicken
½ cup finely minced celery
¼ cup finely chopped blanched almonds
mayonnaise
1 teaspoon lemon juice
salt and pepper to taste

- Combine chicken, celery, almonds, lemon juice, and enough mayonnaise to moisten.
- Stir until well combined
- Season with salt and pepper to taste.
- Fill toast cups.
- Heat and serve warm or at room temperature.

Appetizers

Mushroom Spread

Filling for 70 Miniature Toast Cups

1 12-ounce can mushroom caps, finely chopped
1 small onion, finely chopped
2 tablespoons butter
1 teaspoon sherry
8 ounces cream cheese, softened
2 tablespoons mayonnaise
salt and pepper to taste

- Sauté mushrooms and onion in butter.
- Add sherry.
- Blend cheese and mayonnaise until smooth.
- Stir cheese into mushroom and onion mixture.
- Add salt and pepper to taste.
- Fill toast cups.
- Heat and serve warm.

Hot Olive Spread

20 servings

Keep this on hand for impromptu entertaining.

1 cup chopped black olives
3/4 cup mayonnaise
1/2 cup chopped green onions
1/2 teaspoon salt
1 1/2 cups shredded sharp Cheddar cheese
1/2 teaspoon curry powder
toasted bread rounds

- Preheat oven to 350 degrees.
- Mix spread ingredients well.
- Spread mixture on bread rounds.
- Bake for 10 minutes or until brown and bubbly.
- Serve hot.
- This spread may be stored in the refrigerator for 6 weeks.

Raspberry Cheese Mold

12 to 15 servings

1 pound sharp Cheddar cheese, shredded
1 cup finely chopped pecans
1 cup finely chopped onions
1 cup mayonnaise
1 12-ounce jar seedless red raspberry jam
butter flavored crackers

- Combine cheese, pecans and onions.
- Add mayonnaise and mix well.
- Place in a 4-cup mold and refrigerate until ready to serve.
- Unmold onto platter.
- Pour raspberry jam over mold or press an indentation in center of mold and fill to overflowing with jam.
- Serve with butter flavored crackers.

Brie Board

Brie cheese
dried apricots
currants
walnuts
raspberries
kiwi fruit, peeled and sliced
seedless grapes
strawberries, hulled
variety of crackers

- A Brie board may consist of as much or as little cheese, nuts and fruit as desired.
- Place wedge or round of Brie on board or desired platter.
- Cover in a wedge pattern with fruit and nuts.
- Fig Jam or Peach Chutney may be substituted for fresh fruit.
- Serve with crackers.

Fruit And Cheese Spread

2½ cups

1 16-ounce can fruit cocktail, drained and crushed
1 8-ounce package cream cheese, softened
1 tablespoon minced green onion tops
2 tablespoons mayonnaise
1 teaspoon curry, optional
4 slices bacon, cooked and crumbled
1 medium pineapple
chopped fresh parsley
bagel rounds, crackers or toast cups

- Combine first 6 ingredients; mix well.
- Chill for 3 hours.
- Cut a lengthwise slice from pineapple, removing about ⅓ pineapple.
- Scoop pulp from remaining portion of pineapple, leaving the shell ½ to ¼ inch thick.
- Reserve pulp for another use.
- Spoon cream cheese mixture into pineapple shell and garnish with parsley.
- Serve with thinly sliced bagel rounds, crackers or use as a filling for Miniature Toast Cups.

Hot Sweet Mustard Sauce
1½ cups

Versatile! Excellent over hot pork tenderloin medallions or mixed with sliced kielbasa.

4 ounces Coleman's dry mustard
1 cup sugar
1 cup cider vinegar
2 eggs

- Place all ingredients in a food processor and process just to combine.
- Transfer sauce to top of a double boiler and cook over simmering water until thick.
- Remove from heat and cool slightly.
- Store in a covered jar in the refrigerator for up to 1 month.
- Let stand at room temperature for 20 minutes before serving if served as a sauce for dipping.

Mexican Layer Dip
15 servings

Teens and adults will love this favorite.

2 large ripe Florida avocados
2 tablespoons lemon juice
½ teaspoon salt
¼ teaspoon pepper
1½ cups sour cream
1 package taco seasoning mix
1 16-ounce can refried beans
¼ cup medium-spiced taco sauce
8 green onions, sliced
2 medium tomatoes, seeded and chopped
1 4½-ounce can ripe olives, drained and chopped
2 cups shredded Monterey Jack cheese
tortilla chips or rounds

- Peel, pit and mash avocados with lemon juice, salt and pepper.
- Combine sour cream and taco seasoning mix.
- Mix refried beans and taco sauce.
- To assemble, spread refried beans on a large shallow serving platter.
- Spread avocado mixture over bean dip.
- Spread sour cream mixture over avocado.
- Sprinkle chopped onion, tomatoes and olives over all.
- Cover with cheese.
- Serve chilled or at room temperature with tortilla chips.

Appetizers

Le Beurre d'Herbes
½ cup

An excellent spread for breads served with wine.

½ cup lightly salted butter
2 tablespoons finely chopped parsley
2 tablespoons finely chopped chives
½ teaspoon oregano
¼ teaspoon salt
¼ teaspoon pepper
1 large clove garlic, crushed
2 tablespoons dry white wine or dry Vermouth
1 teaspoon Worcestershire
variety of crackers or breads

- Beat ingredients except crackers well with mixer until creamy; chill.
- Serve with crackers or a variety of breads.

Fromage Blanc
3 cups

Also delicious piped into blanched snow pea pockets.

2 8-ounce packages cream cheese, softened
1 cup unsalted butter, room temperature
⅓ cup heavy cream
1 tablespoon fresh lemon juice
1 tablespoon minced chives
1 tablespoon flat leaf parsley
¾ to 1 teaspoon mashed garlic
⅛ teaspoon salt
⅛ teaspoon pepper
delicate flavored crackers

- Beat cheese and add butter.
- Gradually beat in cream until smooth.
- Add remaining ingredients except crackers and stir.
- Pack in a 3-cup crock and refrigerate covered until firm, 4 to 6 hours, or up to 1 week.
- Let cheese stand 1 hour before serving.
- Serve with a delicately flavored crisp cracker.

Appetizers

Easy Elegant Grapes 6 to 8 servings

Also an attractive, edible garnish for meat dishes.

2½ cups pecan halves
8 ounces cream cheese, softened
4 ounces Camembert cheese, rind removed
1 tablespoon heavy cream
1 pound green or red seedless grapes

- Preheat oven to 300 degrees.
- Toast pecan halves until golden, about 15 minutes.
- Cool nuts and chop coarsely.
- Beat cheeses and heavy cream together until smooth.
- Coat grapes in cheese mixture.
- Roll grapes in nuts and place on a wax paper lined plate.
- Refrigerate until ready to serve.

Veggie Spread 1½ pints

2 cucumbers, peeled and quartered
2 carrots, peeled and halved
1 green pepper, seeded and halved
1 medium onion, quartered
½ cup diced celery
1 envelope unflavored gelatin
2 tablespoons lemon juice
1 pint mayonnaise
2 teaspoons dried dill
8 ounces cream cheese, softened

- Combine all vegetables in a food processor and finely mince.
- Put through cheese cloth or towel to remove moisture and set aside.
- Dissolve gelatin in ¼ cup water.
- Combine gelatin and remaining ingredients and mix until smooth.
- Stir in vegetable mixture until well blended.
- Spread on bread for great finger sandwiches.
- Combine light and dark bread for interest.
- Store for up to 1 week in refrigerator.

Remember This:

Prepare sandwiches the day before and cover with wax paper and damp kitchen towel to retain freshness.

Appetizers

Sweet Bleu Cheese Dip

Approximately 2 cups

Makes a wonderful salad dressing also.

- *1 cup mayonnaise*
- *½ cup salad oil*
- *2 tablespoons vinegar*
- *2 tablespoons sugar*
- *¼ cup catsup*
- *1 tablespoon prepared mustard*
- *½ teaspoon garlic powder*
- *¼ cup finely minced onion*
- *1 teaspoon celery seed*
- *½ teaspoon tarragon*
- *½ teaspoon freshly ground pepper*
- *4 to 6 ounces bleu cheese, crumbled*
- *1 red cabbage or bread round*

- Mix all ingredients except cabbage or bread round together and stir well.
- Store in refrigerator in a tightly sealed container.
- Shake well before pouring in a hollowed-out cabbage or bread round.
- Best when refrigerated for a few days.
- Serve as a vegetable or bread dip.

Georgia Popcorn

8 appetizer or 6 side dish servings

A Southern finger food.

- *2 pounds fresh okra*
- *1 teaspoon water*
- *4 eggs, beaten*
- *white cornmeal*
- *vegetable oil for deep frying*
- *salt and freshly ground pepper*

- Remove tops of okra and slice okra about ½-inch thick.
- Add water to eggs.
- Dip okra in beaten eggs and roll in cornmeal to coat.
- Fry in 3 inches of oil in a heavy skillet over medium heat (350 degrees on deep-fry thermometer) until golden brown, about 2 minutes.
- Drain on paper towels.
- Season with salt and pepper as desired.
- Serve immediately as an appetizer or vegetable side dish.

Appetizers

Chutney Cheese Ball
10 servings

11 ounces cream cheese, softened
3 tablespoons golden raisins
3 tablespoons sour cream
3 teaspoons curry powder
¾ cup chopped roasted peanuts
½ cup chutney
4 tablespoons crisp cooked bacon, crumbled
1 tablespoon minced onion
¼ cup toasted coconut
green onion brushes

- Mix all ingredients except coconut.
- Chill for 1 hour or until firm enough to shape into a ball.
- When ready to serve, roll in toasted coconut and garnish with green onion brushes.
- May be prepared one day ahead without coconut.

Bourbon Fruited Cheese
10 to 12 servings

Double this recipe and prepare days in advance for large crowds.

½ cup dried chopped apricots
¼ cup chopped dates
¼ cup golden raisins
¾ cup quality bourbon
16 ounces sharp Cheddar cheese, shredded
8 ounces cream cheese, softened
½ cup almonds, ground
⅔ cup toasted almonds, ground
dried whole apricots for garnish
crackers or gourmet ginger snaps

- Soak fruit in bourbon for 1 hour.
- Using metal blade in a food processor, combine cheese, bourbon-marinated fruits and ½ cup ground almonds, being careful not to over process.
- Lightly grease an 8-inch cake pan and line with wax paper.
- Press cheese mixture into prepared pan.
- Cover and refrigerate to chill thoroughly, preferably overnight.
- To serve, remove cheese from pan and spread toasted almonds on top.
- Garnish with a flower designed from whole dried apricots and holly leaves.
- Serve with crackers or gourmet ginger snap cookies.

Appetizers

Parmesan Twists
20 to 30 twists

Great with salads and soups.

1 pound frozen puff pastry
1 cup grated Parmesan cheese, divided
½ teaspoon cayenne pepper
½ cup sesame seeds or poppy seeds

- Allow puff pastry to thaw for 30 minutes.
- Preheat oven to 350 degrees.
- Roll out to 20x24 inches with a rolling pin.
- Mix ½ cup cheese with cayenne pepper and sprinkle over pastry.
- Use rolling pin to mix cheese into the pastry.
- Fold dough in half and roll again to 20x24 inches.
- Sprinkle with remaining cheese and seeds and roll once more.
- Cut into ⅓-inch strips, then twist into cork screws by holding both ends of the strip and twisting.
- Lay twists side by side on an ungreased baking sheet to prevent untwisting.
- Bake for 15 to 20 minutes or until puffed and brown.
- Cool for 5 minutes.
- Cut apart with a sharp knife.

Fresh Dill Dip
2 cups

1 cup sour cream
1 cup mayonnaise
1 tablespoon fresh lemon juice
salt and freshly ground black pepper
½ cup finely minced fresh dill

- Combine all ingredients and refrigerate until ready to serve.
- Serve in a hollowed-out red or green cabbage surrounded by a variety of blanched vegetables.
- Suggested vegetables include snow peas, whole green beans, asparagus spears, brussel sprouts, carrots cut into julienne strips, cauliflower and broccoli florets.

Elegant Cucumber Bites

40 to 50 bites

8 ounces cream cheese, softened
1 cucumber, peeled, seeded, minced and squeezed dry
2 green onions, finely minced
1 loaf thinly sliced, fine grain bread
2 to 3 cucumbers, thinly sliced
3 ounces cream cheese, softened

- Combine first 3 ingredients and chill.
- Cut bread into small circles.
- Spread bread with cream cheese and vegetable mixture.
- Top with a cucumber slice and store in refrigerator covered with wax paper and a slightly damp kitchen towel until ready to serve.
- Decorate with a cream cheese piped design.

Sweet And Salty Almonds

3 cups

Always a hit!

3½ tablespoons lightly salted butter
½ cup sugar
⅛ teaspoon cayenne pepper
3 cups whole blanched almonds
1¼ teaspoons regular or coarse salt

- In a heavy bottomed skillet, melt butter over moderate heat.
- Add sugar and cayenne pepper.
- Increase heat to high and cook for 1 minute, stirring constantly.
- Add almonds and reduce heat to medium high and cook 6 to 8 minutes, stirring and shaking pan constantly until almonds are dark brown and pop.
- Spread almonds on baking sheet and sprinkle with salt.
- Toss almonds as they cool.
- Store in an airtight container until ready to serve.

Pecan Tasties
5 dozen

1 egg white, room temperature
¾ cup brown sugar, loosely packed
½ teaspoon vanilla extract
2 cups pecan halves

- Preheat oven to 250 degrees.
- Beat egg white until stiff.
- Gradually add brown sugar and vanilla.
- Fold in nuts and coat well.
- Place in small clusters, 2 halves to a cluster, on a greased cookie sheet.
- Bake for 30 minutes.
- Turn oven off and let sit for another 30 minutes.
- Store in an airtight container.
- May be prepared 3 to 4 days in advance.

Cashew Wafers
75 wafers

A delicate, rich wafer.

1 pound extra sharp Cheddar cheese, shredded
1 cup unsalted butter, room temperature
1 teaspoon salt
¾ teaspoon cayenne pepper
1 cup sifted flour
2 cups dry roasted cashews or macadamia nuts, finely chopped

- Preheat oven to 325 degrees.
- Bring cheese to room temperature and beat until smooth.
- Beat in butter, one tablespoon at a time.
- Add salt and cayenne.
- Stir in flour, 2 tablespoons at a time.
- Add nuts and form a ball.
- Chill dough and form into small balls.
- Place on lightly greased cookie sheets, spaced 1 inch apart.
- Flatten with fork tines dipped into flour.
- Bake for 20 to 25 minutes.
- Cool and store in an airtight container until ready to serve.

Beverages

Orange Almond Punch

25 to 30 servings

Freeze a portion of punch for an ice mold.

4 cups water
2 cups sugar
1 3-ounce package orange flavored gelatin
1½ cups fresh or frozen lemon juice
1 46-ounce can unsweetened pineapple juice
1 tablespoon almond extract
½ gallon water

- In a small saucepan, bring 4 cups water to a boil.
- Add sugar and cook over high heat until sugar is dissolved, stirring occasionally.
- Remove from heat and stir in gelatin until dissolved.
- Pour gelatin and water mixture into a large bowl.
- Add lemon juice, pineapple juice, almond extract and half gallon water.
- Stir well and refrigerate until thoroughly chilled.

Birthday Party Punch

8 cups

This punch is similar to an ice cream soda.

3 cups pineapple juice, chilled
2½ cups fresh orange juice, chilled
¼ cup chilled fresh lemon juice
½ teaspoon vanilla extract
1 pint pineapple or orange sherbert
ice ring of orange juice, pineapple juice or a combination

- A day in advance prepare an ice ring with orange and pineapple juice.
- In a large punch bowl, combine pineapple, orange and lemon juice; stir in vanilla.
- Add frozen ice ring and garnish with scoops of sherbet.

Beverages

Reception Punch 28 cups

1 12-ounce can frozen orange juice
1 6-ounce can frozen lemonade
1 6-ounce can frozen limeade
2 46-ounce cans pineapple juice
6 cups water
2 2-liter bottles ginger ale, chilled
lemon and lime slices

- Combine all juices with water.
- Refrigerate to chill punch or freeze until ready to serve.
- When ready to serve, thaw punch if frozen and add ginger ale.
- Garnish with fruit slices.

Golden Tea Punch 18 servings

6 small teabags
½ cup sugar
1 cup fresh lemon juice
1 cup pineapple juice
¼ cup grenadine
1 quart ginger ale, chilled
additional fruit juices for ice ring
orange slices

- A day in advance, prepare an ice ring with additional fruit juices and orange slices.
- Add 2 cups boiling water to tea bags and steep; discard bags.
- Add sugar and stir to dissolve.
- Add fruit juices and grenadine; chill.
- To serve, place ice ring in a punch bowl, pour in punch and add ginger ale.
- Garnish with orange slices and place a small flower on top of each orange.

Remember This:

For a colorful variation, substitute frozen fruit for ice.

Beverages

Holiday Cranberry Punch

20 servings

Delicious served before holiday dinners and perfect for a Valentine's party.

2 cups orange juice
1/3 cup lemon juice
1/2 cup sugar
1 48-ounce bottle cranberry juice
2 pints raspberry sherbet
2 28-ounce bottles ginger ale, chilled

- Combine first 3 ingredients; stir until sugar dissolves.
- Add cranberry juice; mix well and chill.
- When ready to serve, pour mixture into a punch bowl and spoon scoops of sherbet on top.
- Add ginger ale and gently stir to blend.

Champagne Holiday Punch

20 servings

1 64-ounce bottle cranberry juice, chilled
1 cup sugar
1 bottle rosé wine, chilled
1 bottle champagne, chilled
mint leaves

- Add sugar to cranberry juice and refrigerate for at least 1 hour or until ready to serve.
- In a large bowl, combine cranberry juice-sugar mixture, rosé wine and champagne.
- Serve in a punch bowl or in fluted champagne glasses.
- Garnish with mint leaves.

Champagne Cocktail

6 servings

2 ounces Cointreau
2 ounces lime juice
2 tablespoons sugar
1 bottle champagne, chilled

- In a large pitcher combine Cointreau, lime juice and sugar.
- Stir to dissolve sugar; add champagne and stir to combine.
- Serve over ice in champagne glasses.
- If desired, before filling glasses dip rims first in lime juice and then sugar.

Classic Eggnog

12 to 15 servings

This recipe will taste good the next day – if you are lucky enough to have any left!

12 large eggs, separated
2 cups sugar
3 tablespoons vanilla extract
2½ cups quality bourbon
⅔ cup quality brandy
4 cups milk
2 cups well-chilled heavy cream
freshly grated nutmeg

- Allow yolks and whites to reach room temperature.
- Beat yolks in an electric mixer until pale yellow.
- Beat in sugar, 2 tablespoons at a time, until all sugar is added and mixture is thick.
- Using a hand-held whisk, add vanilla extract, bourbon, brandy and milk.
- Pour into a large bowl.
- In a separate mixing bowl, beat egg whites until soft peaks form.
- Fold beaten egg whites into yolk mixture.
- Whip cream until soft peaks form and fold into yolk mixture.
- Chill eggnog for 3 to 5 hours.
- Stir gently before serving and sprinkle with freshly grated nutmeg.

Remember This:

Separate yolks and whites while eggs are cold for easier separation.

Beverages

Wassail
16 cups

A delicious fall beverage served to Wickery customers for years.

1 quart hot tea
1 quart cranberry juice
1 quart apple juice
3 cinnamon sticks
12 cloves
1 cup sugar, optional
2 cups orange juice
3/4 cup lemon juice
1 orange, sliced
1 lemon, sliced

- Mix together all ingredients and simmer for at least 1 hour before serving to give the flavors time to mull.
- Serve hot.

Fruited Champagne Punch
46 1/2-cup servings

For a non-alcoholic punch, substitute ginger ale for champagne.

2 cups water
1 1/2 cups sugar
1 46-ounce can unsweetened pineapple juice
1 1/2 cups orange juice
1/2 cup fresh lemon juice
3 ripe bananas, mashed
2 quarts ginger ale, chilled
1 bottle champagne, chilled
4 strawberries, hulled
fresh mint leaves or sliced kiwi

- Combine sugar and water in a saucepan.
- Bring to a boil to dissolve sugar.
- Remove from heat and cool slightly.
- In a very large bowl, combine sugar syrup, fruit juices and mashed bananas.
- Divide mixture evenly into two 3-quart shallow dishes; cover and freeze.
- Twenty minutes before serving, cut frozen mixture into cubes and place in a punch bowl.
- Pour ginger ale and champagne over cubes.
- As the cubes melt, stir punch occasionally.
- Garnish with strawberries, mint leaves or sliced kiwi.

Beverages

Williamsburg Punch
32 cups

A Southern favorite.

1 gallon strong coffee
1 gallon chocolate milk
2 quarts vanilla ice cream
1 pint heavy cream, whipped
freshly grated nutmeg, optional

- Mix coffee, milk and ice cream in a punch bowl.
- Add whipped cream and sprinkle with nutmeg.

Melon Shake
4 to 5 servings

A refreshing drink made with watermelon, cantaloupe or honeydew.

3 cups cubed, seedless melon
1 cup milk
1 pint vanilla ice cream
½ teaspoon vanilla extract
melon balls
mint leaves

- Place melon in a blender.
- Add milk, ice cream and vanilla extract.
- Blend well, scraping down sides occasionally.
- Serve immediately in stemmed wine glasses.
- Garnish each serving with melon balls and mint leaves on a toothpick.

Strawberry Banana Margaritas
2 servings

Beautiful served in fluted champagne glasses.

1 small banana
1 cup chopped frozen strawberries
4½ ounces tequila
1½ ounces Triple Sec
3 tablespoons lime juice
2 tablespoons confectioner's sugar
1 cup cracked ice

- Peel and break banana into pieces.
- In a blender, purée strawberries and banana with tequila and Triple Sec.
- Add lime juice, sugar and cracked ice.
- Blend well, scraping down sides occasionally, until mixture is smooth but still frozen.

Beverages

Summer Cooler

20 servings

1 cup sugar
2½ cups crushed pineapple with juice
2 cups bananas, mashed
2 cups fresh orange juice
2 tablespoons fresh lemon juice
½ teaspoon vanilla extract
pinch of salt
10 to 12 maraschino cherries
4 quarts ginger ale, room temperature

- Combine all ingredients except ginger ale in a blender.
- Blend until fluffy.
- Pour into ice cube trays and freeze.
- When ready to serve, place 2 to 3 frozen cubes in stemmed glasses and cover with ginger ale.
- Or, place ice cubes in a punch bowl and add ginger ale.
- For variation, add 1-ounce vodka or rum to each glass.

Sherry Slush

18 servings

Perfect for brunch.

3 cups water
1 cup sugar
1 cup grape juice
½ cup lemon juice
3 cups orange juice
1 cup sherry

- To make syrup, boil water and sugar for 10 to 15 minutes; remove from heat and cool.
- Mix fruit juices and sherry with sugar syrup and freeze.
- Thaw to slush before serving.

Beverages

White Sangria

20 servings

Elegant served in wine glasses over cracked ice.

1 large orange
1 large lemon
1 large lime
2 to 3 cinnamon sticks
2 bottles dry white wine, chilled
½ cup sugar
1 cup Triple Sec
1 cup vodka
1 quart club soda, chilled
lemonade ice ring

- A day in advance, prepare an ice ring with lemonade.
- Thinly slice fruit and remove seeds.
- Place fruit and cinnamon sticks in a bowl and add Triple Sec.
- Refrigerate for 4 to 12 hours.
- Pour chilled wine and sugar in a glass container; stir.
- To serve, discard cinnamon sticks and stir together remaining ingredients in a large punch bowl; add lemonade ice ring.

Hot Buttered Rum

25 cups

2 cups butter, softened
1 pound confectioner's sugar
1 pound brown sugar
1 tablespoon ground cinnamon
1 tablespoon ground nutmeg
1 quart vanilla ice cream, softened
light rum
hot water
thin slices of butter for garnish

- Beat butter, sugars and spices together.
- Add ice cream, stirring until well blended.
- Spoon into a 2-quart freezer container and freeze.
- To serve, thaw slightly.
- Place a heaping tablespoon of butter mixture and 1 jigger of rum in a large mug.
- Fill with hot water.
- Stir well and garnish with a thin slice of butter.
- Any unused butter mixture may be refrozen.

Beverages

Cafe Olé 1 servings

An elegant ending for any meal.

ground cinnamon
sugar
1 wedge of lemon
3 ounces strong, hot coffee
1½ ounces French brandy
1½ ounces coffee liqueur
whipped cream
1 cinnamon stick

- Combine equal amounts of sugar and cinnamon.
- Rub the rim of a long-stemmed, tulip-shaped water goblet with lemon.
- Dip goblet in cinnamon and sugar mixture.
- Place a metal spoon in glass to prevent cracking and pour in hot coffee.
- Add brandy and coffee liqueur.
- Stir and add a generous amount of whipped cream to fill glass.
- Garnish with a cinnamon stick.

Savory Juice Cocktail 4 servings

Particularly pretty served in stemmed wine glasses.

4 cups clam and tomato cocktail juice
2 tablespoons fresh lime juice
3 teaspoons drained bottled horseradish, or to taste
1 teaspoon Worcestershire sauce
6 to 10 drops Tabasco or to taste
4 small celery stalks with leaves for garnish

- Combine juices, horseradish, Worcestershire and Tabasco in a pitcher.
- Stir well and pour over ice.
- Garnish with celery stalks and serve.

Breads

Orange Upside Down Biscuits
6 to 8 servings

Topping:
¼ cup butter
½ cup orange juice
½ cup sugar
2 teaspoons grated orange rind
Biscuit Dough:
2 cups flour
3 teaspoons baking powder
1 teaspoon salt
¼ cup shortening
¾ cup milk
Filling:
2 to 4 tablespoons butter, melted
¼ cup sugar
½ teaspoon cinnamon

- Preheat oven to 425 degrees.
- To prepare topping, melt butter in an 8-inch square pan.
- Add orange juice, sugar and orange rind; stir.
- To prepare dough, stir flour, baking powder and salt in a mixing bowl.
- Cut in shortening until dough is consistency of coarse cornmeal.
- Stir in most of the milk.
- If dough is not pliable, add milk to make it soft, puffy, and easy to roll.
- Turn onto floured board and knead 20 to 25 times.
- Roll in a rectangle about ¼-inch thick and brush with 2 to 4 tablespoons melted butter.
- Combine ¼ cup sugar and cinnamon and sprinkle over melted butter.
- Roll dough as for jelly roll and pinch seam to seal.
- Cut ½-inch slices dipping knife in water after each cut.
- Place cut side down in orange mixture.
- Bake for 20 to 25 minutes.
- When done, turn pan upside down on plate.
- Serve warm.

Pimento Cheese Biscuits

15 biscuits

2 cups flour
3 teaspoons baking powder
1 tablespoon sugar
1 teaspoon salt
1/8 to 1/4 teaspoon cayenne pepper
1 1/2 cups shredded sharp Cheddar cheese
4 tablespoons butter
4 tablespoons shortening
3/4 to 1 cup milk
1/4 cup chopped pimento, drained
1/4 cup finely chopped green bell pepper, optional

- Preheat oven to 450 degrees.
- Combine flour, baking powder, sugar, salt, and cayenne pepper.
- Add cheese and mix well.
- Cut shortening and butter into flour with pastry blender until consistency of coarse cornmeal.
- Add pimento and green pepper, if desired.
- Make a well in the dry ingredients and add 3/4 cup milk.
- Using a fork, stir to combine until mixture forms a ball.
- Add additional 1/4 cup of milk as needed.
- Turn dough onto a floured surface and knead 8 to 10 times.
- Roll out to a 1/2-inch thickness and cut into 2-inch rounds.
- Bake biscuits on an ungreased cookie sheet for 12 to 15 minutes.

Sour Cream Biscuits

30 mini biscuits

A quick, rich biscuit that does not require butter when served.

1 cup margarine, melted
1 cup sour cream
2 cups self-rising flour

- Preheat oven to 400 degrees.
- Combine melted margarine and sour cream.
- Measure self-rising flour into a large bowl.
- Combine butter and sour cream with flour stirring to mix thoroughly.
- Fill ungreased mini-muffin pans with heaping tablespoons of batter.
- Bake 15 minutes.
- Cool baked biscuits for 3 minutes before removing from pan.

Breads

Angel Biscuits 50 rolls

The pocket shape makes these rolls ideal for serving with sliced meat as an appetizer.

2 packages dry yeast
2 tablespoons lukewarm water
2 cups buttermilk
5 cups self-rising flour
¼ cup sugar
1 cup shortening
½ cup melted butter

- Mix yeast and water.
- Let sit for 3 to 5 minutes.
- Add yeast mixture to buttermilk.
- In a large mixing bowl, combine flour and sugar.
- Cut in shortening until mixture resembles coarse meal.
- Add liquids and mix well.
- Dough mixture may be refrigerated in a plastic bag and used as needed.
- Will keep for 2 weeks in refrigerator.
- To form biscuit, knead dough 2 to 3 minutes on floured board.
- Roll out dough to ½-inch thickness and cut into 2-inch rounds.
- Brush melted butter on tops and fold over, making into pocketbook rolls.
- Place on greased cookie sheets.
- Let rise for 1 hour.
- Bake at 400 degrees for 15 minutes, or until brown.

Remember This:

To prepare Angel Biscuits 1 day in advance, refrigerate after shaping. Remove rolls 1 hour before baking.

Breads

Yeast Rolls 4 dozen

A yeast dough that may be stored in the refrigerator for days.

2 packages yeast
¾ teaspoon ground ginger
1 teaspoon sugar
1 cup lukewarm water, 110 to 115 degrees
¾ cup sugar
1 cup shortening
1 cup boiling water
2 eggs, room temperature
6 cups unsifted flour
1 tablespoon salt
melted butter

- Dissolve yeast, ginger, and 1 teaspoon sugar in lukewarm water.
- Cream shortening and sugar; add boiling water.
- When moderately cool, beat in eggs; add yeast mixture and beat again.
- Stir in flour and salt.
- Store covered in refrigerator.
- Mixture can be used in 3 hours or will keep up to 5 days in refrigerator.
- Roll dough to ¼-inch thickness.
- Cut, dip into melted butter and fold over.
- Let rise 2 hours before baking.
- Bake at 350 degrees for 10 to 15 minutes.
- If baked ahead for freezing, reduce baking time by 3 to 5 minutes, to compensate for reheating.

Blueberry Muffins 24 muffins

2½ cups flour
¾ cup sugar
1 tablespoon baking powder
½ teaspoon salt
6 tablespoons butter
¾ cup chopped walnuts or pecans
2 eggs
1 cup milk
1 teaspoon vanilla extract
1½ cups fresh blueberries

- Preheat oven to 400 degrees.
- Mix first 4 ingredients in a large bowl.
- Cut in butter with knife or pastry blender until consistency of fine crumbs.
- Stir in nuts.
- In a small bowl, combine eggs, milk and vanilla extract; beat.
- Stir egg mixture into flour, just until moist.
- Gently fold in blueberries.
- Spoon into greased muffin tins.
- Bake 10 to 12 minutes or until brown.

Almond Muffins 24 muffins

A rich filling makes this muffin a specialty.

Filling:
12 ounces cream cheese, softened
2 eggs
2 tablespoons sugar
1 tablespoon grated orange rind
Muffin:
1 cup butter
1½ cups sugar
4 eggs
3 cups flour
2 teaspoons baking powder
1 cup milk
1 teaspoon almond extract
1 cup chopped almonds, toasted

- Preheat oven to 400 degrees.
- Beat cream cheese, eggs, sugar and orange rind together; set aside.
- Cream butter and sugar until light and fluffy.
- Add eggs one at a time, beating after each addition.
- Stir flour and baking powder together.
- Add flour and milk alternately to butter and sugar mixture, beginning and ending with flour.
- Add almond extract and fold in almonds.
- Fill each lightly greased muffin tin half full with muffin batter.
- Spoon approximately 1½ tablespoons of filling in each muffin tin.
- Top filling with muffin batter.
- Bake muffins for 15 to 20 minutes or until muffin just bounces back when pressed.

Mini Pumpkin Muffins 5 dozen

1½ cups sugar
½ cup oil
1 16-ounce can pumpkin
2 eggs, slightly beaten
2 cups flour
1 teaspoon baking soda
½ teaspoon ground cinnamon
½ teaspoon ground nutmeg

- Preheat oven to 375 degrees.
- Combine sugar, oil, pumpkin and eggs.
- Mix together dry ingredients and stir into pumpkin mixture.
- Pour batter into greased and floured mini-muffin pans.
- Bake 8 to 12 minutes.
- Let cool 5 minutes before removing from pan.

Breads

Banana Snack Muffins

12 muffins

A nutritious snack for children and adults.

½ 6-ounce can frozen orange juice concentrate, thawed
2 ripe bananas, mashed
2 eggs
¼ cup vegetable oil
2 tablespoons honey
1 teaspoon ground cinnamon
1 teaspoon ground allspice
2 cups biscuit mix
½ cup raisins

- Preheat oven to 400 degrees.
- Combine juice, bananas, eggs, oil, honey and seasonings in a large mixing bowl.
- Beat with mixer until light and fluffy.
- Fold in biscuit mix and raisins.
- Stir until dry ingredients are moistened.
- Fill greased or lined muffin cups ¾ full.
- Bake for 20 minutes.

Hearty Bran Muffins

12 muffins

Not too sweet, not too heavy.

2 large eggs
¼ cup packed light brown sugar
1 cup milk
¼ cup vegetable oil
1½ cups wheat bran cereal
½ cup oat bran
½ cup flour
2 teaspoons baking powder
½ cup raisins
½ cup sunflower seeds, optional

- Preheat oven to 375 degrees.
- Grease muffin tins, or use paper or foil baking cups.
- Beat eggs and brown sugar in a medium size bowl until smooth.
- Whisk in milk and oil.
- Stir in wheat bran cereal and let soak for at least 15 minutes.
- Mix oat bran, flour, baking powder, raisins and sunflower seeds in a large bowl.
- Add soaked bran mixture to dry ingredients and fold until dry ingredients are just moistened.
- Spoon batter into muffin tins.
- Bake for 20 to 25 minutes or until firm in center and browned.
- Turn out onto rack to cool.

Herb Bread
2 round loaves

A flavorful bread recipe from Lorrie Guttman, Food Editor.

2 packages yeast
½ cup warm water
1½ cups scalded milk
4 tablespoons sugar
6 tablespoons shortening
3 teaspoons salt
2 eggs, beaten
1 teaspoon ground nutmeg
2 teaspoons rubbed sage
4 teaspoons caraway seeds
6½ to 7 cups sifted flour
softened butter or vegetable oil
1 egg white, slightly beaten
2 teaspoons caraway seeds

- Dissolve yeast in warm water.
- Combine milk, sugar, shortening and salt; let cool.
- Add softened yeast.
- Stir in eggs, nutmeg, sage, 4 teaspoons caraway seeds and 4 cups flour.
- Beat until smooth with a wooden spoon.
- Add more flour to make a soft dough, approximately 2 to 2½ cups.
- Sift ½ cup flour on a pastry cloth or board and knead dough until smooth and elastic, approximately 8 to 10 minutes.
- Rub butter or oil over dough and place in a large, greased bowl.
- Cover and let rise in a warm place until doubled in size, approximately 1 hour.
- Punch down dough and let rise 10 minutes.
- Divide into two balls and place each in a greased 9-inch pie pan.
- Cover and let rise 45 minutes.
- Brush with egg white and sprinkle generously with 2 teaspoons caraway seeds.
- Bake at 400 degrees for 30 to 40 minutes.
- If tops start to brown, cover with foil.

Breads

Zucchini Carrot Bread
2 loaves

A nutritious, light bread.

2½ cups flour
1 teaspoon baking powder
1 teaspoon baking soda
1 teaspoon salt
1 tablespoon ground cinnamon
¾ cup vegetable oil
3 eggs
1½ cups packed brown sugar
2 teaspoons vanilla extract
1 cup shredded zucchini
1 cup shredded carrots
1 cup sunflower seeds
½ cup bran flake cereal

- Preheat oven to 350 degrees.
- Combine first 5 ingredients in a bowl; set aside.
- Beat oil, eggs, sugar and vanilla extract in a large bowl.
- Stir in zucchini and carrots.
- Add flour mixture and stir until just moistened.
- Stir in sunflower seeds and cereal.
- Pour into 2 greased 9x5x3-inch loaf pans.
- Bake for 1 hour, or until toothpick inserted in center comes out clean.
- Cool for 10 minutes in pan; remove and place on wire racks until completely cooled.

Cheddar And Parmesan Bread
8 servings

Tasty with barbecue.

3 ounces extra sharp Cheddar cheese, cut into 1-inch cubes
3 ounces Parmesan cheese, cut into 1-inch cubes
¼ cup olive oil
1 teaspoon freshly ground pepper
1½ teaspoons prepared mustard
1 loaf French bread

- Preheat oven to 350 degrees.
- Coarsely chop cheeses in a food processor.
- Continue processing until finely chopped.
- Add oil, pepper and mustard and mix in processor about one minute until paste forms.
- Slice bread in half length-wise, leaving one side attached.
- Spread cheese mixture evenly over each side of bread, leaving a ½-inch border around the outside edges.
- Place halves together and wrap in foil.
- Bake for 30 minutes, or until cheese melts.
- Serve warm.

Sausage Bread

12 servings

Excellent for breakfast, hot or cold.

1 cup raisins
1 pound hot bulk sausage
1½ cups brown sugar
2 eggs
1 cup chopped walnuts
3 cups flour or 2½ cups flour, plus 1 cup oats
½ to 1 teaspoon ginger
1 teaspoon pumpkin pie spice
½ teaspoon ground cinnamon
¼ teaspoon ground cloves
¼ teaspoon nutmeg
1 teaspoon baking powder
1 cup cold coffee
1 teaspoon baking soda

- Preheat oven to 350 degrees.
- Place raisins in a saucepan and cover with water.
- Simmer for 5 minutes; drain.
- Mix uncooked sausage, brown sugar, and eggs.
- Stir in raisins and nuts.
- Mix flour, spices and baking powder.
- Stir baking soda into coffee.
- Blend coffee and flour mixture into sausage mixture.
- Pour into a greased and floured 9-inch tube pan.
- Bake for 1¼ hours or until tested done.

Corn, Corn Bread

10 servings

This is a perfect accompaniment to salads.

¾ cup yellow cornmeal
¾ cup flour
1 teaspoon salt
3 teaspoons baking powder
1 cup sour cream
2 eggs
1 cup fresh corn kernels
½ cup oil
½ cup butter, melted

- Preheat oven to 400 degrees.
- Grease a 13x9-inch pan.
- Combine dry ingredients.
- Add sour cream, eggs, corn and oil; stir to mix.
- Bake for 25 to 30 minutes, until center springs back when touched.
- Pour melted butter over corn bread.

Breads

Southern Corn Bread

6 to 8 servings

3 tablespoons shortening
2 cups white self-rising cornmeal
3 heaping teaspoons baking powder
½ teaspoon salt
2 eggs, beaten
2½ cups milk

- Preheat oven to 450 degrees.
- Melt shortening in a 12-inch cast iron skillet in preheating oven.
- Sift dry ingredients together.
- Add beaten eggs to milk.
- Add milk and egg mixture to dry ingredients and mix.
- Add 1 tablespoon of melted shortening to batter, stirring constantly.
- Pour batter into hot skillet.
- Bake for 15 to 20 minutes.
- Turn corn bread out of skillet onto a large plate.
- Slice and serve hot.

Orange French Toast

6 servings

¼ cup butter
⅓ cup sugar
¼ teaspoon ground cinnamon
1 teaspoon grated orange rind
4 eggs, slightly beaten
⅔ cup orange juice or ⅓ cup orange juice and ⅓ cup Grand Marnier
8 slices firm white bread
confectioner's sugar

- Preheat oven to 325 degrees.
- Melt butter in 10x15-inch jelly roll pan.
- Combine sugar, cinnamon and orange rind.
- Sprinkle cinnamon mixture in jelly roll pan.
- In a separate bowl, mix eggs and juice.
- Dip bread in egg and juice mixture, soaking well.
- Arrange bread on top of butter and sugar mixture.
- Bake for 20 minutes.
- Remove pan from oven, flip bread and bake an additional 5 minutes.
- Sprinkle with confectioner's sugar.

Sticky Coffee Cake

8 to 10 servings

Prepared in a jiffy, eaten in seconds!

- *½ cup sugar*
- *½ cup brown sugar*
- *2 teaspoons cinnamon*
- *4 10-ounce cans refrigerated biscuits*
- *¾ cup coarsely chopped pecans*
- *6 tablespoons margarine, melted*

- Preheat oven to 325 degrees.
- Combine sugars and cinnamon in a plastic bag.
- Separate biscuits and cut into quarters.
- Place quartered biscuits in bag and shake to thoroughly coat with sugar.
- Grease a bundt pan and sprinkle bottom of pan with pecans.
- Place sugar-coated biscuits in pan and drizzle with margarine.
- Bake for 30 to 35 minutes.
- Turn coffee cake carefully onto a large round plate while still hot.
- Serve immediately.

Sour Cream Coffee Cake

10 servings

Easy to freeze for later.

- *1 cup butter, softened*
- *2 cups sugar*
- *2 eggs*
- *1 cup sour cream*
- *½ teaspoon vanilla extract*
- *2 cups flour*
- *1 teaspoon baking powder*

Topping:

- *½ cup sugar*
- *2 teaspoons cinnamon*
- *1 cup finely chopped nuts*

- Preheat oven to 350 degrees.
- Cream butter and sugar together.
- Add eggs one at a time.
- Fold in sour cream and vanilla extract.
- Sift flour and baking powder together.
- Add flour mixture to egg mixture.
- Combine topping ingredients.
- Pour half of batter into a 10-inch tube pan; add topping.
- Cover with remaining batter.
- Bake for 40 to 50 minutes, or until browned.
- Store in refrigerator.

Danish Puff

8 to 10 servings

This pastry may be prepared as a loaf or as individual puffs.

Dough:
½ cup butter or margarine, softened
1 cup flour
2 tablespoons water

Batter:
½ cup butter or margarine
1 cup water
1 teaspoon almond extract
1 cup flour
3 eggs

Glaze:
1½ cups confectioner's sugar, sifted
2 tablespoons butter or margarine, softened
1½ teaspoons vanilla extract
1 to 2 teaspoons warm water
3 tablespoons lightly toasted sliced almonds

- Preheat oven to 350 degrees.
- To prepare dough, cut butter into flour with pastry blender until the mixture resembles meal.
- Sprinkle water over mixture and mix with a fork.
- Divide dough in half and pat each into 12x3-inch strips.
- Place on an ungreased baking sheet.
- Strips should be 3 inches apart.
- To prepare batter, heat butter and water to a rolling boil.
- Reduce heat and quickly stir in almond extract and flour.
- Stir vigorously over low heat until mixture forms a ball, about 1 minute.
- Remove from heat.
- Beat in eggs one at a time with a wooden spoon and continue beating until smooth.
- Divide puff batter over each dough strip.
- Bake one hour; cool.
- To prepare glaze, stir confectioner's sugar, butter, vanilla extract and water until mixture is smooth.
- Spread over puff and sprinkle with almonds.
- To prepare as individual puffs, spread a rounded tablespoon of batter over a round of dough, extending the batter just beyond the edge.
- Bake 30 minutes or until crisp; cool and frost.

Fig Jam

8½ pints

6 quarts boiling water
6 quarts fresh figs
sugar
1 quart water
8 slices lemon

- Pour boiling water over figs, let stand 15 minutes.
- Drain and thoroughly rinse in cold water.
- Pat dry; remove stems.
- Crush and measure figs; place in a large pan.
- Add ½ cup sugar for each cup of crushed figs.
- Add 1 quart water.
- Bring to a rapid boil; reduce heat and simmer uncovered 3 hours or until thickened, stirring occasionally.
- Ladle jam into hot sterilized jars, leaving ¼-inch space at top.
- Add a slice of lemon to each jar.
- Cover at once with metal lids and screw on bands.
- Process in a boiling water bath for 10 minutes.

Remember This:

If liners are used, remove muffins from pan to cool. Cool unlined muffins in pan for 5 minutes, then remove.

Salads

Spinach And Orange Salad

8 servings

3 tablespoons red wine vinegar
1 tablespoon sugar
1 tablespoon fresh orange juice
½ teaspoon salt
½ teaspoon celery salt
¼ teaspoon dry mustard
⅓ cup vegetable oil
1 clove garlic
5 medium valencia oranges
10 ounces fresh spinach, washed and trimmed
½ medium purple onion, thinly sliced and separated into rings
1 cup chopped celery
8 slices bacon, cooked and crumbled

- To prepare dressing, combine first 7 ingredients in a blender or food processor and process well.
- Transfer dressing to a jar and add garlic.
- Refrigerate dressing to chill and combine flavors.
- Peel oranges removing all the white membrane.
- Slice oranges crosswise into ¼-inch slices and save any juices.
- Cut slices in half and remove seeds.
- Tear spinach into bite-size pieces.
- Combine oranges, onion, celery, and spinach in a large bowl.
- Remove garlic clove before dressing the salad.
- Pour dressing over salad and toss.
- Sprinkle with bacon and serve immediately.

Zesty Poppy Seed Dressing

For a variation, substitute berry-flavored vinegar.

2 cups

½ cup sugar
1 teaspoon dry mustard
¼ teaspoon salt
½ cup vinegar
1½ tablespoons finely chopped onion
1 cup salad oil
1½ tablespoons poppy seeds

- Mix sugar, dry mustard, salt and vinegar.
- Gradually blend in onion and oil.
- Add poppy seeds and stir.
- Refrigerate for up to 2 weeks.

Hearts Of Palm Salad

6 servings

2 heads Bibb lettuce
2 14-ounce cans hearts of palm, drained
1 pound mushrooms, sliced
1 cup chopped walnuts
Dressing:
1 egg
1 teaspoon salt
1½ teaspoons sugar
¼ teaspoon paprika
1½ tablespoons brown spicy mustard
1 teaspoon Worcestershire sauce
1 clove garlic, crushed
¼ cup water
½ cup wine vinegar
1 cup vegetable oil

- To prepare dressing, combine all ingredients except oil and mix together well.
- Slowly add oil, beating constantly; chill.
- Rinse and drain lettuce leaves; tear into bite-size pieces.
- Arrange lettuce evenly on 6 salad plates.
- Arrange hearts of palm in spoke formation on lettuce.
- Sprinkle each salad evenly with mushrooms and nuts.
- Spoon desired amount of dressing over salads.

Remember This:

Garnish or perk up salads with edible, insecticide-free flower petals. Gently rinse and drain nasturtiums, chrysanthemums, daisies, geraniums, marigolds, pansies or violets. Refrigerate petals or blossoms until ready to use.

Salads

Lemon Vinaigrette Salad

6 servings

1 medium head red leaf lettuce
2 small heads Bibb lettuce
1 pink grapefruit, peeled and sectioned
1 small red onion, thinly sliced
Lemon Vinaigrette:
⅓ cup fresh lemon juice
grated rind of two lemons
⅔ cup vegetable oil
salt
freshly ground black pepper

- Rinse lettuce leaves under cold running water and drain well.
- Wrap leaves in a kitchen towel and shake to remove excess water.
- Refrigerate towel-wrapped leaves until ready to assemble salad.
- Tear lettuce into bite-size pieces and place in a large bowl.
- Add sectioned grapefruit pieces and onion slices.
- Mix all vinaigrette ingredients in a jar with a tight fitting lid.
- Shake vigorously to combine well.
- Pour Lemon Vinaigrette over salad and toss.

Exotic Spinach Salad

4 servings

Good with a light summer meal!

10 ounces spinach, torn and stems removed
½ pint strawberries, hulled and sliced
3 kiwi, peeled and sliced
½ cup walnuts, chopped
⅓ cup salad oil
3 tablespoons red wine vinegar
½ teaspoon sugar
¼ teaspoon salt
⅛ teaspoon pepper

- Wash spinach, drain and pat dry with paper towels.
- In a medium bowl, combine strawberries, kiwi, and walnuts.
- Combine oil, vinegar, sugar, salt, and pepper in a small jar with tight fitting lid.
- Shake well until blended.
- Just before serving, gently toss spinach leaves with about half the dressing in a large bowl.
- Divide leaves among 4 salad plates.
- Arrange strawberries, kiwi and walnuts over spinach leaves.
- Drizzle remaining dressing over fruit.

Salads

Chutney Dressing 6 servings

Especially tasty on spinach salads.

¼ cup wine vinegar
4 tablespoons chutney
2 cloves garlic, crushed
2 tablespoons coarsely ground French mustard or Dijon mustard
3 teaspoons sugar
½ cup vegetable oil
salt and freshly ground pepper

- Combine vinegar, chutney, garlic, mustard and sugar in a food processor or blender; process until smooth.
- With the machine running, slowly add oil and process until thick and smooth.
- Season with salt and pepper.

Florida Citrus Salad 6 servings

Very refreshing and different.

2 cups torn green leaf lettuce
2 cups torn romaine lettuce, ribs removed
½ cup watercress leaves
3 navel oranges, peeled and sectioned
2 grapefruit, peeled and sectioned
1 medium avocado, peeled, seeded, and cubed
2 cups Jarlsberg cheese, cubed
½ cup salad oil
3 tablespoons red wine vinegar
3 tablespoons chopped parsley
1 clove garlic, minced
¼ teaspoon tarragon, crushed
½ medium purple onion, sliced and separated into rings

- In a large bowl, combine green leaf lettuce, romaine lettuce, watercress, oranges, grapefruit, avocado and Jarlsberg cheese.
- In a small bowl, combine salad oil, red wine vinegar, parsley, garlic and tarragon; blend well.
- Top salad with purple onion slices.
- Pour dressing over salad and toss just before serving.

Dilled Summer Salad

8 servings

1 large cucumber, peeled and thinly sliced
3 large ripe tomatoes, cut into 1-inch cubes
1 medium head cauliflower, separated into small florets
1 medium sweet red pepper, seeded and cut into julienne strips
1 medium green bell pepper, seeded and cut into julienne strips
⅓ cup vegetable oil
3 tablespoons white wine vinegar
2 tablespoons fresh dill
¼ teaspoon sugar
salt and freshly ground pepper
1 head Boston lettuce

- Place cucumber, tomatoes, cauliflower and peppers in a 3-quart shallow dish.
- In a small jar with tight fitting lid, combine vegetable oil, wine vinegar, dill, sugar, salt and pepper to taste.
- Shake vigorously.
- Pour dressing over vegetables and toss gently.
- Cover and chill for 2 hours, stirring occasionally.
- To serve, place 2 Boston lettuce leaves on individual salad plates.
- Spoon vegetables on lettuce-lined plates and pour remaining dressing over servings.

Remember This:

Refrigerated dressing will keep for several weeks.

Cheese And Fruit Salad

6 servings

4 small heads Boston or Bibb lettuce (about 1/4 to 1/3 pound each)
2 cups fresh cubed pineapple
1 cup fresh blueberries
1 cup cottage cheese
1 cup shredded Cheddar cheese
1/3 cup raisins
1/3 cup chopped pecans or walnuts
2 bananas, peeled and sliced
1 cup red seedless grapes
Cheese Dressing:
1 3-ounce package cream cheese, softened
1 8-ounce carton sour cream
2 tablespoons honey
1 teaspoon vanilla extract

- Prepare lettuce by trimming blemished outer leaves; thoroughly wash and drain lettuce heads.
- Pat dry with paper towels.
- Cut out center leaves using tip of a sharp knife, leaving core and outer leaves intact.
- Set lettuce shells aside and shred center leaves into 1/4-inch wide strips and set aside.
- Combine pineapple, blueberries, cottage cheese, Cheddar cheese, raisins, nuts, and bananas.
- Toss well; cover and refrigerate for 1 hour.
- Beat cream cheese in a small bowl until fluffy.
- Beat in remaining ingredients; cover and chill thoroughly.
- To serve, spread lettuce shells open, place lettuce strips in centers and mound with cheese and fruit mixture.
- Place grapes on top.
- Serve with Cheese Dressing.

Remember This:

To prepare lettuce in advance, rinse leaves and drain well. Wrap in a kitchen towel and store in refrigerator until ready to assemble salad.

Salads

Cherry Salad Supreme

10 servings

Lovely as a holiday salad!

1 3-ounce package raspberry flavored gelatin
1 20-ounce can lite cherry pie filling
1 3-ounce package lemon flavored gelatin
1 3-ounce package cream cheese, softened
⅓ cup mayonnaise
1 8-ounce can crushed pineapple
½ cup heavy cream, whipped
2 tablespoons chopped pecans
lettuce leaves

- Dissolve raspberry flavored gelatin in 1 cup boiling water.
- Stir in pie filling.
- Pour into a 9x9x2-inch pan.
- Chill until partially set.
- Dissolve lemon flavored gelatin in 1 cup boiling water.
- Beat together cream cheese and mayonnaise.
- Gradually add lemon gelatin to cream cheese mixture.
- Stir in undrained pineapple.
- Fold in whipped cream and spread over cherry mixture.
- Sprinkle with nuts and chill until set.
- When ready to serve, cut into squares and serve on lettuce leaves.

Sherry Fruit Salad Dressing

1 cup

Dress a Florida fruit salad of watermelon, cantaloupe, mangoes, papaya and kiwi with this!

1 egg
1 teaspoon cornstarch
¼ cup pineapple juice
¼ cup sherry
¼ teaspoon salt
3 tablespoons lime juice
3 tablespoons sugar
½ cup sour cream

- Beat egg with cornstarch.
- Add pineapple juice, sherry, salt, lime juice, and sugar.
- Cook over simmering water in a double boiler, stirring constantly until thickened.
- Remove from heat and cool.
- Fold in sour cream and refrigerate until ready to dress fruit salad.

Watercress, Pear And Bleu Cheese Salad 4 servings

A spectacular salad!

1 small head Boston lettuce, torn into pieces
10 ounces watercress leaves
2 ripe pears, sliced
½ cup bleu cheese, crumbled
½ cup walnut halves
Dressing:
1 teaspoon salt, or to taste
½ teaspoon freshly ground black pepper
¼ teaspoon sugar
½ teaspoon dry mustard
juice of ½ lemon
1 clove garlic, minced
5 tablespoons tarragon vinegar
½ cup vegetable oil
2 tablespoons extra virgin olive oil
1 egg, slightly beaten
¼ cup light cream

- Divide greens among plates and arrange pear slices over greens.
- Top with bleu cheese and walnuts.
- Prepare dressing by combining all ingredients in a jar and shaking vigorously to blend.
- When ready to serve, pour dressing over salad.

Remember This:

Put a dry sponge in vegetable or crisper drawer of refrigerator to absorb moisture.

Salads

Apricot Nectar Salad
6 servings

12 ounces apricot nectar
1 3-ounce package lemon flavored gelatin
1/3 cup water
1 tablespoon lemon juice
1 11-ounce can mandarin oranges, drained
3/4 cup seedless green grapes
1/2 cup diced, unpeeled apple
sliced apples, optional
seedless green grapes, optional
additional mandarin orange sections, optional

- Bring apricot nectar to a boil; add gelatin and stir until dissolved.
- Blend in water and lemon juice.
- Chill until consistency of unbeaten egg white.
- Stir in next 3 ingredients.
- Pour into a lightly oiled 4-cup mold.
- Chill until firm.
- Unmold salad and garnish with apple slices, grapes and orange sections if desired.

Sweet Basil Oil
2 cups

Great way to preserve the fresh flavor of basil leaves.

1/4 cup chopped basil leaves
2 cups olive oil

- Pound basil briefly with a mortar and pestle.
- Add a little olive oil and pound again.
- Mix with remaining oil and pour into a wide-mouthed bottle.
- Seal tightly.
- Let sit for 2 weeks, shaking every 2 or 3 days.
- Do not strain.
- Use in salad dressing or drizzle over pizzas just before serving.

Salads

Poppy Seed Toss
10 servings

1 bunch broccoli
1 head cauliflower
1 medium yellow squash
1 medium zucchini
5 bananas
½ cup walnuts, halved
2 red apples
½ cup raisins
Poppy Seed Dressing:
⅓ cup red wine vinegar
¾ cup sugar
1 teaspoon salt
1 teaspoon dry mustard
1 small onion, minced
2 tablespoons poppy seeds
1 cup vegetable oil

- Separate broccoli and cauliflower into florets, chopping some broccoli stems.
- Thinly slice squash and zucchini.
- Place in a large container and set aside.
- In a blender or food processor, mix all dressing ingredients, except oil.
- Add oil slowly while processing or blending.
- Dressing will thicken.
- Pour generous amount of dressing over broccoli, squash, cauliflower and zucchini; reserve remaining dressing.
- Toss, cover and marinate salad in refrigerator overnight.
- When ready to serve, drain and discard dressing.
- Slice bananas and cut unpeeled apples into 1-inch cubes.
- Combine fruit, nuts and vegetables.
- Add reserved dressing; toss and serve.

Zesty Artichoke Salad
4 servings

⅓ cup salad oil
2 teaspoons red wine vinegar
4 teaspoons fresh lemon juice
1½ teaspoons salt
1 teaspoon sugar
¼ teaspoon pepper
1 head romaine or Bibb lettuce
1 14-ounce can artichoke hearts
¼ cup crumbled bleu cheese

- In a large bowl, combine first 6 ingredients and mix well.
- Remove 6 outer leaves from lettuce; rinse and set aside.
- Rinse and tear remaining lettuce into small pieces; drizzle with dressing.
- Drain artichokes and halve; add to lettuce.
- Add bleu cheese; stir well.
- Line a bowl with reserved lettuce leaves.
- Spoon salad into bowl and serve.

Summer Salad 6 servings

1 pound small zucchini, cut into julienne strips
1 pound small yellow summer squash, cut into julienne strips
1 large head romaine lettuce
½ red onion, sliced and separated into rings
salt and freshly ground pepper
freshly grated Parmesan cheese
Vinaigrette Dressing:
grated rind of 2 lemons
⅓ cup fresh lemon juice
½ cup salad oil
2 tablespoons chopped fresh parsley
salt and freshly ground pepper

- Blanch squash in boiling water about 1½ minutes; drain and rinse with cold water; drain again and pat dry.
- Cover and refrigerate until ready to toss salad.
- Clean lettuce leaves under cool water, drain well.
- Reserve outer leaves for garnish.
- Remove ribs and tear leaves into bite-size pieces.
- Place all dressing ingredients in a jar with a tight fitting lid and shake.
- Mix onion, squash, and ½ cup Vinaigrette Dressing in large bowl.
- Marinate for 10 minutes.
- Mix in lettuce leaves and onions; add enough Vinaigrette Dressing to coat.
- Season with salt and pepper.
- Line a serving tray with reserved lettuce leaves, mound salad in center, grate cheese over all and serve.

Herbal Oil 2 cups

2 cups olive oil or walnut oil
2 branches rosemary
6 sprigs thyme
1 large clove garlic
1 green chili pepper
5 to 6 small red chili peppers
6 whole black peppercorns
6 juniper berries

- Place all ingredients in a jar with cork stopper.
- Place on a sunny window sill for 1 to 2 weeks and stir occasionally.
- Do not remove herbs.
- Use in dressings as a flavorable substitute for vegetable oil.

Salade Niçoise

6 servings

4 medium red potatoes
½ teaspoon salt
2 cups cauliflower florets
1 cup diced green beans
8 asparagus spears
⅓ cup diced red bell pepper
½ cup extra virgin olive oil
¼ cup vegetable oil
¼ cup fresh lemon juice
½ teaspoon Dijon mustard
salt and freshly ground pepper
¼ cup sliced black olives
1 tablespoon drained capers
leaf lettuce
cracked black pepper
chopped fresh parsley

- Cut potatoes into 1-inch cubes.
- Cook in a small amount of salted water until tender.
- Remove from heat and drain.
- Steam cauliflower and green beans for 8 minutes or until tender crisp.
- Rinse under cold water and drain well.
- Pare asparagus spears and cut into ½-inch pieces.
- Steam asparagus for 5 minutes, or until tender crisp, adding red bell pepper the last 2 minutes.
- Rinse with cold water and drain.
- Whisk oils, lemon juice and mustard in a small bowl until smooth.
- Season to taste with salt and pepper.
- If desired, the vegetables and dressing may be separately covered and refrigerated overnight.
- At least 4 hours before serving, pour dressing over vegetables and stir in olives and capers.
- Refrigerate covered and gently toss twice during chilling time.
- Serve cold on leaf lettuce leaves with cracked black pepper and a sprinkle of fresh parsley.

Remember This:

When cooking cauliflower, avoid odors by adding a slice of bread.

Salads

Steak And Mushroom Salad

4 servings

1 head Boston lettuce, torn into bite-size pieces
12 small fresh mushrooms, sliced
1½ pounds cooked steak or roast beef, sliced thin
12 cherry tomatoes, halved
1 14-ounce can artichoke hearts, drained and halved
2 tablespoons chopped fresh parsley
3 tablespoons bleu cheese, crumbled
Dressing:
½ cup olive oil
¼ cup red wine vinegar
2 tablespoons Dijon mustard
freshly ground pepper
1 garlic clove, crushed
1 teaspoon salt
½ teaspoon sugar

- Arrange lettuce on salad plates and top with remaining salad ingredients.
- Combine dressing ingredients in a jar with a tight fitting lid and shake well.
- Drizzle dressing over salad just before serving.

Arabic Salad

6 to 8 servings

Fast and fabulous!

1 head cabbage
1½ teaspoons salt
2 cloves garlic
1½ tablespoons fresh lemon juice
¼ to ½ cup olive oil

- Finely slice or shred cabbage.
- Grind salt and garlic cloves with a mortar and pestle.
- Add lemon juice and mix.
- Pour over cabbage and toss.
- Drizzle olive oil over cabbage and toss again.

Salads

Sesame, Beef And Broccoli Salad

4 servings

1 bunch broccoli, 1½ pounds
½ cup sesame oil, divided
8 ounces fresh mushrooms, sliced
¼ cup white vinegar
¼ cup soy sauce
1 tablespoon honey
1 clove garlic, finely chopped
1 pound deli roast beef or cooked steak, sliced
1 8-ounce can sliced water chestnuts, drained
1 tablespoon toasted sesame seeds

- Divide broccoli into florets; cut stems diagonally into ½-inch lengths.
- Stir fry broccoli stems in ¼ cup oil in a large skillet for 2 minutes.
- Add florets, cover and cook for 4 minutes or until tender crisp.
- Transfer to a large serving bowl.
- Stir fry mushrooms in remaining ¼ cup oil for 4 minutes.
- Add to broccoli.
- Stir together vinegar, soy sauce, honey and garlic.
- Pour over vegetables and mix well.
- Slice beef into ¼-inch strips.
- Stir in beef and water chestnuts and mix well; chill.
- Sprinkle with sesame seeds just before serving.
- May be prepared 1 day ahead.

Our Favorite Mayonnaise

1 cup

1 large egg, room temperature
1 teaspoon sugar
1 teaspoon salt
1 teaspoon prepared mustard
½ teaspoon celery seed
¼ to ½ teaspoon freshly ground pepper
1 tablespoon white wine vinegar or lemon juice
1¼ cups vegetable oil

- In a food processor or blender, process first 7 ingredients for 2 or 3 seconds, continue to process or blend while slowly adding oil in a steady thin stream.
- Do not turn off machine during the addition of oil.
- Mayonnaise will thicken.
- Cover and refrigerate until ready to use.

Herbed Vinegar

½ gallon

Create a piquant combination of herbs and spices for zestier salad dressings.

2 heaping cups chopped fresh herbs (green basil leaves, purple basil leaves, tarragon, chervil, shallots, or garlic chives)
½ gallon white vinegar
2 to 3 cloves garlic

- Note: Chervil and shallots or garlic chives may be combined to measure 2 cups.
- Using a half gallon jar with non-metallic lid, fill with herbs.
- Heat white vinegar to almost boiling.
- Pour vinegar in herb-filled jar and let cool for several hours.
- Screw on lid and shake jar.
- Let vinegar steep in a cool dark place for at least 3 weeks shaking jar once a week.
- Strain vinegar through a cheese cloth to remove herbs.
- Return herb-flavored vinegar to jar and place a fresh identifying sprig of herb in jar.
- Use for dressing or as desired.
- If using rosemary, sage or oregano, substitute red wine vinegar.

French Dressing

2½ cups

½ cup vegetable oil
⅓ cup catsup
¼ cup cider vinegar
⅛ cup fresh lemon juice
1 small onion, quartered
¾ teaspoon garlic salt
⅓ cup sugar
1 teaspoon paprika

- Place all ingredients in a food processor fitted with a metal blade.
- Process until onion is minced.
- Refrigerate until completely chilled.
- Will keep in a covered jar for 2 weeks.

Salads

Creole Shrimp Salad

8 servings

2 pounds large shrimp, cooked and shelled
⅔ cup finely chopped celery
¼ cup thinly sliced green onions
2 tablespoons finely chopped chives
2 cups salad oil
½ cup chili sauce
3 tablespoons lemon juice
2 tablespoons horseradish
1 tablespoon prepared mustard
½ teaspoon paprika
½ teaspoon salt
1 or 2 dashes Tabasco
lettuce

- Refrigerate cooked shrimp until chilled.
- Add celery, onion and chives to shrimp.
- Combine salad oil, chili sauce, lemon juice, horseradish, prepared mustard, paprika, salt and Tabasco.
- Pour over shrimp, mix gently, and cover.
- Refrigerate for 12 hours, stirring 2 or 3 times.
- Serve in lettuce cups or on a bed of shredded lettuce.

Chicken Asparagus Salad

6 to 8 servings

3 cups cooked chicken breast, cubed
1½ cups chopped celery
½ cup chopped onion
¾ cup mayonnaise
1 teaspoon fresh lemon juice
½ teaspoon curry powder
¼ teaspoon salt
⅛ teaspoon white pepper
1 pound fresh asparagus, cooked and chilled

- Combine chicken, celery and onion; toss well.
- Combine mayonnaise, lemon juice, curry, salt and white pepper.
- Add to chicken mixture and stir.
- Chill for 3 to 4 hours.
- Spoon over asparagus and serve.

Paella Salad

8 servings

1 7-ounce package yellow rice mix
2 tablespoons tarragon vinegar
⅓ cup oil
⅛ teaspoon salt
⅛ teaspoon dry mustard
salt to taste
1 teaspoon Old Bay Seasoning
1 cup shrimp
2 cups chicken, cooked and diced
1 tomato, peeled, seeded, and chopped
1 green bell pepper, chopped
½ cup minced onion
⅓ cup sliced celery
1 tablespoon salt
1 pound smoked sausage, cooked and sliced, optional
½ cup sliced ripe olives, optional
1 cup frozen baby English peas, optional

- Cook rice according to package directions.
- Combine vinegar, oil, and ⅛ teaspoon salt.
- Mix with cooked rice and cool to room temperature.
- Add mustard, salt and Old Bay Seasoning to 2 quarts boiling water.
- Cook shrimp in seasoned water until just pink; drain, shell and devein.
- Add chicken, shrimp, tomato, green bell pepper, onion, celery, 1 tablespoon salt, and any or all of optional ingredients to rice.
- Toss and chill before serving.

Remember This:

Tomatoes are more flavorful when served at room temperature. Ripening tomatoes at room temperature is best since cool temperatures stop the ripening process.

Salads

Wild Rice And Chicken Salad

10 servings

2 6-ounce packages long grain and wild rice
3½ cups cooked and cubed chicken
1 4¼-ounce can ripe olives, drained and chopped
½ cup chopped green onions, tops included
½ cup chopped pecans
1 cup chopped celery
1½ cups mayonnaise
salt and pepper to taste

- Cook rice according to package directions and cool.
- Combine chicken, olives, onions, pecans, celery and mayonnaise.
- Add mixture to rice.
- Mix well and season with salt and pepper.
- Refrigerate salad to chill.
- Remove from refrigerator 20 minutes before serving.

Chicken Salad Supreme

10 servings

10 chicken breast halves, boned and skinned
1 teaspoon rosemary, crushed
1 teaspoon thyme
1 teaspoon salt
¼ teaspoon freshly ground pepper
2 packages Italian salad dressing mix
1 cup crumbled, cooked bacon (about ½ to ¾ pound)
¼ cup slivered almonds
1⅓ cups green grapes, halved
3 tablespoons mayonnaise
2 teaspoons prepared mustard
lettuce leaves or cantaloupe slices

- In a large skillet filled almost half full of water, place chicken, rosemary, thyme, salt and pepper.
- Cook over medium heat until chicken is done.
- Prepare Italian dressing according to package directions and pour dressing into a 3-quart shallow dish.
- Place hot chicken in dressing and marinate for at least 3 hours; remove and cube chicken.
- Discard dressing reserving 2 tablespoons; toss with cubed chicken.
- Combine chicken, bacon, almonds and grapes.
- Stir together mayonnaise and mustard and add to salad, one tablespoon at a time, until salad holds together.
- Serve over cantaloupe slices or on lettuce.

Curried Turkey Salad

6 servings

May substitute chicken for turkey.

2 cups turkey, cooked and cubed
1 large celery stalk, thinly sliced
½ cup slivered almonds
¼ cup golden raisins
1 green onion, thinly sliced
2 tablespoons mango chutney
4 tablespoons curry mayonnaise
Curry Mayonnaise:
3 tablespoons mayonnaise
1 tablespoon curry powder
1 tablespoon Dijon mustard
1 teaspoon fresh lemon juice
1 large clove garlic, minced
red leaf lettuce
mayonnaise
Garnishes:
hard-cooked eggs, halved; boiled new potatoes sliced thin; cucumber slices; fresh pineapple or melon chunks; tart apple slices; blanched vegetables

- Combine turkey, celery, almonds, raisins, green onion and chutney in a medium bowl.
- Mix Curry Mayonnaise ingredients in a small bowl.
- Add 2 tablespoons Curry Mayonnaise to salad and toss to blend.
- Spoon turkey mixture over lettuce leaves.
- Arrange any or all garnishes in pairs around salad.
- Thin remaining 2 tablespoons Curry Mayonnaise with mayonnaise and pass as a sauce for garnishes.

Remember This:

For perfect hard-cooked eggs, cover eggs with cold water and bring to a boil. Remove from heat and place a tight fitting lid on sauce pan. Set timer for 20 minutes.

Salads

Elegant Turkey Salad
12 servings

2 cups mayonnaise
2 tablespoons soy sauce
2 tablespoons curry powder
2 tablespoons fresh lemon juice
2 quarts cooked turkey breast, (2½-3 pound breast) coarsely cut
1 20-ounce can water chestnuts, sliced and drained
2 cups sliced celery
½ teaspoon paprika
4 8-ounce cans well-drained pineapple tidbits
⅔ cup toasted slivered almonds
1 head Bibb or Boston lettuce
toasted almonds and pineapple

- Make dressing by combining mayonnaise, soy sauce, curry powder, and lemon juice in a small bowl; mix well.
- Combine turkey, water chestnuts, celery, paprika, pineapple and almonds; toss with dressing.
- Chill for 2 to 3 hours.
- Spoon into nests of Bibb or Boston lettuce.
- Garnish with toasted almonds and pineapple tidbits.
- Seedless grapes may be substituted for pineapple, or 1 pound each of pineapple and grapes may be used.

Broccoli And Walnut Salad
6 to 8 servings

1 large bunch broccoli
6 to 8 oranges, peeled and sectioned
1 8-ounce bag walnut halves
Dressing:
1 tablespoon Dijon mustard
4 tablespoons red wine vinegar
1 teaspoon sugar
½ teaspoon salt
½ teaspoon freshly ground pepper
½ cup olive oil
fresh chopped parsley and/or chives to taste

- Cut broccoli into florets, and steam for 4 minutes or until emerald green and crispy..
- Place broccoli in a bowl and cool.
- Add orange sections to broccoli.
- Coarsely chop walnuts and add to salad; chill.
- To prepare dressing, mix together all ingredients in a covered container and shake.
- Add dressing to salad just before serving and toss.
- Dressing will keep for several days in refrigerator.

Popular Potato Salad

8 servings

3 pounds red potatoes, halved
salt and freshly ground pepper
5 green onions, finely chopped, including 1/3 green tops
1 cup frozen baby green peas, thawed
1 cup chopped celery
1/4 cup fresh chopped parsley
1 3-ounce jar real bacon bits
3/4 cup mayonnaise
1 teaspoon Dijon mustard

- Cook potatoes until tender, about 15 to 20 minutes.
- Drain and let cool.
- Cube potatoes and season with salt and pepper.
- Add onions, peas, celery, parsley and bacon.
- Mix mayonnaise and mustard together.
- Stir into salad.
- Refrigerate to combine flavors for several hours.

Yellow Rice Salad

8 servings

1 10-ounce package yellow rice mix
2 14-ounce cans artichoke hearts, drained and coarsely chopped
5 green onions, sliced (including 1/3 of green tops)
1/2 cup diced red bell pepper
1/2 cup sliced black olives
tomato wedges for garnish
Dressing:
2 tablespoons extra virgin olive oil
1 tablespoon basil vinegar
2 tablespoons minced fresh parsley
1/2 teaspoon paprika
1 to 2 cloves garlic, pressed
1/2 teaspoon salt
1/8 teaspoon freshly ground pepper

- Prepare rice according to package directions and cool.
- Prepare dressing by combining all ingredients in a blender.
- Pour dressing over artichokes and marinate for at least 1 hour.
- Mix cooled rice with all ingredients and toss to combine.
- Chill for several hours to combine flavors.
- Allow salad to stand at room temperature for 30 minutes before serving.
- Garnish with tomato wedges.

Coleslaw With Celery Seed Dressing

10 servings

1 large head cabbage
1 carrot, peeled
1 small onion, finely chopped
1½ tablespoons salad oil
¾ cup mayonnaise
¼ cup sugar
2 tablespoons cider vinegar
½ teaspoon celery seed
1½ tablespoons prepared mustard
¼ teaspoon salt

- Remove outer loose leaves of cabbage.
- Rinse, drain and reserve.
- Shred cabbage and carrot.
- Combine cabbage, carrot, and onion; toss.
- In a medium bowl, whisk oil, mayonnaise, sugar, cider vinegar, celery seed, mustard, and salt.
- Pour dressing over slaw and toss well.
- Cover and refrigerate to chill thoroughly before serving.
- Line serving bowl with reserved leaves.
- With slotted spoon, transfer slaw into bowl and serve.
- If preparing slaw 5 to 6 hours before serving, toss cabbage, carrot and onion with oil, cover and refrigerate.
- Mix dressing as directed omitting oil and refrigerate.
- Dress slaw 1 hour before serving.

Twenty-Four Hour Coleslaw

8 servings

Stores well for a week in the refrigerator.

1 head cabbage, green or purple
1 onion
1 green bell pepper, seeded
1 cup apple cider vinegar
1½ cups sugar
1 cup salad oil
1 tablespoon celery seed
1 teaspoon salt

- Hand grate cabbage, onion and green bell pepper.
- Combine next 5 ingredients together and bring to a boil.
- Pour over cabbage mixture and marinate in refrigerator overnight.

Salads

Herb Tomatoes

10 servings

6 medium ripe tomatoes
2/3 cup salad oil
1/4 cup Herbed Vinegar
2 to 3 tablespoons sugar
1/4 cup fresh chopped parsley
1/4 cup finely chopped green onions
1 to 2 teaspoons salt
1/4 teaspoon pepper
2 tablespoons dried thyme
1/4 tablespoon dried marjoram
1 clove garlic, minced

- Peel and cut tomatoes into wedges; set aside.
- In a blender, combine oil, vinegar, and sugar.
- Remove from blender and add parsley, green onions, salt, pepper, thyme, marjoram and garlic.
- Pour over tomatoes and refrigerate for 1 to 2 hours.

Tomato And Feta Salad

8 servings

2 cloves garlic, peeled
2 pints cherry tomatoes, halved
1/2 cup pitted ripe olives
1 1/2 cups crumbled feta cheese
1/3 cup olive oil
1/2 cup plus 2 teaspoons wine vinegar
1 teaspoon dried whole oregano
1 teaspoon dried whole thyme
salt and pepper to taste

- Rub inside of salad bowl with garlic; discard garlic.
- Combine tomatoes, olives, and cheese in salad bowl.
- Combine remaining ingredients in a jar, cover tightly and shake vigorously.
- Pour over tomato mixture, tossing gently.
- Refrigerate for at least 4 hours.

Lighter Entrées

Spinach Lasagna

10 servings

Distinctive enough for company.

3 tablespoons olive oil
1 bell pepper, seeded and chopped
3 cloves garlic, chopped
2 28-ounce cans whole tomatoes, chopped
2 6-ounce cans tomato paste
1 tablespoon dried oregano
1 tablespoon Italian herbs
1 tablespoon thyme
½ teaspoon black pepper
2 bay leaves
pinch of sugar and salt
2 10-ounce packages frozen chopped spinach
2 cups freshly grated Parmesan cheese, divided
2 pounds mozzarella cheese, shredded
8 to 10 fresh spinach or plain lasagna noodles, cooked

- To prepare tomato sauce, heat olive oil in a Dutch oven.
- Sauté garlic and bell pepper until tender.
- Add chopped whole tomatoes and paste.
- Add seasonings and simmer for several hours.
- Cook spinach according to package directions; drain well.
- Mix with 1 cup Parmesan cheese and set aside.
- To assemble, spread approximately 1 cup tomato sauce in a 9x13-inch baking dish.
- Layer with two spinach noodles, 6 to 9 tablespoons spinach mixture, and ⅓ mozzarella cheese.
- Repeat layers ending with tomato sauce.
- Top with noodles, tomato sauce and 1 cup Parmesan cheese.
- Bake at 350 degrees for 30 minutes.

Remember This:

When cooking pasta, add a small amount of vegetable oil to water to reduce splashing and prevent sticking. Add pasta all at once to boiling water.

Fettuccine Cabonara

4 to 8 servings

4 eggs
1/4 cup butter
1/4 cup heavy cream
1 pound fettuccine
1 cup crumbled, cooked bacon or 2 3 1/2 ounce packages pepperoni, cut into strips
1 cup freshly grated Parmesan cheese
1/4 cup chopped parsley
cracked pepper, to taste
1/2 cup mushrooms, sautéed (optional)

- Allow eggs, butter, and cream to come to room temperature.
- Beat together eggs and cream until blended.
- Cook pasta 10 to 12 minutes in boiling, salted water or if fresh fettuccine is used, cook for 2 minutes.
- Drain pasta and toss with butter, bacon, or pepperoni in a preheated 3-quart baking dish.
- Pour egg mixture over and toss.
- Add cheese, parsley and cracked pepper; toss to mix.
- Serve immediately topped with mushrooms, if desired.

Shrimp And Artichoke Fettuccine

4 servings

3 tablespoons butter
1 tablespoon olive oil
1 pound medium fresh shrimp, shelled and deveined
3 to 4 cloves garlic, crushed
1 14-ounce can artichoke hearts, drained and quartered
1/4 cup white wine
dash of salt and pepper
7 ounces fresh spinach fettuccine
4 tablespoons freshly grated Parmesan cheese

- Melt butter in a large skillet and add oil.
- Sauté shrimp and garlic in butter and oil for 1 to 2 minutes.
- Add artichokes and heat through.
- Add white wine, salt and pepper; and cook for 10 minutes.
- Drain shrimp and artichokes reserving liquid.
- Cook fettuccine; drain and place on a heated platter.
- Toss fettuccine with 1 cup reserved liquid, shrimp and artichokes.
- Sprinkle generously with Parmesan cheese.
- Serve immediately.

Eggplant And Salami Shells

4 to 6 servings

The sauce makes this an outstanding dish!

1½ pounds eggplant, peeled and cut into ½-inch pieces
1 teaspoon salt
2 2-ounce jars pimento, drained
⅓ cup chicken broth
¼ cup olive oil
1 clove garlic, minced
2 tablespoons freshly minced basil
1 tablespoon fresh lemon juice
½ teaspoon salt
½ teaspoon freshly ground pepper
1 small onion, chopped
3 tablespoons olive oil
1 15-ounce container ricotta cheese
¾ cup chopped Genoa salami
1 cup coarsely grated mozzarella cheese
3 tablespoons Parmesan cheese
1 large egg
⅓ cup freshly minced basil
¾ pound dried jumbo pasta shells

- Preheat oven to 350 degrees.
- Toss eggplant with salt in a colander.
- Cover with a plate and press; let drain for 30 minutes.
- In a blender, purée pimento with broth, ¼ cup olive oil, garlic, 2 tablespoons basil, lemon juice, salt and pepper.
- Store sauce, covered.
- In a large skillet over moderate heat, cook onion in 3 tablespoons olive oil until soft.
- Add eggplant and cook until thoroughly heated.
- In a bowl, combine ricotta, salami, mozzarella, Parmesan, egg, ⅓ cup basil, and eggplant mixture; correct seasonings.
- Cook shells in boiling water until al dente; drain.
- Spread half of sauce in bottom of a large baking dish.
- Stuff shells with eggplant mixture and arrange over sauce.
- Bake, tightly covered, for 30 minutes.
- Serve with remaining sauce.

Remember This:

To cook pasta in advance, drain well and toss with oil. Cover with a damp cloth and refrigerate. Just before serving, dip pasta in boiling water for 1 to 2 seconds.

Vegetable Pizza 4 servings

A showcase of color and flavor.

2 cups carrots, sliced on the diagonal
3 tablespoons butter
1 small onion, chopped
1 large clove garlic, minced
4½ cups sliced zucchini (about 4 small)
½ teaspoon salt
¼ teaspoon pepper
¼ teaspoon dried basil
¼ teaspoon dried oregano
¼ teaspoon dried thyme
2 rounds pita bread
2 medium tomatoes, seeded and chopped
12 ounces mozzarella or Havarti cheese, sliced or shredded

- Preheat oven to 425 degrees.
- Place carrots in a saucepan with a small amount of water.
- Bring to a boil and reduce heat to medium-low; cook for 8 minutes.
- In a large skillet, melt butter and sauté onion and garlic.
- Add zucchini, carrots, salt, pepper and herbs to skillet and stir.
- Cover vegetables and simmer for 15 minutes.
- Stir occasionally.
- Slice pita bread in half to make 4 rounds and place on a cookie sheet.
- For a crisp pizza crust, lightly brown one side of sliced pita bread.
- Stir tomatoes into vegetable mixture and divide between the 4 pita rounds.
- Cover with cheese and bake for 3 to 5 minutes or until cheese melts.

Classic Pesto 6 servings

⅓ cup pine nuts
1 large clove garlic, coarsely chopped
2 cups fresh basil leaves
½ cup extra virgin olive oil
½ cup freshly grated Parmesan cheese
salt to taste

- Place pine nuts and garlic in food processor; process until finely chopped. Add half the basil and process until coarsely chopped.
- Add remaining basil.
- With machine still running, pour oil in steady, thin stream through feed tube.
- Transfer pesto to mixing bowl and fold in cheese and salt with spatula.

Garden Frittata   6 servings

Substitute your favorite vegetables.

6 tablespoons butter, divided
1 medium onion, thinly sliced
1 cup peeled and cubed potatoes
salt and pepper to taste
1 tablespoon minced fresh basil
2 cups cubed zucchini
1 cup tomatoes, peeled, seeded, chopped and well drained
1 cup coarsely chopped red or green bell pepper, or ½ cup of each
6 eggs
dash of Tabasco
2 cups shredded Monterey Jack cheese

- In an ovenproof skillet, melt 3 tablespoons butter.
- Add onions and potatoes and cook until slightly tender and browned.
- Stir in salt, pepper and basil.
- Add zucchini; cook for 5 minutes.
- Blend in tomatoes and peppers and cook for 10 minutes until most of the liquid has evaporated.
- Add remaining butter to bottom of pan.
- Beat eggs well and add Tabasco.
- Preheat broiler in oven.
- Pour eggs over vegetables, lifting vegetables so eggs can settle.
- Cook for 5 minutes, until eggs are set.
- Sprinkle cheese over mixture and place under broiler until cheese bubbles.
- Let cool for 5 minutes; cut into wedges and serve.

Sausage Egg Casserole   8 servings

Must be prepared a day ahead.

6 large eggs
2 cups milk
1 teaspoon salt
6 slices thin bread
1 pound bulk sausage, cooked and drained
1½ cups shredded Colby or Longhorn cheese

- Beat eggs, milk and salt together.
- Cube bread.
- Combine bread and egg mixture.
- Add cheese and cooked sausage.
- Stir and pour into a greased 9x13-inch baking dish.
- Cover and refrigerate overnight.
- Bake in preheated oven at 350 degrees for 45 minutes.

Spanakopeta 8 servings

1 10-ounce package frozen chopped spinach
16 ounces ricotta cheese
8 ounces feta cheese, crumbled
½ cup freshly grated Parmesan cheese
4 eggs, beaten
1 cup sour cream
2 tablespoons flour
¾ cup chopped fresh parsley
½ cup chopped green onion
½ teaspoon salt
½ teaspoon pepper
dash nutmeg
1½ cups butter, melted
20 sheets phyllo dough, thawed

- Preheat oven to 325 degrees.
- Prepare spinach according to package instructions.
- Drain and squeeze water from spinach.
- Blend spinach with the ricotta, feta, Parmesan, eggs, sour cream, flour, parsley, onion, salt, pepper and nutmeg; set aside.
- Clear a large working area; assemble melted butter, phyllo dough, pastry brush and 9x13-inch greased baking dish.
- Layer overlapping phyllo in a clockwise direction, brushing each sheet with butter.
- Extend half of each sheet over edge of pan.
- Continue until all dough is used.
- Keep unused dough covered with a damp cloth to prevent drying out.
- Pour spinach mixture into phyllo.
- Fold each sheet over the spinach, working counterclockwise, brushing each sheet with butter.
- Freeze at this point if desired.
- Allow to thaw overnight in refrigerator.
- Bake for 45 minutes until golden.
- Let cool for 10 minutes before serving.

Walnut Soufflé 4 to 6 servings

A dramatic dish that will appeal to all tastes.

2 tablespoons butter
1 clove garlic, pressed
½ medium onion, minced
pinch of thyme
3 tablespoons flour
1 cup tomato purée
½ cup half and half
¾ cup finely ground walnuts
1 cup shredded Cheddar cheese, Colby or Longhorn may be substituted
¼ teaspoon dry mustard
salt and freshly ground pepper to taste
4 egg yolks, slightly beaten
6 egg whites
⅛ teaspoon cream of tartar
pinch of salt

- Preheat oven to 400 degrees.
- Melt butter in a heavy saucepan.
- Sauté garlic and onion until transparent.
- Stir in pinch of thyme and flour.
- Let cook for 2 to 3 minutes, then stir in tomato purée and half and half.
- Whisk to smooth sauce.
- When heated and thick, add walnuts and cheese while beating with whisk.
- Remove from heat and beat in mustard, salt, pepper and egg yolks; set aside.
- Beat egg whites, cream of tartar and salt until whites are stiff, but not dry.
- Stir ⅓ of whites into sauce.
- Fold remaining whites gently into sauce.
- Spoon soufflé into a 6 cup, buttered soufflé dish.
- Place in oven on lowest rack and turn oven down immediately to 375 degrees.
- Bake for 35 to 40 minutes.
- Serve immediately.

Remember This:

To reduce mold growth on cheese, wipe cheese with vinegar and store in an airtight container with two lumps of sugar.

Green Chili Cheese Bake

6 servings

A melt in your mouth texture!

1 pound medium Cheddar cheese, shredded
1 pound Monterey Jack cheese, shredded
2 4-ounce cans green chilies, chopped and drained
2 tablespoons flour
1 12-ounce can evaporated milk
4 eggs, slightly beaten
1 teaspoon salt
1 large tomato, sliced

- Preheat oven to 325 degrees.
- Layer cheese and peppers in a 9x13-inch shallow dish.
- Mix flour and enough milk to make a paste; add remaining milk.
- Stir together eggs, flour mixture and salt.
- Pour over cheese and peppers.
- Bake for 30 minutes.
- After 30 minutes, top with sliced tomato and bake for an additional 15 minutes.
- Serve warm or at room temperature.

Breakfast Burritos

6 servings

Too delicious to reserve only for breakfast

1 pound hot, bulk sausage
½ medium onion, finely chopped
1 jalapeño pepper, finely chopped
1 medium potato, diced
salt and pepper to taste
6 eggs, beaten
6 to 8 flour tortillas
Salsa or Picante sauce

- Brown sausage in a heavy skillet, stirring to break sausage apart.
- When sausage is slightly browned, add onion and jalapeño pepper and cook for 2 to 3 minutes.
- Stir in diced potatoes and cook for about 10 more minutes, until sausage is thoroughly cooked.
- Drain off all excess fat.
- Add eggs, salt and pepper and scramble all ingredients until eggs are cooked.
- Spoon filling into tortillas and roll up burrito style.
- May be served with Salsa or Picante sauce.

Perfect Cheese Soufflé

4 servings

½ cup butter
¼ cup flour
½ teaspoon salt
1 cup milk
½ pound sharp Cheddar cheese, shredded
4 large eggs, separated

- Preheat oven to 325 degrees.
- Melt butter in a heavy skillet over medium heat.
- Add flour and salt; cook stirring constantly for 2 minutes.
- Slowly add milk, stirring constantly, until all milk is combined and mixture is thick.
- Add cheese and stir until melted.
- Remove skillet from heat.
- Beat egg whites until stiff, but not dry, and set aside.
- Beat egg yolks in a medium mixing bowl.
- Slowly add cheese sauce to egg yolks while beating.
- Fold egg whites into yolk mixture.
- Pour into an ungreased 2½-quart soufflé or baking dish and place on lowest rack in a 325 degree oven for 1 hour.
- Serve immediately.

Remember This:

Sharp cheese is a must for a rich tasting soufflé.

Swiss Cheese Mushroom Quiche

6 servings

1 9-inch pie pastry, unbaked
1½ cup shredded Swiss or Cheddar cheese
1 medium onion, chopped
¼ pound mushrooms, chopped
salt and pepper to taste
dash of thyme
3 tablespoons butter, melted
4 eggs
1½ cups milk
3 tablespoons flour
½ teaspoon salt
¼ teaspoon dry mustard
paprika

- Preheat oven to 375 degrees.
- Cover bottom of pie crust with cheese.
- Sauté onions, mushrooms, salt, pepper and thyme in melted butter until onions are transparent.
- Cover cheese with mushroom mixture.
- Beat together eggs, milk, flour, salt and dry mustard.
- Pour over mushroom layer and sprinkle with paprika.
- Bake for 40 to 45 minutes, or until firm in the center.
- Set aside for 5 to 10 minutes before serving.
- Other vegetables such as broccoli or cauliflower may be substituted for the mushrooms for variety.

Feta Cheese And Leek Tart

4 to 6 servings

A specatcular meatless main dish.

Cheese Crust:
1⅓ cups flour
1 bunch chives or 3 scallions, thinly sliced
½ teaspoon paprika
8 ounces feta cheese
¼ cup butter
3 to 4 tablespoons ice water

- To prepare crust, place flour, half of chives or scallions and paprika in a medium mixing bowl; stir to combine.
- Add 2 ounces feta cheese and butter.
- Cut in cheese and butter with pastry blender until mixture resembles coarse crumbs.
- Lightly mix in enough ice water for the dough to hold together.

Continued

Feta Cheese And Leek Tart (continued)

Filling:
1 tablespoon olive oil
6 small or 3 large leeks (white part only), rinsed and coarsely chopped
1 clove garlic, minced
½ teaspoon salt
freshly ground pepper to taste
1 cup half and half
2 large eggs
pinch of cayenne pepper

- Knead dough lightly and gather into a ball.
- Roll dough out to an 11-inch circle on a lightly floured surface.
- Coat a 10-inch tart or 9-inch pie pan lightly with butter or vegetable spray.
- Line pan with dough and press sides.
- Refrigerate until cold; at least 1 hour.
- To prepare filling, heat oil in a medium skillet.
- Add leeks and garlic; reduce heat.
- Cook covered until soft and golden.
- Stir in salt and pepper to taste.
- Remove from heat and set aside.
- Prick chilled crust with fork.
- Bake crust for 10 minutes at 375 degrees.
- While crust is baking, whisk half and half, eggs and cayenne pepper together until smooth.
- Brush crust with a little egg mixture and bake for another 2 minutes.
- Sprinkle leek mixture and remaining chives in shell.
- Crumble remaining cheese and sprinkle evenly into shell.
- Pour egg mixture over all.
- Bake on baking sheet for 25 to 30 minutes until puffed and golden.

Fresh Tomato Sauce

3 to 3½ cups

This makes a light summer meal.

5 to 6 large ripe tomatoes
¼ cup olive oil
3 cloves garlic, minced
2 tablespoons minced fresh basil or 1 teaspoon dried basil
1 teaspoon dried oregano
salt and freshly ground pepper
1 pound fresh pasta
freshly grated Parmesan or Romano cheese

- Peel tomatoes by submerging whole tomatoes in boiling water for 1 minute.
- Drain tomatoes and slip off skins.
- Cut out the stem end of each tomato; seed and chop coarsely.
- Heat olive oil in a heavy skillet over medium heat.
- Add garlic and sauté for 4 minutes.
- Add tomatoes, basil, oregano, salt and pepper.
- Simmer tomato sauce for 15 minutes, stirring occasionally.
- Serve sauce over favorite fresh pasta and sprinkle with freshly grated cheese.

Cheddar And Bacon Soup

2 quarts

5 slices bacon
½ cup grated carrots
½ cup finely chopped celery
½ cup finely chopped onion
½ cup finely chopped green pepper
¼ cup flour
4 cups chicken stock
3 cups shredded sharp Cheddar cheese
2 cups milk
1 tablespoon dry sherry
5 ounces pimento-stuffed olives, chopped
salt and pepper to taste

- In a large pan, fry bacon until crisp; drain and reserve drippings.
- Crumble bacon and set aside.
- Sauté carrots, celery, onion and green pepper in bacon drippings until tender, not brown.
- Blend in flour and gradually add stock.
- Cook over low heat until mixture thickens and boils.
- Continue cooking about 5 minutes.
- Add cheese and stir until melted.
- Stir in milk, sherry and olives; simmer for 10 minutes.
- Season to taste and serve garnished with crumbled bacon.

Asparagus Soup

4 servings

24 to 30 pencil-thin asparagus spears
1/4 cup butter
1 cup chopped onions
2 cloves garlic, minced
1 tablespoon flour
2 cups chicken stock or broth, warmed
1/8 teaspoon freshly ground pepper
1/2 teaspoon salt
1/2 cup finely minced parsley
2 fresh basil leaves
1/2 cup whipping cream
1 small seeded and peeled tomato, chopped for garnish (optional)

- Trim woody ends of asparagus and cut stalks into 2-inch lengths.
- Trim and reserve tips.
- Steam asparagus tips for 3 to 5 minutes.
- Rinse tips in cold water.
- Drain well and refrigerate for garnish.
- Melt butter in a large saucepan.
- Add onions and garlic.
- Sauté over medium-low heat, until onions are transparent, about 10 minutes.
- Add flour and cook, stirring constantly for 3 minutes.
- Add warmed broth slowly, stirring constantly.
- Add asparagus stems, parsley, seasonings, and basil.
- Bring to a boil.
- Reduce heat to a simmer and cook covered for 30 minutes.
- Cool asparagus soup slightly and purée in batches.
- Strain in a medium sieve to remove woody pieces.
- Add cream and reheat gently if serving hot, refrigerate if serving cold.
- Garnish servings with several of reserved asparagus tips and chopped tomato, if desired.
- May be made the day before.

Carrot Soup
6 to 8 serivngs

Chef Jack Shoop's special recipe.

½ cup clarified butter
(½ cup butter and ½ cup oil may be substituted)
8 carrots, peeled and sliced
2 medium white onions, sliced
1 medium turnip root, peeled and sliced
1½ quarts chicken stock
1 large potato, peeled and sliced
1 pint whipping cream
salt and pepper

- To clarify butter, melt over low heat.
- When completely melted, remove from heat.
- Let stand for a few minutes, allowing milk solids to settle to the bottom.
- Skim butter fat from the top and place in a container.
- Discard milk solids.
- Put ¼-inch to ½-inch clarified butter in bottom of a large Dutch oven.
- Add carrots, onions, and turnips.
- Cook covered without boiling for 10 minutes.
- Add potato and stock and cook until tender, about 45 minutes.
- Drain and reserve liquid.
- Purée vegetables and return to stock.
- Add cream, salt and pepper.
- Serve warm.

Remember This:

Use ice cube trays to freeze small amounts of stock. Pop out when frozen and store in freezer bags.

Cold Yellow Squash Soup

6 servings

1½ pounds small yellow squash
2 packages Martha Washington Golden Seasoning
white pepper
2 to 2½ cups half and half
fresh dill
sour cream

- Wash squash and remove bloom and stem ends.
- Cook whole squash in a small amount of water in a covered skillet until very tender.
- Place cooked squash in a food processor fitted with a metal blade.
- Sprinkle Golden Seasoning over all.
- Add pepper to taste and purée hot squash.
- Chill mixture well or freeze until ready to use.
- Stir half and half into chilled squash until desired consistency is achieved.
- Garnish individual servings with fresh dill sprigs and dollops of sour cream.

Corn And Sausage Chowder

6 servings

A hearty soup from the restaurant Annella's.

1 pound mild bulk sausage
1 large onion, chopped
3 large potatoes, peeled and cubed
2 teaspoons salt, or to taste
½ teaspoon pepper
1 teaspoon dried basil
2 cups water
1 17-ounce can cream style corn
1 16½-ounce can whole kernel corn, drained
1 12-ounce can evaporated milk

- Shape sausage into a large patty and brown for 5 minutes on each side in a large skillet.
- Drain off fat and break sausage into pieces.
- Put sausage pieces into a soup kettle.
- Return 2 tablespoons of fat to skillet and sauté onions.
- Add onions, potatoes, salt, pepper, basil and water to soup kettle.
- Cover and simmer for 15 minutes.
- Stir in corn and evaporated milk.
- Cover and heat thoroughly.

Cream Of Squash Soup

10 cups

The flavor is enhanced if made several days ahead.

¼ cup butter or margarine, melted
2 tablespoons vegetable oil
1 large onion, minced
2 cloves garlic, minced
3 pounds yellow squash, thinly sliced
3½ to 4 cups chicken stock
1 cup half and half
1½ teaspoons salt
½ teaspoon white pepper
chopped fresh parsley

- Combine butter and oil in a large Dutch oven.
- Add onion and garlic; sauté until tender.
- Stir in squash and chicken stock.
- Cover and simmer 15 to 20 minutes, or until squash is tender.
- Spoon ⅓ of squash mixture into container of electric blender, and process until smooth.
- Repeat with remaining squash mixture.
- Return squash mixture to Dutch oven.
- Stir in half and half, salt and pepper.
- Cook over low heat, stirring constantly until well heated.
- Serve hot or chilled and garnish with parsley.

Chilled Strawberry Soup

4 to 5 servings

Try serving in a Crimson Sweet carved watermelon.

2 cups unsweetened pineapple juice
⅓ cup sugar
2 cups strawberries, stems removed
½ cup claret or other wine
½ cup sour cream
mint leaves
whipped cream

- Place in a blender 1 cup of pineapple juice, sugar and strawberries.
- Cover and blend on high speed until smooth.
- Pour mixture into a bowl and add remaining pineapple juice, wine and sour cream.
- Serve in a large wine goblet or champagne glass.
- Garnish with mint leaves and top with a dollop of whipped cream.

Avocado Soup
6 servings

A unique combination of flavors that will delight your dinner guests.

½ cup chopped onion
⅓ cup minced celery
2 tablespoons butter
1 tablespoon flour
2 teaspoons curry powder, or to taste
2 cups chicken stock, warmed
1 Granny Smith apple, peeled, cored and chopped
1 ripe Florida avocado, peeled, pitted and cubed
2 cups half and half
salt to taste
avocado slices
red caviar, optional

- Sauté onion and celery in butter until limp.
- Stir in flour and curry powder.
- Cook, stirring constantly until blended for 1 minute.
- Slowly add chicken stock, stirring constantly.
- Add apple and reduce heat to low.
- Cook until apple is soft; about 15 minutes.
- Transfer mixture to a food processor and add avocado.
- Process mixture until smooth.
- Pour processed mixture into a large bowl.
- Add half and half and salt; stirring well.
- Cover soup with plastic wrap and refrigerate to chill thoroughly.
- Serve chilled and garnish with avocado slices and red caviar.

Cream Of Spinach Soup
6 servings

Perfect fare for light eating.

3 tablespoons sliced green onions
3 tablespoons butter
3 tablespoons flour
2 cups milk, warmed
1 cup half and half
salt and pepper to taste
dash nutmeg
2 cups cooked fresh spinach or 2 10-ounce packages frozen spinach, cooked and well drained
paprika

- Sauté onions in butter until soft.
- Add flour and stir until smooth; about 2 minutes.
- Stir in milk and cream slowly until sauce becomes thick.
- Add salt, pepper and nutmeg.
- Put spinach in a food processor and chop into small pieces.
- Mix with cream sauce.
- Reheat to serve.
- Garnish with paprika.

Beef Barley Vegetable Soup

8 to 10 servings

1½ to 2 pounds lean beef
vegetable oil
2 quarts water
4 teaspoons salt
¼ teaspoon pepper
1 tablespoon chopped fresh parsley
1 large onion, chopped
½ cup sliced celery
1 28-ounce can whole tomatoes, drained and cut up
1 8-ounce can tomato sauce
1 cup sliced carrots
2 potatoes, diced
1 cup sliced okra, peas or green beans
¼ cup barley

- Cut beef into ½-inch pieces.
- Brown in hot oil.
- Transfer browned meat to a large pot.
- Add water, seasonings, parsley, onion, celery, tomatoes and tomato sauce.
- Bring to a boil, reduce heat and simmer for 1 hour.
- Add carrots, potatoes and okra.
- Cook for another hour.
- Add barley and cook according to package directions.
- Does not freeze well.

Crab Bisque
4 to 6 servings

Serve with fresh baked Herb Bread and lots of butter.

- *1 medium onion, chopped*
- *2 tablespoons butter*
- *1 tablespoon flour*
- *1 10¾-ounce can tomato soup*
- *1½ quarts half and half*
- *2 tablespoons Bay Seasonings*
- *1 pound lump crabmeat, crumbled*
- *salt and freshly ground pepper to taste*
- *1 tablespoon dry sherry*

- Sauté onion in butter; do not brown.
- Add flour, stirring constantly to make a paste.
- Stir in tomato soup, half and half, Bay Seasonings and crabmeat.
- Blend in salt and pepper; heat until very hot, without boiling.
- Add sherry just before serving.

Shrimp Étoufée
4 servings

- *1 cup margarine*
- *1 cup finely chopped white onion*
- *½ cup finely chopped celery*
- *1 cup finely chopped green onions, including tops*
- *1 teaspoon minced garlic*
- *2 tablespoons flour*
- *1 16-ounce can tomatoes, drained mashed*
- *2 cups clam juice*
- *1 teaspoon salt*
- *¾ teaspoon pepper*
- *1 tablespoon Worcestershire sauce*
- *2 pounds uncooked medium shrimp, shelled and deveined*
- *1 cup long grain rice, cooked*

- In a large saucepan or skillet, melt margarine and sauté onions, celery and green onions until tender.
- Add garlic and cook for 1 more minute.
- Stir in flour, stirring constantly until golden brown.
- Add tomatoes and brown.
- Blend in clam juice and simmer for 10 minutes.
- Add salt, pepper, Worcestershire and shrimp.
- Cook over low heat for 15 to 20 minutes or until shrimp turn pink.
- Serve in bowls over rice.

Florida Fish Chowder

6 servings

½ pint oysters
1 tablespoon vegetable oil
1 cup diced potatoes
1 cup diced onions
¾ cup diced celery
¾ cup diced carrots
1 tablespoon fresh lime juice
1 teaspoon dried dill
¼ teaspoon salt
⅛ teaspoon cayenne pepper
2 tablespoons Tabasco
1 quart half and half
½ cup heavy cream
2 egg yolks, well beaten
½ pound flounder fillets or other fish fillets
¼ pound fresh bay scallops
¼ pound uncooked shrimp, shelled and deveined

- Drain oysters, reserving liquid.
- Remove any remaining shell particles.
- In a large preheated saucepan, sauté vegetables in oil until tender, but not brown.
- Add reserved oyster liquid, lime juice, dill, salt, cayenne pepper, Tabasco, and half and half.
- Simmer for 10 minutes.
- In a small mixing bowl, blend heavy cream and egg yolks well.
- Add oysters, flounder fillets, scallops, shrimp and cream-egg mixture to vegetables in saucepan, stirring constantly.
- Do not boil chowder.
- Simmer for 20 minutes, or until seafood is done.

Remember This:

Always simmer soups, never boil them.

Salad Boats
6 to 8 servings

3 cups coarsely chopped cabbage
1 8¾-ounce can whole kernel corn, drained
1 cup cooked diced ham
½ cup diced Cheddar cheese
¼ cup sliced pitted ripe olives
1 small green pepper, coarsely chopped
1 2-ounce jar diced pimento, drained
½ teaspoon salt
½ cup Italian dressing
6 to 8 large hard rolls
¼ cup Italian dressing
lettuce leaves
variety of raw vegetables

- Combine first 9 ingredients; mix well and let stand 30 minutes.
- Cut off top of each roll and hollow out remaining half leaving a ⅛-inch shell.
- Break bread removed from rolls into small pieces; toss with ¼ cup Italian dressing.
- Spread bread pieces on a lightly greased baking sheet.
- Bake at 350 degrees for 12 minutes or until golden, stirring occasionally.
- Fill shells with ham mixture; top with toasted bread.
- Serve on lettuce leaves.
- Garnish plate with raw vegetables.

Barbecue Sandwiches
8 servings

2 pounds pork, Boston butt
2 pounds beef, roast of choice
1 cup catsup
4 large onions, finely chopped
½ cup Worcestershire sauce
2 14½-ounce cans stewed tomatoes
4 tablespoons sugar
2 tablespoons butter
2 teaspoons chili powder
salt to taste
buns

- Remove fat from beef and pork.
- Cook meat until tender about 2 hours at 350 degrees.
- Tear meat into small pieces.
- Combine meat with remaining ingredients and simmer for 1 to 1½ hours.
- Serve over split toasted buns.

The Gourmet Hen

4 servings

In a word, magic!

4 chicken breast halves, boned and skinned
4 slices pumpernickel bread
mayonnaise
4 slices Muenster cheese
4 tablespoons toasted slivered almonds
½ to ¾ cup Peach Chutney

- Place chicken in a skillet, cover with water.
- Bring to a boil, reduce heat and simmer until tender.
- Transfer chicken to platter and cool.
- Slice cooked breast and set aside.
- Lightly spread each slice of bread with mayonnaise.
- Layer sliced chicken, cheese and sprinkle with toasted almonds.
- Broil 4 to 5 minutes until cheese melts and bubbles.
- Remove from oven and liberally cover each sandwich with Peach Chutney, about 2 to 3 tablespoons.
- May substitute mango chutney.

Apple Sandwiches

6 servings

A sandwich combination to delight children and adults.

2 apples, finely chopped
¼ cup raisins
6 to 8 ounces cooked ham, finely diced
¼ cup shredded mild Cheddar cheese
½ cup mayonnaise
2 teaspoons lemon juice
12 slices hot buttered toast
6 lettuce leaves

- Combine apple, raisins, ham, cheese, mayonnaise, and lemon juice; mix well.
- Spread about ½ cup apple mixture on 6 slices of toast.
- Top with lettuce leaves and remaining toast.
- Cut sandwiches in half and serve.

Hawaiian Sandwiches

4 servings

½ cup mashed ripe banana
1 3-ounce package cream cheese
1 cup crushed pineapple, drained
¼ cup chopped pecans
8 slices bread
¼ cup milk
1 egg, beaten
dash of salt
¼ cup butter or margarine

- Make sandwich filling by mixing banana, cream cheese, pineapple and pecans.
- Spread filling on bread slices to make 4 sandwiches.
- Combine milk, egg and salt in a shallow dish.
- Dip each side of sandwich into egg mixture.
- Brown quickly on both sides in hot butter.
- Serve hot.

Iced Crab Sandwich

12 servings

Great for brunch or lunch.

24 slices white bread
Filling:
1 pound fresh claw crabmeat, well picked to remove shells
2 to 3 tablespoons chopped ripe olives
4 hard-cooked eggs, chopped
⅔ cup mayonnaise
1 teaspoon dried dill
Frosting:
2 5-ounce jars sharp Old English cheese
1 cup butter
2 eggs
1 teaspoon Beau Monde seasoning
dash of Tabasco

- Lightly grease 2 large cookie sheets.
- Trim crusts from bread.
- Mix together ingredients for filling.
- Beat all frosting ingredients together until fluffy.
- Spread half of bread with filling, top with remaining slices.
- Frost top and sides of sandwiches.
- May be frozen at this point.
- Place sandwiches on cookie sheets and refrigerate until frosting is firm.
- Preheat oven to 425 degrees.
- Bake sandwiches for 8 to 10 minutes.
- If frosting runs, trim for a more attractive sandwich.

Entrées

Entrées

Valley Châteaubriand
4 servings

tenderloin of beef, 2 pounds
salt and freshly ground pepper
½ pound fresh mushrooms, sliced
3 tablespoons butter
1 tablespoon chopped chives
1 tablespoon chopped fresh parsley
2 small shallots, chopped
½ teaspoon salt
dash of pepper
1 teaspoon Worcestershire sauce
½ cup dry sherry
2 tablespoons brandy

- Salt and pepper meat as desired.
- Grill to desired doneness.
- Melt butter in a skillet over medium-high heat and sauté sliced mushrooms.
- Add chives, parsley, shallots and simmer for 5 minutes.
- Add seasonings and Worcestershire sauce; stir to combine.
- Blend in sherry and simmer.
- Add brandy just before serving and thin sauce with more sherry if desired.
- Spoon sauce over grilled meat.

Steak With Tarragon Butter
6 servings

Tarragon butter is also delicious on vegetables and baked potatoes.

2 medium shallots, peeled and halved
2 tablespoons chopped fresh parsley
4 teaspoons tarragon vinegar
½ teaspoon dried tarragon
½ teaspoon freshly ground pepper
8½ tablespoons butter, well chilled and cut into small pieces
6 beef tenderloin steaks

- Combine shallots, parsley, vinegar, tarragon and pepper in a food processor.
- Add butter and blend well.
- Shape into a roll and wrap in wax paper; refrigerate until firm.
- Grill, broil or pan fry steaks.
- Slice butter roll into 6 slices and place 1 slice on each steak.
- Serve immediately.

Entrées

Beef Wellington
10 to 12 servings

A specialty of the Wedge and Wineglass.

1 beef tenderloin, peeled
freshly ground pepper
½ pound liver pâté or pork pâté
¼ cup butter
¼ cup vegetable oil
2 sheets of 10x14-inch frozen puff pastry
1 egg
1 tablespoon water

- Cut tenderloin into 10 to 12 rounds, 1½ to 2 inches thick.
- Season meat with pepper.
- Melt butter in a skillet and sear both sides of each beef round.
- Cool and spread a light coating of pâté over each round.
- Lightly brush with coating of vegetable oil.
- Thaw pastry according to package directions.
- Cut both puff pastry sheets into 6 rectangles.
- Prepare egg wash by beating egg and water.
- Place meat on pastry pâté side down.
- Fold pastry over beef and brush with egg wash to seal seams.
- Be sure there are no breaks in the bottom of folds.
- Place wrapped beef on a greased cookie sheet, seam side down.
- Lightly brush the tops of puff pastry with egg wash and bake at 425 degrees until golden brown.
- Serve immediately.
- This dish is best served medium to medium rare because longer baking will burn the puff pastry.

Grilled Steak With Mushroom Sauce

6 servings

A wonderful culinary experience.

2 flank steaks, 1¼ to 1½ pounds each

Marinade:

- *½ cup soy sauce*
- *½ cup vegetable oil*
- *3 tablespoons red wine or balsamic vinegar*
- *freshly ground pepper*
- *2 medium cloves garlic, crushed*

Mushroom Sauce:

- *3 tablespoons butter*
- *3 tablespoons vegetable oil*
- *1 pound mushrooms, sliced*
- *1 cup beef broth*
- *4 teaspoons Dijon mustard*
- *3 teaspoons coarse-grained mustard*
- *½ cup heavy cream*
- *salt and freshly ground pepper*

- Place steaks in a non-aluminum pan.
- Whisk together soy sauce, oil, vinegar, pepper and garlic.
- Pour over steaks, turning to coat all sides.
- Cover pan tightly and refrigerate for 24 hours, turning occasionally.
- To prepare sauce, melt butter with oil in a large skillet over medium-high heat.
- Sauté mushrooms for 3 minutes.
- Mix in beef broth and mustards.
- Increase heat to high and boil until reduced by half, about 5 minutes.
- Stir in cream and boil until sauce coats a spoon, about 3 minutes.
- Season with salt and pepper if needed.
- Mushroom sauce may be prepared 1 day ahead.
- Grill steaks over hot coals, cooking about 4 minutes per side for medium-rare.
- Cut steaks in diagonal slices and serve with mushroom sauce.

Grilled Flank Steak

4 servings

- *1 cup dry red wine*
- *2 tablespoons olive oil*
- *2 tablespoons balsamic vinegar*
- *3 cloves garlic, minced*
- *4 tablespoons minced chives*
- *1½ pounds flank steak*

- Combine wine, oil, vinegar, garlic and chives in a shallow glass dish.
- Add steak and turn several times to coat.
- Cover and refrigerate for 24 hours, turning occasionally.
- Grill drained steak over hot coals for 5 minutes on each side for medium-rare.
- Slice steak thinly across grain and serve.

Whipped Horseradish Sauce

1⅓ cups

This light and tangy sauce compliments grilled beef.

¼ cup prepared horseradish
¼ teaspoon Tabasco
salt
1 tablespoon chopped chives
½ cup heavy cream, whipped

- In a small bowl, stir horseradish, Tabasco, salt and chives together.
- Fold mixture into whipped cream.
- Refrigerate until ready to serve.
- Whip sauce with a wire whisk several times before serving.

Mushroom Stuffed Tenderloin

10 servings

An elegant company fare.

4 pounds beef tenderloin or sirloin
¼ cup margarine
1 pound fresh mushrooms, chopped
½ cup chopped celery
½ cup chopped onion
¼ green bell pepper, chopped
1 teaspoon salt
⅛ teaspoon pepper
⅛ teaspoon rubbed sage
⅛ teaspoon ground thyme
2 tablespoons flour

- Cut a pocket the full length of the tenderloin, being careful not to cut through the other side.
- Melt margarine in a skillet and sauté mushrooms.
- Add celery, onion, green bell pepper, salt, pepper, sage and thyme.
- Saute until vegetables are tender and blend in flour.
- Stuff prepared tenderloin with vegetable mixture.
- Fasten opening with skewers and lace with cord.
- Roast meat at 325 degrees for 25 minutes per pound or to 150 degrees on a meat thermometer for medium rare.

Sirloin Stroganoff
8 servings

A fabulous buffet dish.

4 pounds lean sirloin tip
4 tablespoons butter
2 medium Bermuda onions
1 pound fresh mushrooms, sliced
salt and pepper to taste
1 clove garlic, crushed
2 8-ounce cans tomato sauce
1 pint sour cream
2 cups rice, cooked

- Cut meat into ½-inch strips, then into bite-size pieces.
- Sear in a large frying pan with butter, onions and mushrooms.
- When meat has browned add salt, pepper, garlic and tomato sauce.
- Simmer for 10 minutes.
- Stir in sour cream and transfer to a covered baking dish.
- Bake for 1½ hours at 300 degrees.
- Remove cover for last 15 minutes to brown.
- Serve over rice.

Chili Con Carne
15 servings

5 pounds ground beef
2½ cups chopped onion
2 cloves garlic, crushed
½ teaspoon pepper
1 teaspoon sugar
2 tablespoons salt
1 teaspoon cumin
3 tablespoons chili powder
2 28-ounce cans peeled, crushed tomatoes
1 46-ounce can tomato juice
2 15-ounce cans tomato sauce
2 bay leaves
2 30-ounce cans kidney beans
2 cups shredded Cheddar cheese
1½ cups sliced green onions, include ⅓ of tops

- In a large soup kettle, brown beef in batches over medium-high heat stirring to break up meat.
- Drain fat and add onion and garlic.
- Sauté onion and garlic with meat, stirring frequently until onion is limp.
- Stir in pepper, sugar, salt, cumin and chili powder.
- Add tomatoes, tomato juice, tomato sauce, bay leaves and beans.
- Stir and bring chili to a boil.
- Reduce heat to a simmer.
- Cover and cook for 3 to 6 hours, stirring occasionally.
- Serve hot with bowls of shredded Cheddar cheese and sliced green onions.

Tostados Con Carne

6 servings

For casual impromptu entertaining, keep one of these in the freezer.

2 pounds ground chuck
1 large onion, chopped
1 to 2 cloves garlic, minced
1½ tablespoons chili powder
2 15-ounce cans tomato sauce
1 teaspoon sugar
2 teaspoons salt
1 4-ounce can green chilies, drained and diced
½ cup black olives, sliced
8 corn tostados, broken into large pieces
2 cups dry cottage cheese
1 egg, beaten
8 ounces Monterey Jack cheese, shredded
1 cup chopped green onions, tops included
1 cup sour cream
1 cup sliced black olives

- Brown meat in 2 batches in a large skillet.
- Sauté onion and garlic with last batch of meat.
- Return all meat to skillet.
- Add next 6 ingredients and mix well.
- Heat mixture thoroughly and reduce heat to a simmer for 15 minutes.
- Combine egg and cottage cheese; set aside.
- Spread one third of meat mixture in a shallow 3-quart baking dish.
- Cover with half of the sliced cheese, cottage cheese and tostados.
- Repeat with another one third of meat and remaining sliced cheese, cottage cheese and tostados.
- Top layers with remainder of meat mixture.
- Sprinkle with Cheddar cheese and bake at 350 degrees for 30 minutes.
- Serve with sour cream, green onions and sliced black olives as toppings.
- May be frozen before baking; bring to room temperature and bake as directed.

Remember This:

Freeze individual spoonfuls of chili on cookie sheets. When frozen, put in freezer bags to use later for chili dogs.

Pork Crown Roast With Celery Wild Rice Stuffing

14 to 16 servings

1 pork crown roast, 14 to 16 ribs
1 tablespoon salt
¼ teaspoon freshly ground pepper
2 6-ounce boxes long grain and wild rice
2 cups thinly sliced celery
¼ cup finely chopped onion
8 ounces fresh mushrooms, sliced
1 cup butter
1 teaspoon sage
½ teaspoon salt
¼ cup chopped parsley
½ teaspoon poultry seasoning
1 cup chopped pecans
2 eggs, well beaten
mint leaves
red and green grapes
red and green apple slices

- Preheat oven to 325 degrees.
- Sprinkle pork crown roast with 1 tablespoon salt and pepper.
- Place roast, rib ends down, in a roasting pan and roast for 2 hours.
- Meanwhile, cook rice according to package directions and set aside.
- In a large skillet, sauté celery, onions and mushrooms in butter until tender, but not brown.
- Remove from heat and add sage, ½ teaspoon salt, parsley, poultry seasoning and pecans.
- Add eggs slowly, while beating continually.
- Gently mix with cooked rice.
- After 2 hours, remove roast from oven and carefully invert so that ribs face up.
- Fill cavity of roast with stuffing.
- Save any remaining stuffing and bake in a greased, covered baking dish during last 30 minutes of roasting time.
- Insert meat thermometer between 2 ribs, being careful not to touch a bone.
- Return stuffed roast to oven and cook for 45 minutes to 1½ hours or until meat thermometer reaches 170 degrees.
- If stuffing becomes too brown, cover with foil.
- Place roast on platter and let stand 15 minutes before carving.
- To carve, slice between ribs.
- Garnish with mint leaves and clusters of grapes and apple slices.

Pork Roast With Tomato Sauce

6 servings

1 boneless pork roast, $3\frac{1}{2}$ to 4 pounds
1 clove garlic, thinly sliced
salt and freshly ground pepper
2 cups chopped onions
1 green bell pepper, seeded and chopped
1 tablespoon bacon drippings
1 6-ounce can tomato paste
2 $14\frac{1}{2}$-ounce cans whole tomatoes
2 cups water
Tabasco to taste
1 pound angel hair pasta or vermicelli, cooked
$\frac{1}{4}$ cup freshly chopped parsley

- Insert slices of garlic in roast.
- Generously salt and pepper surface of meat.
- Place meat in a roasting pan and cook at 325 degrees until juices of meat run clear, 30 to 35 minutes per pound.
- To prepare tomato sauce, lightly sauté onions and green bell pepper in bacon drippings.
- Add tomato paste to mixture when onions are transparent.
- Stir over medium heat until mixture browns, about 5 to 8 minutes.
- Add canned tomatoes, water and Tabasco.
- Stir to blend ingredients.
- Simmer over low heat $1\frac{1}{2}$ hours uncovered, breaking up whole tomatoes as the sauce simmers.
- At end of roasting time, remove meat from oven and pour off excess grease.
- Set meat aside.
- Add enough tomato sauce to deglaze roasting pan.
- Return tomato sauce to skillet and stir to combine.
- Serve sliced roast in the center of a large platter.
- Surround meat with pasta, topped with tomato sauce and sprinkled with parsley.
- Serve remaining sauce on the side.

Porc Au Poivre
6 servings

1/3 cup Dijon mustard
2 to 3 tablespoons vegetable oil
1 teaspoon dried tarragon
1 1/2 pounds pork tenderloin
1/2 cup flour
1/2 cup bread crumbs
1/4 cup cracked pepper
vegetable oil

- Combine mustard, oil and tarragon.
- Cut tenderloin into 1/2-inch slices.
- Spread each slice with mustard, oil and tarragon mixture.
- Refrigerate for 4 hours or longer.
- Combine flour, bread crumbs and cracked pepper.
- Coat pork slices with flour and bread crumb mixture.
- In a large skillet, add enough oil to cover bottom of skillet.
- Warm oil over medium-high heat.
- Cook meat until done, about 4 minutes on each side.

Chutney Chops
4 servings

Simply delicious!

4 lean pork chops, 1/2 to 3/4-inch thick
salt and freshly ground pepper
1 tablespoon olive oil
1/2 clove garlic, crushed
1/4 cup Major Grey's Chutney
juice and zest of 1/2 orange

- Season chops with salt and pepper.
- In a large skillet, heat olive oil and sauté garlic.
- Add chops and brown.
- Reduce heat and cook until chops are done, about 30 minutes.
- Transfer meat to a heated platter.
- Add chutney, orange juice and zest to skillet.
- Over low heat, cook until mixture is thoroughly heated.
- Return chops to skillet and coat.
- Serve on a platter with sauce spooned over chops.

Entrées

Marinated Pork Chops
4 to 8 servings

Delicious with wild rice.

1 cup soy sauce
¼ cup Worcestershire sauce
¼ cup red wine vinegar
½ cup brown sugar
½ teaspoon crushed garlic
8 pork chops, ½-inch thick

- Mix soy sauce, Worcestershire, vinegar, brown sugar, and garlic.
- Pour over chops.
- Marinate for at least 24 hours, rearranging chops to thoroughly coat.
- Grill over medium to hot coals about 5 to 10 minutes per side.

Heritage Ham And Asparagus
10 to 12 servings

Perfect for a buffet meal.

32 stalks fresh asparagus
16 ⅛-inch thick slices fully cooked ham
½ pound Gruyère cheese, shredded
4 tablespoons flour
4 tablespoons butter
2 cups warm milk
¼ teaspoon nutmeg
2 tablespoons Dijon mustard, optional

- Cook asparagus in boiling water until tender-crisp.
- Drain and slice in half.
- Sprinkle ham slices with 1 tablespoon cheese.
- Place 4 asparagus pieces on a ham slice and roll up.
- Place in a 3-quart shallow baking dish, seam side down.
- Prepare cream sauce by melting butter over medium heat; stir in flour.
- Cook for 2 minutes, stirring constantly.
- Slowly stir in warm milk and cook until thickened.
- Add nutmeg and mustard if desired and pour over ham rolls.
- Sprinkle with remaining cheese.
- Bake at 350 degrees until browned.

Honey Glazed Ham

Glaze for 1 whole ham

Pack this ham for weekend excursions.

1 smoked, fully cooked ham
1 tablespoon grated orange rind
1 cup fresh orange juice
1 cup orange blossom honey
whole cloves
10 thin orange slices

- Preheat oven to 300 degrees.
- Remove tough rind from ham and cut away all but 1/8-inch layer of fat.
- Diagonally score remaining layer of fat, being careful not to cut into meat.
- Place ham, fat side up, on a rack in a shallow roasting pan.
- Blend orange rind, orange juice and honey.
- Baste ham with glaze and bake for 15 minutes per pound.
- Occasionally brush ham with glaze while baking.
- Place cloves over ham, where diagonal lines of scoring intersect, 45 minutes before ham is ready.
- Using cloves or toothpicks broken into small pieces, secure orange slices over ham.
- Carefully brush glaze over ham and orange slices.
- Return to oven, increase heat to 325 degrees and bake for final 45 minutes.
- Baste frequently with glaze.
- Cover scored surface of ham with a tent of aluminum foil if ham browns too quickly.

Sausage Fettuccine 8 servings

A savory combination of herbs make this a delectable pasta dish.

1½ pounds mild Italian bulk sausage
½ cup butter
½ pound fresh mushrooms, sliced
½ cup diced green bell pepper
½ cup sliced green onion (use ⅓ of tops)
½ cup chopped fresh parsley
2 tablespoons chopped fresh cilantro
2 cloves garlic, pressed
1 teaspoon dried or 1 tablespoon fresh basil
1 teaspoon dried oregano
1 pound fettuccine, cooked and drained
freshly grated Parmesan cheese

- Cook sausage in a large skillet over medium-high heat until browned, crumbling with a spoon.
- Drain sausage on paper towels and pour off any fat remaining in skillet.
- Melt butter in skillet and add mushrooms, green bell pepper, onion, parsley, cilantro, garlic, basil and oregano.
- Sauté mixture for about 10 minutes or until tender.
- Remove skillet from heat and stir in cooked sausage mixture.
- Serve over pasta and sprinkle with Parmesan cheese.
- Sausage and herb mixture may be served with Lebanese flat bread or pita bread.

Remember This:

Pasta should be cooked al dente or firm to the bite.

Rack Of Lamb

8 to 10 servings

This unique roasting technique yields a succulent entrée.

leg of lamb, 5 to 6 pound
4 garlic cloves
salt and freshly ground pepper
flour
2 onions, unpeeled
4 carrots, unpeeled
1 leek
1 celery stalk
1/4 teaspoon thyme
1 bay leaf

- Preheat oven to 350 degrees.
- Place garlic cloves in joints of lamb, nearest to main bones.
- Rub lamb well with salt and pepper and dust with sifted flour.
- Place lamb directly on oven rack, fat side up.
- Place roasting pan with vegetables, thyme and bay leaf on bottom oven rack beneath meat to collect drippings.
- Roast for 30 minutes per pound to desired doneness.
- Discard drippings and vegetables.
- Slice and serve with Currant Sauce.

Currant Sauce

10 servings

1/2 cup butter
3/4 cup currant jelly
1/4 cup cognac
1/4 cup catsup
1/4 cup fresh mint leaves
1 tablespoon finely chopped orange zest
watercress or parsley for garnish

- In a small saucepan over moderately low heat, melt butter.
- Add currant jelly, cognac, catsup, mint leaves and orange zest.
- Stir and simmer for 10 minutes.
- Arrange sliced lamb on a heated platter.
- Pour sauce over the lamb or serve in a heated sauceboat.
- Garnish with watercress or parsley bouquets.

Veal Strips Paprika

4 servings

Serve with rice or pasta.

8 thin veal slices
salt and freshly ground pepper
1 tablespoon olive oil
1 tablespoon butter
1/4 cup finely chopped onion
2 teaspoons paprika
1/4 cup dry white wine
1/2 cup half and half
1/2 cup sour cream

- Cut veal into thin strips and sprinkle with salt and pepper.
- Heat olive oil and butter in a skillet until bubbling.
- Add veal and cook for approximately 30 seconds.
- Add onions and cook, stirring constantly for 1 minute.
- Sprinkle with paprika.
- Using a slotted spoon, transfer veal to a platter.
- Add wine to skillet to deglaze and stir for 3 minutes.
- Pour in half and half and cook for 1 minute.
- Stir in sour cream and cook for 1 additional minute.
- To serve, pour sauce over veal.

Remember This:

Partially freeze raw meats before slicing thinly.

Veal Jardinière 6 servings

Bouquet Garni:
3 to 4 sprigs parsley
1 bay leaf
¼ teaspoon dried or 1 teaspoon fresh thyme leaves
2 sprigs celery leaves

6 veal loin chops
salt and pepper to taste
½ cup butter
4 onions, finely sliced
¼ cup dry white wine
3 pounds fresh green peas, shelled
½ pound baby carrots, peeled
½ pound button onions
½ pound small new potatoes, sliced
2 cups stock
1 teaspoon sugar
fresh parsley

- To prepare bouquet garni, place sprigs of parsley, bay leaf, thyme and celery leaves in tea ball or cheesecloth bag and set aside.
- Trim and season chops with salt and pepper.
- Melt ¼ cup butter in a heavy skillet.
- Brown meat on all sides over moderate heat; transfer meat to a platter.
- Add sliced onions and cook until tender.
- Return meat to skillet, moisten with wine and cook until sauce begins to carmelize slightly.
- Cover and cook over low heat for approximately 1 hour.
- In a separate saucepan, melt remaining butter over low heat.
- Add peas, carrots, button onions, potatoes and bouquet garni.
- Cover and cook for 15 minutes, stirring occasionally.
- Add stock and sugar to vegetables.
- Bring to a boil and simmer for 10 minutes.
- Add vegetable stock to veal as needed.
- Arrange meat in center of a serving dish and surround with vegetables.
- Discard bouquet garni.
- Pour juices over meat and sprinkle with parsley.

Entrées

Veal Marsala 4 servings

Very quick and absolutely delicious!

1 pound veal, thinly sliced or pounded
flour
½ cup butter
¼ cup olive oil
1 tablespoon chopped fresh garlic
1 cup fresh mushrooms
½ cup Marsala wine
1 cup chicken stock
¼ cup fresh lemon juice
1 tablespoon sugar
¼ cup chopped fresh parsley
lemon slices and parsley

- Lightly flour meat.
- Melt butter with olive oil in a skillet over medium-high heat.
- Sauté meat quickly without browning and transfer to a serving platter.
- Sauté garlic and mushrooms in skillet and spoon over meat.
- Add Marsala wine, chicken stock, lemon juice, sugar and parsley to skillet and bring to a quick boil, reducing liquid slightly.
- Pour over meat.
- Garnish with sliced lemons and parsley.

Chicken Divine 12 servings

Ease of preparation and delicate flavor make this a specialty.

2 cups sour cream
¼ cup fresh lemon juice
4 teaspoons Worcestershire sauce
1 teaspoon celery salt
2 teaspoons paprika
2 cloves garlic, finely minced
½ teaspoon freshly ground pepper
6 whole chicken breasts, split, boned, and skinned
3 cups dried bread crumbs
½ cup butter, melted

- In a medium bowl, combine sour cream, lemon juice, Worcestershire sauce, celery salt, paprika, garlic and pepper.
- Divide mixture into 2 large plastic bags; add chicken and refrigerate overnight.
- Remove chicken from bags and roll in bread crumbs.
- Arrange chicken in a single layer in a large baking dish.
- Spoon half of butter over chicken.
- Bake uncovered at 350 degrees for 35 minutes.
- Spoon remaining butter over chicken and bake for 5 to 10 minutes or until browned.

Old-Fashioned Chicken And Dumplings

6 servings

1 3 to $3\frac{1}{2}$ pound chicken
2 stalks celery, halved
2 chicken bouillon cubes
salt
Dumplings:
2 cups flour
2 teaspoons baking powder
1 teaspoon salt
$\frac{1}{3}$ cup shortening
$\frac{1}{2}$ cup milk

- Remove giblets from chicken cavity and reserve for another use.
- Place chicken in a Dutch oven and add enough water to almost cover.
- Add celery, bouillon cubes and salt.
- Bring to a boil; reduce heat to low and cook about $1\frac{1}{2}$ hours or until tender.
- Remove chicken from cooking liquid and cool slightly.
- Reserve liquid in Dutch oven and discard celery.
- Debone chicken; cover and set aside.
- To prepare dumplings, combine flour, baking powder and salt.
- Cut in shortening until size of small peas.
- Make a well in the flour mixture.
- Add milk and stir with a fork to form a stiff dough.
- On a floured surface, roll dough to $\frac{1}{8}$-inch thickness and cut into 1-inch squares, $1\frac{1}{2}$-inch strips or diamonds.
- Sprinkle dumplings lightly with flour and drop 1 at a time into rapidly boiling chicken stock.
- Cover and boil gently for 3 to 5 minutes.
- Return deboned chicken to liquid.
- Heat for 1 minute more and serve immediately.

Chicken Mushroom Sauté

6 servings

A tempting combination.

1 3 pound chicken, cut into 8 serving pieces
2 tablespoons oil
4 tablespoons butter
salt and freshly ground pepper
½ pound fresh mushrooms, sliced
¼ cup chopped onion
½ cup dry white wine, optional
1 tablespoon flour
1 cup chicken stock or broth, warmed
4 ripe tomatoes, peeled, seeded and chopped
1 tablespoon finely minced parsley
1 teaspoon dried tarragon

- Rinse chicken and pat dry with paper towels.
- Heat oil and 1½ tablespoons butter in a large skillet over high heat.
- Brown chicken a few pieces at a time, turning as needed.
- Return chicken to skillet and season with salt and pepper; cover.
- Reduce heat and simmer for 15 minutes or until tender.
- Transfer chicken to a platter and keep warm.
- In a separate skillet, melt remaining butter and sauté mushrooms for 5 minutes.
- Cover and set aside.
- Spoon all except ½ teaspoon fat from chicken skillet.
- Add onion to skillet and cook over medium heat until lightly browned.
- If desired add wine, increase heat and cook until wine has evaporated.
- Stir in flour and cook stirring constantly for 1 minute.
- Remove skillet from heat and stir in warmed chicken stock.
- Return to heat and cook, stirring frequently until thickened.
- Stir in tomatoes, herbs and mushrooms; season with salt and pepper.
- Return chicken to pan, cover and simmer for 3 minutes.
- May be served over steamed rice.

Pecan Fried Chicken

5 servings

1 2 to 2½ pound chicken, cut into serving pieces
1 cup buttermilk
1 cup flour
1 teaspoon salt
½ teaspoon paprika
½ cup finely chopped pecans
2 tablespoons chopped fresh parsley
1 teaspoon dried oregano, crushed
vegetable oil

- Skin chicken if desired.
- Place chicken in a shallow 3-quart baking dish and cover with buttermilk.
- Cover with plastic wrap and refrigerate for 1 to 2 hours.
- Combine flour, salt, paprika, pecans, parsley and oregano in a shallow dish.
- Remove chicken from buttermilk and roll in flour mixture.
- Fry chicken in deep oil for approximately 15 minutes or until done.
- Drain and serve hot.
- If oven-fried chicken is desired, brown pieces in ¼ cup oil and ¼ cup butter on all sides.
- Place chicken in a 3-quart baking dish and drizzle with ⅓ cup butter.
- Bake for 40 to 50 minutes at 350 degrees.

Lake Iamonia Barbeque

A tangy barbeque sauce.

Sauce for 3 to 4 chickens

1¼ cups fresh lemon juice, about 10 lemons
1½ cups butter
½ cup Worcestershire sauce
dash of Tabasco
2 tablespoons dry mustard
2 tablespoons catsup
1 clove garlic, crushed

- Melt butter in a small saucepan over medium heat.
- Add lemon juice, Worcestershire sauce, Tabasco, dry mustard, catsup and garlic.
- Whisk to combine and simmer for 15 to 20 minutes.
- Baste chicken frequently during grilling.

Chicken Curry

15 servings

Makes serving a crowd easy!

5 onions, finely chopped
2 cloves garlic, minced
½ cup butter
¼ to ½ cup curry powder
½ cup flour
3 cups applesauce
5 cups chicken broth
3 tablespoons tomato paste
juice of 1 lemon
3 3-pound chickens, cooked and boned
4 cups rice, cooked
Toppings:
1 cup chopped salted peanuts
2 8-ounce jars chutney
2 bunches green onions, sliced
6 hard-cooked eggs, chopped
1 4-ounce can flaked coconut
1 pound bacon, cooked, drained, and crumbled

- Sauté onions and garlic in butter until soft, but not brown.
- Stir in curry powder and flour.
- Cook gently over low heat for 5 minutes.
- Add applesauce, chicken broth, tomato paste and lemon juice; blend well.
- Simmer for 45 minutes over low heat, stirring often.
- Pour through a sieve into a saucepan.
- Add chicken and heat thoroughly, but do not boil.
- Serve chicken over rice with toppings.

Artichoke Chicken Casserole

6 servings

3 chicken breasts, halved, skinned and boned
salt and lemon pepper to taste
flour
olive oil
2 bunches spring onions
1 green bell pepper, chopped
1 14-ounce can artichoke hearts in water
1 pound fresh mushrooms, sliced
3 cups chicken stock
1 pint cherry tomatoes, halved
½ cup parsley, freshly snipped
1 10-ounce package yellow rice mix

- Season chicken with salt and lemon pepper.
- Dredge seasoned chicken in flour.
- Brown chicken in olive oil and drain on a paper towel.
- In remaining oil, sauté onion and green bell pepper.
- Add artichokes and sliced mushrooms.
- Add about 1 cup of chicken stock and cherry tomatoes to vegetables.
- Arrange chicken in a 3-quart baking dish.
- Pour vegetable mixture over chicken and sprinkle with parsley.
- Cover with foil and cook at 350 degrees for 40 to 45 minutes.
- Prepare rice according to package directions substituting chicken stock for water.
- Serve chicken over yellow rice.

Barbeque Chicken Marinade

6 servings

1 cup vegetable oil
1½ cups cider vinegar
1½ tablespoons salt
1 teaspoon poultry seasoning
2 eggs
1 teaspoon freshly ground pepper
½ cup water
2 chickens, quartered

- Place all marinade ingredients in a blender.
- Whip until well blended.
- Place chicken in a non-metallic dish.
- Pour marinade over chicken and cover with plastic wrap.
- Refrigerate for at least 4 hours or overnight.
- Remove chicken from marinade and barbeque.
- Baste chicken with marinade during grilling.

Sherried Chicken

10 servings

2 3-pound chickens, cut into pieces
1½ cups water
1½ cups sherry
salt
1 medium onion, peeled
1½ teaspoons curry powder
1 cup chopped celery
1 pound fresh mushrooms, sliced thick
¼ cup butter
1 6-ounce box long grain and wild rice
1 10¾-ounce can cream of mushroom soup
1 cup sour cream

- Place chicken pieces in a Dutch oven.
- Add water, sherry, salt, onion, curry powder and celery.
- Bring to a boil; reduce heat and simmer until chicken is tender.
- Remove chicken and reserve liquid.
- Debone and cut chicken into bite-size pieces and set aside.
- In a large skillet, melt butter and sauté mushrooms.
- Prepare rice according to package directions using reserved liquid.
- In a large bowl, combine mushroom soup, sour cream, chicken, sautéed mushrooms and cooked rice.
- Spoon mixture into a 3-quart baking dish and bake at 350 degrees for 40 minutes.

Remember This:

Use an egg slicer to slice mushrooms.

Greek Chicken
6 servings

6 fryer leg quarters
2 to 3 onions, peeled and quartered
2 to 3 cloves garlic
1 cup yogurt
juice of 2 lemons
¼ cup finely minced parsley
salt and pepper to taste
yellow rice

- Rinse leg quarters and pat dry.
- Trim away excess skin.
- Place in a shallow 3-quart baking dish and set aside.
- In a food processor, purée onion.
- Add garlic and process until finely minced.
- Add yogurt, lemon juice, parsley and seasonings.
- Process several times to combine and pour over chicken.
- Cover and refrigerate for 6 to 8 hours or overnight, turning chicken once.
- Grill chicken, turning twice before basting with yogurt marinade.
- Continue basting until chicken is done.
- Serve with yellow rice.

Herb-Basted Cornish Hens
4 servings

Excellent served with wild rice.

2 Cornish game hens, 1½ pounds each
2 medium limes
2 tablespoons olive oil
2 tablespoons butter
½ teaspoon dried thyme
¾ teaspoon salt
¼ teaspoon freshly ground pepper
1 clove garlic, minced

- Preheat broiler and cut Cornish hens in half.
- Grate ½ teaspoon rind and squeeze 2 tablespoons juice from limes.
- In a 1-quart saucepan over low heat, cook lime peel, juice, olive oil, butter, thyme, salt, pepper and garlic until butter melts.
- Place hens, skin-side down in a broiler pan.
- Broil for 25 minutes, brushing occasionally with butter.
- Turn hen skin-side up and broil for 20 minutes or until tender.
- Brush with remaining butter.

Festive Fruit Sauce
6 cups

A delicious accompaniment to turkey or game.

2 12-ounce packages fresh cranberries
3 apples, pared, cored and diced
2 pears, pared, cored and diced
2 cups sugar
2 cups golden raisins
1 cup fresh orange juice
1 tablespoon freshly grated orange rind
2 teaspoons ground cinnamon
1/4 teaspoon freshly grated nutmeg
1/2 cup Cointreau or orange flavored liqueur

- Rinse and drain cranberries.
- In a large saucepan, bring all ingredients except liqueur to a boil.
- Reduce heat and simmer uncovered, stirring frequently until mixture thickens, approximately 45 minutes.
- Stir in liqueur.
- Cover and refrigerate for 4 hours or overnight.
- Serve slightly chilled.
- Purée sauce and use as a spread for turkey sandwiches.

Ginger Madeira Mustard
1 1/4 cups

Wonderful served with poultry.

1/4 cup mustard seed
1/4 cup Madeira wine
1/3 cup red wine vinegar
3 tablespoons snipped fresh dill
2 teaspoons honey
2 tablespoons chopped onion
1 teaspoon salt
1/4 teaspoon freshly ground pepper
1 teaspoon peeled and minced fresh gingeroot
2 teaspoons flour

- In a small bowl, mix mustard seed, wine and vinegar; let stand for 3 hours or more.
- In a blender, blend mustard seed mixture well.
- Add dill, honey, onion, salt, pepper, gingeroot, and 1/4 cup water; blend for 1 minute.
- Transfer mixture to a saucepan.
- In a small bowl, mix flour with 2 tablespoons of mustard mixture.
- Add flour mixture to saucepan.
- Cook over low heat, stirring until thick.
- Transfer to a sterilized jar, chill, and keep indefinitely.

Southern Roasted Turkey

16 to 20 servings

1 10 to 14-pound turkey
1 tablespoon salt
1½ teaspoons freshly ground pepper
2 tablespoons seasoned salt
1 tablespoon poultry seasoning
1 teaspoon dried basil
1½ teaspoons garlic powder
1 tablespoon paprika
3 to 4 tablespoons bacon drippings

- Rinse turkey and pat dry with paper towels.
- Combine all seasonings in a small bowl.
- Rub inside and outside of bird with bacon drippings.
- Sprinkle seasonings on outside of bird.
- Cover and roast turkey at 350 degrees for 3½ to 4½ hours or until done.

Seasoned Turkey

10 to 12 servings

1 6 to 8 pound turkey
2 to 3 tablespoons butter
1 teaspoon dried basil
½ teaspoon freshly ground pepper
¼ teaspoon dried rosemary
¼ teaspoon dried marjoram
⅛ teaspoon thyme
1 clove garlic, crushed or ⅛ teaspoon garlic powder

- Rinse bird inside and out under cold water.
- Drain and pat dry with paper towels.
- Rub surface with butter and sprinkle seasonings over buttered turkey.
- Place on a roasting rack and cook at 350 degrees until done.

Remember This:

Turkey will cook faster in a dark roasting pan.

Marinated Duck Wrapped In Bacon

4 entrée or 8 appetizer servings

A hunter's choice.

8 wild ducks, skinned, boned and breasted
2 tablespoons salt
1½ cups Italian dressing
3 tablespoons Worcestershire sauce
¾ teaspoon garlic salt or powder
¾ teaspoon ground cloves
½ cup lemon juice
1 pound sliced bacon

- In a glass dish, cover duck with water.
- Stir in salt and soak in refrigerator for two hours or over night.
- Drain meat and slice into ½-inch strips.
- Combine dressing, Worcestershire sauce, garlic powder, ground cloves and lemon juice.
- Place strips of meat in a shallow dish and cover with marinade.
- Marinate at least 3 hours or overnight in refrigerator.
- Cut bacon in half.
- Before grilling, drain meat and wrap with bacon slices; secure with toothpicks.
- Grill over hot coals for 7 minutes on each side or until bacon is done.

Remember This:

Soaking wild duck in salted water reduces the gamy flavor.

Glazed Apricot Duck
4 servings

1 cup apricot preserves
¼ cup light brown sugar
2 tablespoons brandy
2 tablespoons Cointreau liqueur
4 wild ducks, dressed
4 large onions, peeled
salt and pepper to taste
8 slices bacon

- In a small saucepan, heat first 4 ingredients over medium heat and cook until combined; set aside.
- Preheat oven to 500 degrees.
- Place one whole onion in each duck cavity.
- Sprinkle duck with salt and pepper and wrap with 2 slices of bacon.
- Place breast side up in a roasting pan.
- Roast for 15 to 30 minutes according to size of ducks.
- Baste every 5 minutes with fat from pan.
- Remove from oven and discard onion.
- Reduce heat to 350 degrees.
- Pour glaze over duck and return to oven for 10 to 15 minutes.

Duck Kiev
4 servings

4 whole duck breasts
1 cup butter
2 tablespoons chopped chives
2 tablespoons chopped parsley
1 tablespoon minced garlic
½ teaspoon salt
¼ teaspoon white pepper
3 eggs, beaten
flour
dry cracker crumbs
vegetable oil

- Debone, skin and cut duck breasts in half.
- Pound to ¼-inch thickness.
- Slice butter in pats, equal to one tablespoon.
- Combine chives, garlic, parsley, salt and pepper.
- Roll pat of butter in seasoning and place in center of breast.
- Wrap breast around butter and secure with a toothpick.
- Dip duck in beaten egg, roll in flour, dip in egg again, and roll in cracker crumbs.
- Deep fat fry until golden brown, about 5 to 10 minutes.

Duck and Sausage Gumbo

6 entrée or 10 to 12 first course servings

6 to 8 wild ducks, dressed
2 stalks celery with leaves
1 medium onion, sliced
1 tablespoon salt
chicken broth
½ pound hot smoked sausage, cut into small pieces
½ cup vegetable oil
½ cup flour
¾ cup finely chopped celery
1 large onion, finely chopped
¼ cup chopped green bell pepper, optional
Salt and freshly ground pepper to taste
6 green onions chopped, including tops
2 teaspoons chopped fresh parsley
hot rice
gumbo filé

- Combine ducks, celery, sliced onion and salt in a large Dutch oven.
- Cover with water and bring to a boil.
- Reduce heat and simmer for one hour until duck is tender.
- Remove duck and debone, cutting meat into bite-size pieces.
- Return duck skin and bones to stock and simmer covered for 1 hour.
- Strain stock to remove bones, skin and vegetables.
- Add chicken broth to equal 2½ quarts of stock and set aside.
- Cook sausage for 5 minutes in Dutch oven.
- Drain any fat from Dutch oven and set cooked sausage aside.
- Heat vegetable oil over medium heat in same pan and add flour to make a dark roux the color of pecans, stirring constantly.
- Add chopped celery, chopped onion and green bell pepper and cook over medium heat for 10 minutes, stirring constantly.
- Remove pan from heat and blend in reserved stock slowly, stirring constantly.
- Return pan to heat and bring to a boil; add duck and sausage.
- Reduce heat and simmer gumbo for 20 minutes.
- Add salt, pepper, parsley and green onions; simmer for 20 more minutes.
- Serve gumbo over hot cooked rice and pass gumbo filé for seasoning individually.

Burgundy Game Birds

4 servings

4 pounds pheasant, quail, duck breast or dove
salt and freshly ground pepper
1 cup flour
8 tablespoons butter
¼ cup finely chopped shallots
2 cups thinly sliced mushrooms
1 cup finely chopped cooked ham
2 cups dry red wine
2 tablespoons brandy
½ teaspoon thyme
⅛ teaspoon dried tarragon
½ small bay leaf
pinch of ground nutmeg
2 tablespoons finely chopped parsley

- Wash birds and pat dry with paper towels.
- Season with salt and pepper and roll in flour, shaking each bird to remove excess flour.
- In a large heavy skillet, melt 4 tablespoons butter over moderate heat.
- When foam subsides cook birds, turning frequently to brown on all sides.
- Remove birds from skillet and set aside.
- Melt 2 tablespoons butter in the same skillet.
- Add 3 tablespoons shallots and cook for 4 to 5 minutes over moderate heat, stirring frequently.
- Add mushrooms and ham.
- Cook, stirring occasionally for 4 minutes.
- Transfer mixture to a bowl and set aside.
- Melt remaining 2 tablespoons of butter in skillet and cook remaining shallots for 2 to 3 minutes until soft and lightly colored.
- Add wine and brandy and bring to a boil over high heat, scraping any pan drippings.
- Add thyme, tarragon, bay leaf, nutmeg, salt and pepper.
- Return birds to skillet and baste.
- Reduce heat to low, cover and simmer for 20 to 30 minutes or until birds are tender.

Honeyed Quail

4 servings

12 quail, dressed
Italian dressing
3/4 to 1 cup honey

- Marinate quail in enough Italian dressing to cover for at least 3 hours.
- Remove from marinade and split quail in half down the breast bone.
- Each half should consist of a breast and a leg.
- Heat grill until hot but not flaming.
- Brush quail with a generous amount of honey.
- Place quail on grill breast side up and cook for 3 to 5 minutes, basting with honey.
- Turn quail breast side down and grill for another 8 to 10 minutes, continuing to baste frequently with honey.
- Turn quail and grill for another 5 minutes or until done.
- Serve immediately.

Remember This:

A typical North Florida fare is deep fried quail marinated in milk and dredged in equal portions of flour and bread crumbs.

Country Fried Venison

6 servings

1 boneless venison ham, 2 pounds, cut into ½-inch slices
salt and freshly ground pepper
1 cup flour
3 to 4 tablespoons bacon drippings
2 cloves garlic, halved
4 tablespoons flour
1 cup cold water
¾ cup warm water
3 tablespoons brandy
1½ teaspoons Brown Bouquet Sauce
1 medium onion, sliced
½ pound sliced mushrooms
wild and long grain rice

- Pound slices with a meat mallet to ¼-inch thickness; season with salt and pepper.
- Dredge meat in 1 cup flour and shake to remove excess flour.
- Heat 2 tablespoons bacon drippings in a large skillet and sauté garlic until golden.
- Discard garlic halves and brown venison in batches on both sides regulating heat to brown quickly without burning; add drippings as needed.
- Remove meat when browned and set aside.
- In a jar with a tight fitting lid, stir 4 tablespoons flour into ½ cup cold water to form a smooth paste.
- Gradually add remaining cold water; stir.
- Shake jar vigorously to combine well.
- Add flour-water mixture to skillet and cook over medium-high heat for 2 minutes, stirring constantly; add warm water and bring gravy to a boil.
- When gravy is slightly thickened, add brandy and bouquet.
- Return venison and any juices to skillet; reduce heat to a simmer, correct seasoning.
- Cover and cook for 20 minutes; add sliced onion.
- Cover and simmer for 15 minutes.
- Add mushrooms and simmer for 15 more minutes.
- Serve over steamed rice.

Orange Venison

8 to 10 servings

½ cup catsup
½ cup Worcestershire sauce
¾ cup fresh orange juice
¼ cup red wine, optional
1 cup orange marmalade
⅓ cup vegetable oil
1 venison ham, 6 to 8 pounds
3 cloves garlic, thinly sliced
1 cup fresh orange segments
salt and freshly ground pepper

- In a small saucepan combine catsup, Worcestershire, orange juice, wine, marmalade and oil.
- Bring to a boil; reduce heat and simmer for 15 minutes.
- Pierce meat with a small, sharp knife making cuts approximately 1-inch deep and 1-inch long.
- Press a slice of garlic and one orange segment into each cut.
- Season venison with salt and pepper.
- Place prepared ham in a roasting pan and cover with sauce.
- Cover meat and roast at 300 degrees for 3½ to 4 hours, basting every 30 minutes with sauce.
- At the end of cooking, pour roasting juices into a saucepan.
- Cook over medium heat to reduce by one-third.
- Slice venison and serve with sauce.

Venison Roast With Mustard Pan Sauce

8 servings

Venison Marinade:
½ cup beef stock
½ cup red wine
⅓ cup soy sauce
1½ teaspoons seasoned salt
¼ cup chopped onions
1 tablespoon lime juice
2 tablespoons honey or brown sugar
1 venison roast, 5 to 6 pounds
salt and freshly ground pepper
vegetable oil
2 to 4 cups beef stock
Mustard Pan Sauce:
pan juice from roast (beef, venison, or ham)
¼ cup flour
⅔ cup dry white wine
2¼ cups beef stock
3 tablespoons Dijon mustard
½ teaspoon Worcestershire sauce
salt
freshly ground pepper to taste

- To prepare marinade, combine first 8 ingredients.
- Place venison roast in a shallow dish and cover with marinade.
- Cover roast and marinate overnight; turn meat once.
- Drain and discard marinade before cooking meat.
- Pat roast with paper towels and generously season with salt and pepper.
- Place enough vegetable oil in a roasting pan to just cover the bottom.
- Heat oil over high heat.
- Add roast to hot oil and brown, turning to brown on all sides.
- Watch meat carefully to avoid burning.
- Remove pan from heat and transfer roast to a platter.
- Add 2 to 4 cups beef stock to fill pan to a depth of 1 inch.
- Place roasting rack in pan and position venison on rack.
- Cover and roast meat at 350 degrees for 15 to 20 minutes per pound, or until tender.
- To prepare Mustard Pan Sauce, skim all except 3 tablespoons of fat from pan juices.
- Add flour and cook over moderate heat for about 3 minutes, stirring constantly.
- Blend in wine and stock.
- Bring to a boil and stir for about 3 minutes.
- Add mustard, Worcestershire, salt and pepper.

Continued

Venison Roast With Mustard Pan Sauce (continued)

- Strain into a heated sauce boat.
- Slice roast thin and serve with Mustard Pan Sauce in a chafing dish.
- Serve with small biscuits as an appetizer or over rice or pasta as a main dish.

Peach Chutney 3 pints

Wonderful with game.

5 cups peeled, chopped, stoned peaches (8 to 9 medium-sized peaches)
2½ cups packed brown sugar
1½ cups golden raisins
½ cup chopped crystallized ginger
1 clove garlic, finely minced
1 lemon, seeded and chopped
¼ cup brandy
2 cups cider vinegar
1 teaspoon salt
2 cinnamon sticks, broken in half
5 whole cloves

- Combine all ingredients except cinnamon and cloves in a Dutch oven.
- Tie cloves and cinnamon in a cheese cloth bag and add to saucepan.
- Bring mixtrue to a boil over moderate heat stirring occasionally.
- Reduce heat to a simmer and cook uncovered until chutney is thick, approximately 1½ hours, stirring occasionally.
- Remove cheese cloth bag and ladle chutney into hot, sterilized canning jars.
- Seal jars and process in boiling water bath for 15 minutes.
- Allow chutney to mature 1 month for best flavor.

Remember This:

To remove skins from peaches, blanch in boiling water for about 30 seconds. Remove, cool in cold water, and slip off skins.

Apalachicola Oyster Bake

8 servings

1 slice bacon
½ cup butter
1 cup chopped onion
1 8-ounce package herb stuffing
1 cup sour cream
1 10¾-ounce can cream of mushroom soup
1 pint oysters, drained
1 16-ounce can tomatoes
1 cup shredded sharp Cheddar cheese
½ cup chopped celery
½ cup chopped green bell pepper
½ teaspoon horseradish
1 green bell pepper, sliced in rings and seeded for garnish

- Fry slice of bacon in a large skillet until crisp.
- Remove and reserve for garnish.
- Preheat oven to 350 degrees.
- Melt butter in skillet with bacon drippings; add onion and cook until transparent.
- Add herb stuffing and coat completely with butter.
- In a separate bowl, combine sour cream and soup.
- Blend in tomatoes, cheese, celery, green bell pepper, horseradish and oysters.
- Spread half of herb stuffing in bottom of 9x13-inch baking dish.
- Pour oyster mixture over stuffing.
- Spread remaining stuffing over oyster mixture.
- Garnish with crumbled bacon and green bell pepper rings.
- Bake for 1 hour.

Remember This:

Nearby Apalachicola Bay supplies the nation with some of the world's most delicious oysters.

Entrées

Pine Island Shrimp

6 servings

This sauce is great!

½ cup butter
1 cup sliced fresh mushrooms
¼ cup finely minced onion
dash of garlic powder
3 tablespoons flour
¼ cup white wine
1 cup chicken broth
1 cup sour cream
1 tablespoon chopped parsley
2 pounds medium shrimp, cooked, shelled and deveined
rice or pasta

- Melt butter and sauté mushrooms and onion.
- Add garlic powder and stir in flour.
- Blend in wine and chicken broth; cook until sauce thickens.
- Lower heat and add sour cream.
- Do not boil.
- Add parsley and shrimp just before serving.
- May be served over rice or pasta.

Shrimp and Spinach Pasta

10 to 12 servings

This recipe can be halved.

1 14 or 16-ounce package spinach linguine
3 to 4 pounds shrimp, shelled and deveined
1 cup butter
2 10¾-ounce cans cream of mushroom soup
2 cups mayonnaise
2 cups sour cream
2 tablespoons chopped chives
1 cup Dijon mustard
8 tablespoons dry sherry
1 cup shredded sharp Cheddar cheese

- Preheat oven to 350 degrees.
- Cook noodles according to package directions.
- Line 2 13x9-inch baking dishes with noodles and form nests.
- Sauté shrimp in butter for approximately 5 minutes.
- Cover noodles with shrimp.
- Combine soup, mayonnaise, sour cream, chives, mustard and sherry.
- Pour sauce over shrimp and sprinkle with cheese and bake for 30 minutes.

Shrimp Scampi

4 servings

1 pound large shrimp
½ cup butter
½ teaspoon salt
6 cloves garlic, peeled and crushed
2 tablespoons chopped fresh parsley
1 teaspoon grated lemon rind
1 tablespoon lemon juice
lime or lemon wedge for garnish
1 pound fettuccine; spinach, carrot and plain

- Preheat oven to 400 degrees.
- Shell and devein shrimp.
- Wash under running water; drain well on paper towels.
- Melt butter in a 13x9x2-inch baking dish in oven.
- Add salt, garlic and 1 tablespoon parsley; mix well.
- Arrange shrimp in a single layer in baking dish; bake uncovered for 5 minutes.
- Turn shrimp and top with lemon rind, lemon juice and remaining parsley.
- Bake for 8 to 10 minutes longer or until shrimp are tender.
- Cook fettuccine al dente.
- Arrange shrimp over cooked fettuccine on a heated serving platter.
- Pour sauce over shrimp and garnish with lime or lemon wedges.

Shrimp Light

10 servings

½ cup butter, cut into pats
garlic salt
3 pounds cooked shrimp, shelled and deveined
1 quart cottage cheese
½ to ¾ cup freshly grated Parmesan cheese
1½ cups slivered almonds, toasted
1 cup cracker crumbs

- Preheat oven to 350 degrees.
- Grease a 3-quart baking dish generously with butter and garlic salt.
- Layer shrimp and cottage cheese alternately, sprinkling Parmesan cheese and garlic salt on each layer.
- Top with almonds, cracker crumbs and pats of butter.
- Bake for 30 minutes.

Shrimp Cabourg

6 servings

Can be prepared a few hours ahead and reheated gently.

1 pound mushrooms, sliced
¼ cup finely minced onion
2 tablespoons lemon juice
1 8-ounce bottle clam juice
1 teaspoon salt
1 teaspoon pepper
1 cup water
2 pounds shrimp, shelled and deveined
4 egg yolks, slightly beaten
1½ cups melted butter
3 tablespoons freshly grated Parmesan cheese

- Combine mushrooms, onion, lemon juice, clam juice, salt, pepper and water in a large skillet.
- Bring to a boil; reduce heat and simmer for 2 to 3 minutes, stirring occasionally.
- Add shrimp and cover.
- Simmer for 3 minutes or until shrimp turn pink.
- Remove shrimp and mushrooms with a slotted spoon.
- Boil liquid in skillet until it is reduced to ½ cup.
- Remove from heat and let cool for a few minutes; add egg yolks.
- Beat with a wire whisk over low heat until the consistency of thin white sauce.
- Remove from heat and gradually beat in melted butter; correct seasonings.
- Mix shrimp and mushrooms into sauce.
- Divide among 6 scallop shells or ramekins and sprinkle with cheese.
- Broil until just golden brown.

Remember This:

Two pounds of unpeeled shrimp properly cooked, will yield one pound cooked, peeled, deveined shrimp.

Shrimp Au Gratin

6 to 8 servings

May be served over rice, but certainly stands alone as a dish.

9 cups water
2 tablespoons salt
3 pounds fresh shrimp
1 chicken bouillon cube
1 cup boiling water
¼ cup plus 1 tablespoon butter
3 tablespoons flour
1 cup milk
1 egg, beaten
2 tablespoons sherry
1 teaspoon Worcestershire sauce
4 drops Tabasco
¼ teaspoon pepper
⅛ teaspoon salt
1 cup shredded Cheddar cheese

- Preheat oven to 350 degrees.
- Bring 9 cups water and salt to a boil.
- Add shrimp, reduce heat and cook for 1 to 2 minutes.
- Drain; rinse in cold water; shell and devein.
- Dissolve bouillon cube in 1 cup boiling water.
- In a large saucepan, melt butter over low heat; add flour, stirring until smooth.
- Gradually add bouillon and milk; cook over medium heat stirring constantly.
- Bring to a boil and simmer for 1 minute; stirring constantly.
- Remove from heat.
- Gradually stir ¼ of hot mixture into egg; stir egg into sauce.
- Cook over low heat for 3 to 4 minutes, stirring constantly.
- Remove from heat, stir in sherry, Worcestershire, Tabasco, seasonings and shrimp.
- Pour into a shallow 1½-quart baking dish or 6 individual dishes.
- Top with shredded cheese.
- Cover and bake for 30 minutes.
- May be prepared the night before and refrigerated.

Belgian Style Seafood

8 to 10 servings

Enjoy the bounty of the Gulf.

1 tablespoon butter
1½ pounds medium shrimp, shelled and deveined
1 pound scallops
1 pound crabmeat
6 hard-cooked eggs, coarsely chopped
2 tablespoons flour
2 teaspoons dry mustard
1 teaspoon salt
½ teaspoon pepper
2 cups whipping cream
½ cup shredded Swiss cheese
3 tablespoons chopped fresh parsley
½ cup milk, optional
2 pounds ribbon pasta, cooked al dente

- Preheat oven to 400 degrees.
- In a large buttered baking dish, layer the uncooked seafood and eggs; set aside.
- In a medium saucepan, mix flour, mustard, salt and pepper.
- Gradually add cream and bring to a boil, stirring constantly.
- Remove from heat; add cheese and parsley.
- If necessary, gradually add up to ½ cup milk to thin sauce.
- Pour sauce over seafood.
- Bake for 20 to 25 minutes or until top is golden brown and sauce is bubbly.
- Serve over ribbon pasta.

Pasta With Tomato Shrimp Sauce

4 servings

Light eating at its finest.

1 28-ounce can tomatoes
1 medium onion, sliced
2 teaspoons chopped fresh basil or 1 teaspoon dried basil
3 tablespoons chopped parsley
2 tablespoons olive oil
2 cloves garlic, minced
1 pound pasta, preferably linguine
½ pound medium shrimp, shelled and deveined

- Purée tomatoes in a food processor.
- Transfer to a saucepan and add onion, spices, olive oil and garlic.
- Cook for approximately 20 minutes.
- Add shrimp and simmer until pink, approximately 3 minutes.
- Cook and drain pasta.
- Serve shrimp sauce over pasta with Tabasco.

Chutney Shrimp On Shells Of Pastry
6 servings

Elegant for lucheons.

1 10-inch pie pastry, unbaked
6 5-inch extra deep scallop shells, (available in culinary shops)
vegetable oil
½ cup chopped onion
¼ cup butter
2½ teaspoons curry powder
½ cup chopped mango chutney
3 cups small shrimp, shelled and deveined
1 hard-cooked egg, finely chopped
3 tablespoons minced parsley

- To prepare pastry shells, preheat oven to 375 degrees.
- Prepare a pie pastry, or use ready-made.
- Roll pastry ⅛-inch thick on a lightly floured surface.
- Oil each scallop shell and line with pastry, trimming edges with a dull knife.
- Gently press pastry against shell so all indentations will be imprinted on pastry.
- Place parchment or heavy duty wax paper over pastry and weigh down with one layer of aluminum pellets, dried beans or rice.
- Bake on middle rack of oven for about 10 minutes, or until pastry shells are golden.
- Cool before removing pastry from shell.
- To prepare shrimp filling, sauté onion in butter until golden.
- Stir in curry powder and chutney; mix well.
- Add shrimp, tossing until well coated with sauce and thoroughly heated; do not allow to boil.
- Spoon evenly into pastry shells; sprinkle with egg and parsley.
- Chutney Shrimp may also be served over rice.
- Baked shells may be frozen for 2 weeks when wrapped carefully.
- Allow shells to come to room temperature then freshen at 200 degrees for 10 minutes.

Remember This:
Scallop shells may be purchased in most culinary shops.

Entrées

Shrimp And Artichoke Casserole
6 servings

½ cup butter
¼ pound fresh mushrooms, sliced
⅓ cup flour
1 cup heavy cream
1 cup milk
⅓ cup white wine
1 tablespoon Worcestershire sauce
salt and pepper to taste
1 14-ounce can artichoke hearts, halved and drained
1 pound medium shrimp, cooked, shelled and deveined
⅓ cup freshly grated Parmesan cheese

- Preheat oven to 375 degrees.
- Melt butter; add sliced mushrooms and cook for 2 minutes.
- Stir in flour until blended.
- Add cream and milk and stir constantly with a wire whisk until thickened.
- Add wine and Worcestershire sauce, stirring constantly.
- Season with salt and pepper.
- Arrange artichokes in a 2-quart baking dish and cover with shrimp.
- Pour sauce over shrimp and artichokes, then top with Parmesan cheese.
- Bake for 20 to 30 minutes.

Low Country Boil
6 servings

2 crab boil bags
2 onions, quartered
4 stalks celery, chopped
3 tablespoons salt
1 tablespoon Tabasco
3 tablespoons Worcestershire sauce
4 to 6 cloves garlic
½ cup vinegar
1½ pounds beef sausage, sliced thin
6 to 8 ears fresh corn, halved
3 pounds fresh medium shrimp, washed and unshelled

- Combine first 8 ingredients in a 3 gallon kettle and fill ⅓ of kettle with water.
- Boil for 30 minutes.
- This can be done earlier in the day so seasonings can blend.
- Fifteen minutes before serving, bring to a brisk boil.
- Add sausage and cook for 5 minutes; then add corn and cook for 5 minutes.
- Blend in shrimp and cook for last 5 minutes.
- Strain away pot liquor and serve immediately in a large bowl.
- Serve with cocktail sauce.
- Let guests peel their own shrimp; place small bowls on table for hulls.

Shrimp Creole

6 servings

½ lemon, sliced
4 whole peppercorns
2 pounds shrimp, shelled and deveined
4 slices bacon, cut up
2 tablespoons butter
1 clove garlic, minced
1 cup chopped onion
1½ cups chopped green bell pepper
1½ cups sliced celery
1 28-ounce can tomatoes
1 6-ounce can tomato paste
1 tablespoon lemon juice
¼ teaspoon Tabasco
1 tablespoon sugar
1 teaspoon salt
½ teaspoon pepper
1 bay leaf
½ teaspoon thyme
¼ teaspoon cayenne pepper
1½ cups rice, cooked

- In a large pan, bring 1 quart water to a boil.
- Add lemon slices, peppercorns and shrimp to water.
- Reduce heat and simmer for 3 minutes.
- Drain and reserve 1 cup liquid; discard peppercorns and lemon slices.
- Refrigerate shrimp.
- Melt butter and sauté bacon in a Dutch oven.
- Remove and reserve bacon and add garlic, onion, celery and green bell pepper.
- Cook for approximately 5 minutes.
- Add 1 cup reserved shrimp liquid, tomatoes, tomato paste, bacon and lemon juice.
- Stir in Tabasco, sugar, salt, pepper, bay leaf, thyme and cayenne pepper.
- Bring to a boil and simmer for 1½ hours.
- Add shrimp and serve over hot cooked rice.

Crab And Shrimp Casserole
8 servings

A wonderful combination with the perfect amount of cheeses and seafood.

4 tablespoons butter
2 tablespoons flour
1 cup milk
1 teaspoon horseradish
2 teaspoons lemon juice
1 teaspoon dry mustard
salt to taste
1 pound claw crabmeat
1 pound cooked, diced shrimp
1 cup shredded Longhorn cheese
⅓ cup freshly grated Parmesan cheese
½ cup cracker crumbs
pimento and parsley for garnish

- Preheat oven to 350 degrees.
- Melt butter in a skillet over medium heat.
- Stir in flour and cook for 1 minute.
- Gradually stir in milk.
- Cook until thickened and bubbly; stirring constantly.
- Stir in remaining ingredients and place in a buttered 2-quart baking dish.
- Bake for 20 to 25 minutes.
- Garnish with pimento strips and parsley sprigs.

Best Ever Crab Cakes
6 to 8 servings

1 pound claw crabmeat
2 tablespoons butter
4 tablespoons finely chopped onion
1 cup bread crumbs
1 egg, beaten
1 teaspoon dry mustard
salt and pepper to taste
½ teaspoon grated lemon peel
¼ cup sour cream
flour
2 tablespoons butter

- Pick crabmeat to remove any remaining shells.
- Melt 2 tablespoons butter in a saucepan.
- Add chopped onion and sauté until soft.
- Mix together crabmeat, sautéed onion, bread crumbs, egg, mustard, salt, pepper, lemon peel and sour cream.
- If too dry, add a little milk.
- Shape into cakes and chill well.
- Dredge crab cakes in flour.
- Melt 2 tablespoons butter in a skillet and sauté crab cakes over medium heat until crust is crisp.
- Serve immediately.

Entrées

St. Teresa Crab Casserole

4 to 5 servings

1 pound lump crabmeat
⅔ cup mayonnaise
1 tablespoon prepared mustard
1 tablespoon Worcestershire sauce
1½ tablespoons lemon juice
3 dashes Tabasco
¼ cup milk
½ teaspoon salt
½ teaspoon pepper
1 cup saltine cracker crumbs
¼ cup butter

- Preheat oven to 350 degrees.
- Carefully pick crabmeat to remove any shells without breaking up pieces.
- Prepare sauce with mayonnaise, mustard, Worcestershire sauce, lemon juice, Tabasco, milk, salt and pepper.
- Mix well; add crab and ¼ cup cracker crumbs.
- Pour in a buttered 6-inch baking dish or individual ramekins.
- Top with remaining cracker crumbs and dot with butter.
- Bake for 25 minutes.

Crab Mornay

4 entrée or 8 first course servings

½ cup butter
1 small bunch scallions, chopped
½ cup chopped fresh parsley
2 tablespoons flour
1 pint half and half
½ pound Swiss cheese, shredded
1 tablespoon sherry
red pepper to taste
1 pound claw crabmeat
½ pound cooked shrimp, optional
steamed artichoke leaves, optional

- Melt butter in a heavy saucepan and sauté onions and parsley.
- Blend in flour, cream and cheese until cheese is melted.
- Add sherry and red pepper; gently fold in crabmeat.
- Heat thoroughly.
- If serving in puff pastry shells, serve on a bed of artichoke leaves and garnish with cooked shrimp.

Entrées

Simply Delicious Scallops

4 servings

2 tablespoons butter
1½ pound bay scallops
½ cup butter
1 medium clove garlic, minced
½ teaspoon freshly ground pepper
salt to taste
1 pound plain linguine or ½ pound plain and ½ pound carrot linguine
fresh dill
freshly ground pepper

- Melt 2 tablespoons butter in a large heavy skillet over medium heat.
- Add scallops and stir until just opaque, about 1 minute.
- Transfer to a plate using a slotted spoon.
- Wipe out skillet and add ½ cup butter.
- Melt over medium-low heat; add garlic, pepper and salt.
- Stir for 3 minutes and add scallops.
- Cook pasta until tender but still firm to bite.
- Drain pasta thoroughly and toss with scallops.
- Garnish with fresh dill and season with pepper.
- Serve immediately.

Scallop Kabobs

6 servings

1 pound bay scallops
2 cups cherry tomatoes
2 cups fresh small mushrooms
1 13½-ounce can pineapple chunks, drained
1 green bell pepper, cut into 1-inch squares
¼ cup vegetable oil
¼ cup lemon juice
¼ cup chopped parsley
¼ cup soy sauce
½ teaspoon salt
⅛ teaspoon pepper

- Rinse scallops with cold water to remove any remaining shell particles.
- Place tomatoes, mushrooms, pineapple, green bell pepper and scallops in a bowl.
- Combine oil, lemon juice, parsley, soy sauce, salt and pepper.
- Pour sauce over scallop mixture and let stand for 30 minutes, stirring occasionally.
- Using long skewers, alternate scallops, tomatoes, mushrooms, pineapple and green bell pepper until skewers are filled.
- Cook for approximately 4 minutes over moderately hot coals.
- Baste with sauce; turn and cook for 3 to 4 minutes longer.

Lemon Grilled Red Snapper

4 servings

Deliciously flavored snapper.

½ cup butter, melted
2 tablespoons lemon juice
1 tablespoon chopped parsley
1 teaspoon Liquid Smoke
2 teaspoons salt
dash of pepper
2 pounds red snapper fillets

- Make a pan with aluminum foil and place on grill.
- Spray foil with non-stick spray.
- Mix all ingredients together except fish.
- Place fillets on foil and baste.
- Cook for 8 minutes.
- Turn fillets, baste and cook for 8 to 10 minutes.
- Serve immediately.

Florida Grilled Fish

4 servings

A moist, delicately seasoned dish.

¼ cup butter, divided
2 pounds white fish fillets, grouper, snapper or scamp
salt and pepper
juice of 2 lemons
¼ cup snipped fresh parsley
¼ cup white wine
¼ cup chopped celery
¼ onion, chopped
minced garlic to taste

- Spread foil large enough to make a sealed package for fish.
- Place pats of butter on bottom of foil and top with fish.
- Season with salt and pepper to taste and place remaining butter on top.
- Combine lemon juice, parsley, wine, celery, onion and garlic; pour over fillets.
- Seal foil and place on a heated grill for 15 to 20 minutes.
- Flake with fork to test for doneness.

Remember This:

Fresh fish will remain fresh longest when placed in a plastic bag and packed in ice. Pour off water as ice melts. Stored in this manner, fresh fish will keep for 1 to 2 days in refrigerator.

Gulf Coast Grouper 6 servings

¼ cup milk
2 eggs, slightly beaten
1½ cups Italian bread crumbs
2 pounds grouper fillets
½ cup butter, softened
¼ cup melted butter
¼ cup fresh lemon juice
2 tablespoons chopped fresh parsley

- Combine milk and eggs in a shallow pie plate.
- Dip fillets in egg mixture and roll in bread crumbs.
- Pan fry fish in ½ cup butter at 350 degrees in an electric skillet until fillets are golden and flaky, approximately 8 to 10 minutes on each side.
- Drizzle with melted butter, lemon juice and parsley.

Grouper Parmesan 6 servings

2 pounds grouper fillets, skinned
1 cup sour cream
¼ cup freshly grated Parmesan cheese
1 tablespoon lemon juice
1 tablespoon grated onion
dash of Tabasco
⅛ teaspoon salt
paprika
fresh parsley

- Preheat oven to 350 degrees.
- Place fillets in a single layer in a buttered 9x13-inch baking dish.
- Combine remaining ingredients except paprika and parsley.
- Spread sour cream mixture over fish and sprinkle with paprika.
- Bake for 25 to 30 minutes and garnish with parsley.

Remember This:

Save leftover rinds of Parmesan cheese. A piece added to a pot of vegetable soup adds real gusto.

Grilled Salmon With Wine Sauce

6 servings

The marinade makes this grilled fish special!

3 pounds salmon fillets
Marinade:
¾ cup apple cider
6 tablespoons soy sauce
2 tablespoons unsalted butter
1 large clove garlic, minced
Cream Sauce:
4 tablespoons minced green onion
¼ cup white wine
¼ cup white vinegar
¼ cup heavy cream
6 tablespoons cold unsalted butter

- To prepare marinade, bring cider and soy sauce to a boil over high heat.
- Reduce heat to medium and cook for 3 minutes.
- Add 2 tablespoons butter and garlic; continue cooking until mixture thickens, about 20 minutes.
- Let cool slightly.
- Pour marinade over fillets and let stand at room temperature for 30 minutes.
- Meanwhile, cover rack of broiler pan with heavy aluminum foil and prick foil with a fork.
- Place salmon on prepared rack and grill over hot coals for approximately 20 minutes or until flaky.
- To prepare sauce, bring green onions, wine and vinegar to a boil in a small saucepan.
- Lower heat and simmer until mixture is reduced to almost nothing.
- Add heavy cream and simmer for 1 minute.
- Mix in cold butter, 1 tablespoon at a time, stirring constantly.
- Remove from heat and serve sauce immediately with grilled salmon.

Sherried Crabmeat

Your guests will love this dish!

16 servings

1 cup chopped onion
1 cup chopped green bell pepper
1 cup chopped celery
2 cups butter, divided
3 pounds lump crabmeat
½ cup chopped parsley
4 teaspoons salt, divided
1 to 2 teaspoons Tabasco
juice of 2 lemons
4 pimentos, chopped
1 8-ounce jar sliced mushrooms, drained
½ cup sherry
1 cup flour
1 teaspoon pepper
4 cups milk
½ cup cracker crumbs

- Preheat oven to 350 degrees.
- Sauté onion, celery and green bell pepper in 1 cup butter until tender; remove from heat.
- In a large bowl, combine sautéed vegetables with crabmeat, parsley, 2 teaspoons salt, Tabasco, lemon juice, pimentos, mushrooms and sherry.
- In a large double boiler, combine flour, pepper and remaining salt.
- Gradually stir in milk.
- Cook over hot water, stirring constantly, until mixture is smooth.
- Remove from heat and add remaining butter; stirring until melted.
- Combine sauce with crab mixture and spoon into a 4-quart baking dish.
- Sprinkle with cracker crumbs and bake for 30 minutes.
- Can be divided and baked in two 2-quart baking dishes.

Remember This:

Quickly crush crackers by placing in a zip lock bag and crush with a rolling pin.

Entrées

Hot Crab Salad 6 servings

Tallahassee hostesses serve this salad in deep sea shells collected at nearby beaches.

Salad:
1 tablespoon butter
1 pound claw crabmeat
1 green bell pepper, minced
1 cup mayonnaise
½ teaspoon salt
⅛ teaspoon pepper
1 teaspoon Worcestershire sauce
¼ teaspoon cayenne pepper
¼ teaspoon celery seed
1 teaspoon dry mustard
1 teaspoon lemon juice
1 teaspoon snipped parsley
Topping:
3 tablespoons butter, melted
1 cup bread crumbs

- Preheat oven to 350 degrees.
- Rub bottom of 6 individual sea shells with 1 tablespoon butter.
- Mix all salad ingredients and place salad in shells.
- Stir in butter and bread crumbs together.
- Sprinkle topping over salad.
- Place shells on a cookie sheet and bake until golden.
- Serve immediately.

Linguine With Scallops 2 servings

4 ounces linguine, cooked and drained
½ cup butter
1 clove garlic, minced
½ pound scallops
6 large mushrooms, sliced
½ cup freshly grated Parmesan cheese
salt and pepper to taste
sprig of oregano

- In a large skillet, melt butter.
- Add garlic, scallops, and mushrooms and cook over low heat for 5 minutes.
- Add cooked linguine and sprinkle with cheese, salt and pepper.
- Gently toss linguine and heat until thoroughly warmed.
- Garnish with a sprig of oregano and serve with Parmesan cheese.

Entrées

Baked Flounder Cordon Bleu   6 servings

May be prepared a few hours ahead and chilled prior to cooking.

6 flounder fillets, approximately 2 pounds
6 slices cooked ham, about 6 ounces
6 slices Swiss cheese, about 6 ounces
1 teaspoon grated orange rind
¼ teaspoon white pepper
1 egg, beaten
1 cup bread crumbs
1 tablespoon butter
1 tablespoon flour
1 cup light cream or half and half
¼ cup freshly grated Parmesan cheese

- Preheat oven to 350 degrees.
- Place 1 slice each of ham and cheese in the center of each fillet; cut to fit.
- Sprinkle with grated orange rind and white pepper.
- Roll into pinwheels and secure with toothpicks.
- Gently dip roll in beaten egg and coat with bread crumbs.
- Place in a greased 12x8x2-inch baking dish.
- In a saucepan over medium heat, combine butter and flour.
- Slowly stir in cream; heat until sauce begins to thicken.
- Pour sauce over fish roll-ups and sprinkle with Parmesan cheese.
- Bake at 350 degrees for 20 to 25 minutes or until fish flakes easily when tested with a fork.

Swiss Baked Fish   4 servings

A terrific dish for a busy day.

2 pounds fillet of flounder
1 tablespoon lemon juice
½ cup sour cream
6 ounces Swiss cheese, finely diced
2 scallions, chopped
¼ cup bread crumbs
1 teaspoon seasoned salt
¼ teaspoon pepper
butter

- Preheat oven to 350 degrees.
- Place skinless fish evenly over a baking dish.
- Drizzle lemon juice on fillet and spread with sour cream.
- Cover with Swiss cheese, scallions and bread crumbs.
- Season with salt and pepper; dot with butter.
- Bake for 35 minutes.

Tomato Garlic Sauce 2 cups

2 tablespoons olive oil
2 tablespoons garlic, minced
½ cup onion, chopped
1 16-ounce can plum tomatoes, crushed
1 cup chopped green bell pepper
¼ cup sugar
2 tablespoons fresh or 1 teaspoon dried tarragon leaves, crushed
salt and freshly ground pepper to taste

- Sauté garlic in olive oil until golden.
- Add onion and cook over medium-high heat until tender.
- Add tomatoes, green bell pepper, sugar and tarragon and simmer for 30 minutes.
- Season with salt and pepper.
- Serve warm as an accompaniment to lobster or fish.

Tartar Sauce 1 cup

1 cup mayonnaise
2 teaspoons capers, drained
1 tablespoon fresh parsley, minced
2 teaspoons scallions, minced
2 teaspoons sweet pickles, minced
1 tablespoon white vinegar

- Blend all ingredients and refrigerate to combine flavors before serving.

Cocktail Sauce Approximately 1 cup

½ cup catsup
1 tablespoon fresh lime juice
1 tablespoon prepared horseradish
4 to 6 dashes Tabasco
¼ teaspoon Worcestershire sauce
salt and freshly ground pepper

- Combine all ingredients in a bowl.
- Season with salt and pepper to taste.
- Serve with raw oysters or boiled shrimp.

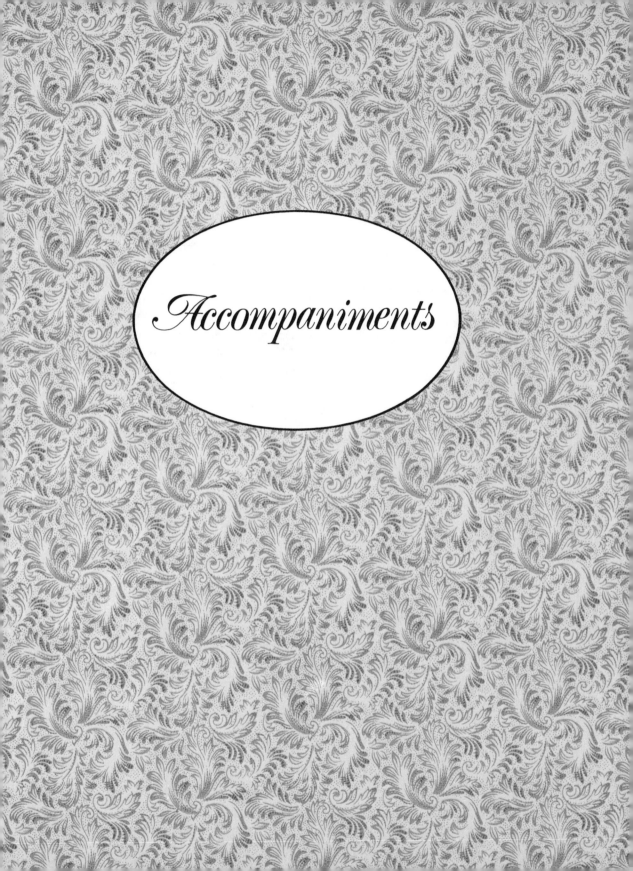

Accompaniments

Zucchini Mushroom Shells

6 servings

6 small zucchini
1 cup minced mushrooms
1 egg, beaten
8 tablespoons grated Parmesan cheese
2 tablespoons chopped fresh or 2 teaspoons dried basil
salt and pepper to taste
1 tablespoon butter

- Trim ends from zucchini and drop zucchini into boiling water for 8 minutes; drain well.
- Slice zucchini in half lengthwise and scoop out pulp leaving a ¼-inch thick shell.
- Combine pulp with mushrooms, eggs, 6 tablespoons cheese and seasonings.
- Place mixture in zucchini shells, sprinkle with remaining cheese and dot with butter.
- Place in a shallow buttered baking dish and bake at 325 degrees for 30 minutes.
- Broil for the last 2 minutes to brown cheese.

Zucchini Rice

6 servings

An outstanding combination of ingredients.

1½ pounds zucchini
1 cup brown rice, cooked
juice of one lemon
¾ cup chopped fresh parsley
1 teaspoon salt
⅛ teaspoon pepper
1 teaspoon dried or 1 tablespoon fresh chopped basil
2 tablespoons olive oil
1 cup low fat cottage cheese
½ cup shredded mild Cheddar cheese
2 tablespoons grated Parmesan cheese

- Preheat oven to 350 degrees.
- Slice and steam zucchini until just crisp.
- Cook brown rice according to package directions.
- Combine rice with lemon juice, parsley, salt, pepper, basil and olive oil.
- Layer a lightly buttered 1½-quart shallow casserole with rice mixture, cottage cheese, and steamed zucchini.
- Sprinkle with Cheddar and Parmesan cheese.
- Bake uncovered for 20 minutes.

Italian Zucchini
8 servings

2 medium onions, finely chopped
3 cloves garlic, minced
3 tablespoons olive oil
2 medium red bell peppers, seeded and sliced thin
3 large tomatoes, peeled and chopped
4 zucchini, diced
salt and pepper to taste

- Sauté onions with garlic in olive oil over medium-high heat.
- When onions are soft, add peppers.
- Cook for 5 minutes over medium heat.
- Add tomatoes and zucchini and season with salt and pepper.
- Cook covered over low heat until peppers are very tender.

Salade Aux Haricots Verts
4 servings

Chez Pierre's savory dish.

1½ pounds green beans
1 clove garlic, finely minced
1 tablespoon Dijon mustard
2 tablespoons red wine vinegar
6 tablespoons oil
salt and pepper to taste
¼ cup chopped fresh parsley
2 thin slices red onion, separated into rings

- Trim or snap off ends of beans and "string", if necessary.
- Drop whole beans into boiling salted water and cook for 5 to 10 minutes, depending on the size of the beans, until tender.
- Watch beans carefully and test for doneness with the tip of a sharp knife.
- Do not overcook.
- Pour beans into a colander and rinse with cold water; drain.
- In a large bowl, add garlic, mustard, and vinegar and mix well.
- Add oil a little at a time, whisking continuously until all oil is added.
- Season with salt and pepper and half of parsley.
- Add green beans to bowl with vinaigrette and toss gently.
- Garnish with remaining parsley and thinly sliced red onion rings.

Green Beans Oriental

4 servings

½ pound green beans, sliced diagonally
½ cup water chestnuts, sliced
½ cup fresh mushrooms
1 clove garlic, minced
2 teaspoons vegetable oil
2½ teaspoons soy sauce
½ teaspoon salt
¼ teaspoon pepper
1 teaspoon sugar
2 teaspoons sesame seeds

- Stir fry beans, water chestnuts, mushrooms and garlic in oil.
- Add remaining ingredients.
- Cover and cook until beans are tender, about 4 to 5 minutes.

Country Green Beans

8 servings

1½ pounds green beans
¼ cup butter
½ cup finely chopped smoked ham
¼ cup minced onion
6 tablespoons minced fresh parsley
¼ cup chopped, toasted almonds
freshly ground pepper

- To trim beans, cut almost through ends of beans and pull to remove any strings.
- Snap beans into 1½-inch pieces.
- Place beans in pan and add water to just cover.
- Add salt if desired.
- Bring water to a boil and reduce heat to medium and cook until beans are tender-crisp.
- Rinse beans under cold water and drain.
- Heat butter in large heavy skillet over medium heat.
- Sauté ham and onion until onion is transparent.
- Add beans and remaining ingredients and cook until thoroughly heated.
- Serve immediately.

Spinach Madeleine
5 to 6 servings

Wonderful over oysters on the half shell for Oysters Rockefeller.

2 10-ounce packages frozen chopped spinach
3 tablespoons butter
4 tablespoons flour
2 tablespoons chopped onion
½ cup evaporated milk
½ cup vegetable broth
½ teaspoon black pepper
¾ teaspoon celery salt
¾ teaspoon garlic salt
salt and red pepper to taste
1 6-ounce package jalapeño cheese, cubed
1 teaspoon Worcestershire sauce
½ cup bread crumbs

- Cook spinach according to package directions.
- Drain and reserve ½ cup vegetable broth.
- Melt butter in a skillet over medium heat.
- Add flour and stir until smooth.
- Add onion and cook until soft, but not brown.
- Add milk and reserved vegetable broth, stirring constantly to avoid lumps.
- Cook until smooth and thick.
- Add seasonings and cheese; stir until cheese melts.
- Combine sauce with cooked spinach.
- Put in a 1½-quart baking dish and bake at 350 degrees for 30 minutes, or top with bread crumbs, refrigerate overnight and bake the next day.

Remember This:

Make bread crumbs in batches using stale breads and crackers. Freeze the unused portion in an airtight container.

Elegant Spinach

6 servings

Elegant indeed!

2 pounds fresh spinach
4 tablespoons butter
1 teaspoon lime or lemon juice
1 teaspoon Worcestershire sauce
½ cup sour cream
¼ pound fresh mushrooms, sliced
4 tablespoons dry sherry
salt and pepper to taste

- Wash spinach thoroughly in cold water several times.
- Place in a saucepan with only the water that is remaining on the leaves.
- Cover and cook over medium heat for about 10 minutes, until just tender.
- Drain well and chop fine.
- Combine 2 tablespoons butter, lime juice, Worcestershire sauce and sour cream in a large skillet.
- Stir in spinach.
- Sauté mushrooms in remaining butter.
- Add sherry, seasonings and mushrooms to spinach.
- Mix and simmer for 2 to 3 minutes.
- Serve at once.

Remember This:

Parsley stays crisp and green for up to 5 days in the refrigerator if stored covered in a plastic container with an apple.

Baked Viennese Spinach

4 servings

1½ pounds fresh spinach or 1 10-ounce package frozen chopped spinach, cooked and drained
1 cup cooked rice
1 cup freshly grated Parmesan cheese
2 tablespoons finely chopped onion
2 eggs, beaten
2 tablespoons butter, melted
½ cup milk
½ teaspoon Worcestershire sauce
½ teaspoon thyme
½ teaspoon salt
½ cup shredded Cheddar cheese

- In a large bowl, combine spinach, rice, Parmesan cheese and onion.
- In a small bowl, combine eggs, melted butter, milk, Worcestershire sauce, thyme and salt.
- Add egg mixture to spinach and stir well.
- Pour mixture into a 1½-quart greased baking dish.
- Sprinkle with Cheddar cheese.
- Bake at 350 degrees for 20 minutes.
- Serve warm.

Almond Asparagus

6 servings

So simple and oh so delectable!

30 thin asparagus spears
4 tablespoons butter
salt and freshly ground pepper to taste
¼ cup lightly toasted sliced almonds

- Rinse asparagus and break off tough ends.
- Slice spears diagonally into 1-inch pieces.
- Melt butter in a medium skillet over medium-high heat.
- Add asparagus, salt and pepper.
- Sauté for 5 to 7 minutes or until tender-crisp, stirring frequently.
- Transfer to a serving dish and sprinkle with toasted almonds.
- Serve immediately.

Marinated Tomatoes And Onions 6 to 8 servings

6 medium ripe tomatoes
1 cup olive oil
1/3 cup white wine vinegar
1 tablespoon freshly chopped basil leaves
1 teaspoon salt
2 teaspoons sugar
1/2 teaspoon dry mustard
1 small garlic clove, minced
1/2 teaspoon freshly ground pepper
1 medium yellow onion, thinly sliced and separated into rings
1/2 cup chopped parsley

- Keep tomatoes at room temperature until fully ripe.
- Remove skins and slice 1/4-inch thick.
- Prepare marinade by combining oil, vinegar, basil, salt, sugar, mustard, garlic and pepper.
- Mix well.
- In a serving bowl, arrange a layer of tomatoes and sprinkle lightly with marinade.
- Arrange a layer of onion rings over tomatoes and sprinkle with parsley and marinade.
- Repeat layers.
- Cover and let stand at room temperature for 1 hour before serving.

Fire And Ice Tomatoes 8 servings

6 large tomatoes
1 large green bell pepper, seeded
1 large onion
3/4 cup vinegar
1 1/2 teaspoons celery seed
1 1/2 teaspoons mustard seed
1/2 teaspoon salt
4 1/2 teaspoons sugar
1/8 teaspoon red pepper
1/8 teaspoon black pepper
1/4 cup water

- Peel tomatoes and onions and cut into quarters.
- Separate onion pieces.
- Cut green pepper into thin strips.
- Place vegetables in a shallow heat-proof dish and set aside.
- Combine vinegar, celery seed, mustard seed, salt, sugar, red pepper, black pepper and water in a small saucepan.
- Bring mixture to a boil and boil for 1 minute.
- Pour hot mixture over vegetables and refrigerate until thoroughly chilled.
- Serve chilled.

Cheddar Tomatoes
4 servings

3 to 4 tomatoes, peeled and sliced
½ cup shredded mild Cheddar cheese
½ cup shredded sharp Cheddar cheese
2 tablespoons chopped green bell pepper
3 tablespoons chopped onion
⅓ cup butter, melted
1 cup butter flavored cracker crumbs
½ cup diced celery
1 teaspoon salt
¼ teaspoon pepper
3 to 4 green bell pepper rings

- Mix all ingredients except pepper rings and pour into a greased 1-quart baking dish.
- Top with pepper rings.
- Bake uncovered at 350 degrees for 20 minutes.

Fresh Tomato Tart
6 servings

1 9-inch pie pastry, unbaked
3 large ripe tomatoes
seasoned salt
freshly ground pepper
1 tablespoon chopped fresh or 1 teaspoon dried basil
½ cup mayonnaise
½ cup freshly grated Parmesan cheese
⅛ teaspoon garlic powder
¼ cup cracker crumbs

- Line a 10-inch tart pan with pie pastry.
- Prick crust well and bake according to package directions; cool.
- Slice tomatoes and place in layers in tart pan.
- Sprinkle with seasoned salt, pepper and basil.
- In a small bowl, combine mayonnaise, Parmesan cheese and garlic powder.
- Spread mixture over tomatoes.
- Mixture will not completely cover tomatoes.
- Sprinkle with cracker crumbs.
- Bake tart at 400 degrees for 15 minutes.

Fried Green Tomatoes
4 to 6 servings

1¼ to 1½ pounds very hard green tomatoes
corn oil
1 egg
1 cup yellow cornmeal
salt and pepper to taste

- Wash and core tomatoes, but do not peel or seed.
- Cut into ½-inch thick slices.
- Heat ½-inch corn oil in a heavy skillet to about 350 degrees, or until a cube of bread browns instantly.
- In small bowl, beat egg well.
- Place cornmeal in a separate bowl.
- When oil is hot, moisten a slice of tomato in beaten egg and dip into cornmeal, coating evenly.
- Place coated tomato slices in hot oil and fry for approximately 1 minute or until edges brown.
- Turn and fry for 1 additional minute.
- Remove from pan and place on a paper towel lined ovenproof platter.
- Do not cover.
- Keep warm until ready to serve.

Summer Palette
6 servings

1½ pounds yellow squash
1 teaspoon seasoned salt
1 teaspoon seasoned pepper
2 cloves garlic, minced
2 small onions, thinly sliced
3 tomatoes, sliced
8 ounces sharp Cheddar cheese, shredded
6 strips bacon

- Halve and slice squash lengthwise.
- Place squash in a greased 13x9-inch baking dish.
- Season with salt, pepper and garlic.
- Layer onions over squash and cover onions with tomatoes.
- Cover with cheese.
- Place uncooked bacon strips on top.
- Bake at 400 degrees for 15 minutes.
- Lower temperature to 375 degrees and bake for 40 minutes.

Sour Cream Yellow Squash

6 servings

2 pounds yellow squash, sliced
½ cup sour cream
¼ cup butter, melted
¼ cup sliced green onions, including tops
½ teaspoon salt
⅛ teaspoon white pepper
1 cup fresh bread crumbs
¼ cup Parmesan cheese
3 tablespoons butter, melted

- Cook squash in small amount of water, until just tender, about 5 to 10 minutes; drain.
- Mash slightly; drain again.
- Combine with sour cream, ¼ cup butter, onions, salt and pepper to taste.
- Place in a buttered 1-quart baking dish.
- Mix together bread crumbs and cheese.
- Toss with 3 tablespoons melted butter and sprinkle over squash.
- Bake in a preheated 350 degree oven for 25 minutes or until bubbly.

Bleu Broccoli

4 servings

A zesty sauce for a favorite vegetable.

1½ pounds fresh broccoli
¼ pound creamy bleu cheese
¼ cup whipping cream
2 teaspoons butter
2 small cloves garlic, minced
¼ cup pine nuts
¼ teaspoon freshly ground pepper

- Cut broccoli into florets.
- Peel top 3 inches of the stems and slice into thin strips, about 1½ inches long.
- Cook florets and stems, covered, in 3 inches boiling water until just tender, 4 to 5 minutes; drain.
- Combine bleu cheese and cream with a fork; stir until smooth.
- Set aside.
- Melt butter in a medium saucepan over medium heat.
- Add garlic and pine nuts.
- Sauté until lightly browned.
- Add broccoli to pine nuts.
- Then add cheese mixture and pepper.
- Toss until just warmed through and serve immediately.

Celebrated Cauliflower

6 servings

1 medium head cauliflower
1½ cups sliced mushrooms
2 tablespoons butter
2 tablespoons flour
¼ teaspoon salt
dash of white pepper
1 cup milk, warmed
1 cup shredded sharp Cheddar cheese
1 teaspoon Dijon mustard
1 tablespoon minced parsley

- Remove outer green leaves from cauliflower and trim stem end.
- Steam whole head of cauliflower in steamer basket for 15 minutes or until tender-crisp.
- In a medium skillet, melt butter over medium heat.
- Add mushrooms and cook until tender; about 4 minutes.
- Stirring constantly, blend in flour, salt and pepper; cook for 1 minute.
- Gradually add milk stirring constantly until thickened.
- Stir in cheese and mustard.
- Heat until cheese melts.
- Place cauliflower on a heated platter; spoon sauce over cauliflower and serve any remaining sauce in a separate dish.
- Sprinkle with parsley.

Cheesy Cauliflower

4 servings

1 large head cauliflower
¾ cup mayonnaise
1 tablespoon Dijon mustard
½ teaspoon horseradish
¾ cup shredded sharp Cheddar cheese

- Remove green stem ends of cauliflower.
- Steam head until tender, about 15 to 20 minutes.
- Place in a shallow baking dish.
- Combine mayonnaise, mustard and horseradish and frost cauliflower with mixture.
- Sprinkle cheese over frosted cauliflower.
- Place cauliflower under broiler until cheese is bubbly.

Marmalade Carrots
4 servings

1 pound carrots
½ cup orange marmalade
1 tablespoon rum
2 tablespoons butter
½ cup toasted slivered almonds

- Peel and slice carrots into rounds.
- Cook carrots until just tender, about 10 minutes.
- Drain any remaining cooking liquids; cover carrots and set aside.
- In a small saucepan, combine marmalade, rum and butter.
- Warm sauce over medium heat until marmalade melts.
- Transfer cooked carrots to a serving dish and cover with sauce.
- Sprinkle almonds over glazed carrots and serve hot.
- Whole baby carrots may be substituted, but the cooking time should be lengthened.

Southern Sweet Potato Casserole
8 servings

A rich topping crowns this casserole.

3 cups cooked sweet potatoes
¾ cup sugar
½ cup milk
2 eggs, beaten
½ teaspoon salt
1 teaspoon vanilla extract
Topping:
1 cup brown sugar
⅓ cup butter, melted
½ cup flour
¾ cup chopped pecans

- Preheat oven to 350 degrees.
- Purée sweet potatoes in a food processor with a metal blade.
- In a large bowl, combine sugar, milk, eggs, salt and vanilla extract.
- Add potatoes to mixture and stir to combine.
- Pour into a greased 2-quart casserole.
- To prepare topping, combine brown sugar, butter, flour and nuts.
- Spread topping over potato mixture.
- Bake at 350 degrees for 40 minutes.

Minted Carrots

8 servings

3 cups water
½ teaspoon salt
2 pounds carrots, peeled
½ cup butter
¼ cup plus 2 tablespoons brown sugar
1 tablespoon cornstarch
¼ cup finely chopped fresh mint leaves

- Combine water and salt in a large saucepan.
- Slice carrots into julienne strips and halve.
- Add carrots to saucepan and bring to boil.
- Reduce heat and cook for 10 to 12 minutes or until tender.
- Drain carrots, reserving 1 cup liquid.
- Set carrots aside and keep warm.
- Melt butter in a heavy saucepan over low heat.
- Add brown sugar and cornstarch, stirring until smooth.
- Cook for 1 minute, stirring constantly.
- Gradually add reserved 1 cup liquid and cook over medium heat, stirring constantly until thickened.
- Stir in mint.
- Pour sauce over carrots and toss.

Remember This:

Vegetables are best steamed using a steamer basket in a saucepan containing 1-inch of water. Bring water to a boil, place vegetables in the basket, cover and reduce heat to medium. Steam until tender-crisp. Serve immediately.

Sweet Potato Pudding

4 servings

A new version of a Southern standard.

2 cups packed shredded sweet potato (about 2 medium peeled sweet potatoes)
3 tablespoons flour
¾ cup sugar
3 eggs, well beaten
1 cup milk
6 tablespoons butter, melted
½ teaspoon grated orange rind
¼ cup finely chopped pecans

- Combine shredded sweet potato with flour in a medium bowl.
- Add sugar, eggs, milk, butter and orange rind.
- Stir to combine.
- Pour mixture into a greased 1-quart shallow baking dish.
- Bake pudding at 350 degrees for 45 minutes.
- Top with chopped pecans and bake for 15 minutes more.

Scalloped Mushrooms

6 servings

1 pound fresh mushrooms, sliced
1 can pitted black olives, chopped
1½ tablespoon flour
½ teaspoon salt
¼ teaspoon pepper
⅓ cup half and half
1½ tablespoons butter
1 cup bread crumbs
1 cup shredded Cheddar cheese

- In a greased 2-quart baking dish, arrange mushrooms, cheese and olives in layers.
- Blend together flour, salt, pepper and cream.
- Pour over mushrooms.
- In a small saucepan, melt butter and stir in bread crumbs.
- Sprinkle over casserole.
- Bake uncovered at 350 degrees for 30 minutes, or until bubbly and golden brown.

Sherried Mushrooms

4 servings

¼ cup butter
3 tablespoons minced shallots
¾ pound mushrooms, sliced
3 tablespoons dry sherry
¾ teaspoon salt
¾ teaspoon freshly grated nutmeg
¼ teaspoon white pepper

- Melt butter in a large heavy skillet over medium heat.
- Add shallots and cook for about 4 minutes, until translucent.
- Add mushrooms and stir until liquid is released.
- Increase heat to high and boil until liquid evaporates, stirring frequently.
- Add all remaining ingredients.
- Stir until all moisture evaporates, about 3 minutes.

Potato Cheese Supreme

4 servings

Rich and cheesy.

3 large baking potatoes
3 tablespoons mayonnaise
¼ cup sour cream
½ cup milk
1½ cups shredded Cheddar cheese
2 tablespoons butter
salt and pepper to taste

- Peel and slice potatoes.
- Boil in a small amount of water until soft; drain.
- Combine mayonnaise, sour cream, milk, 1 cup cheese and butter.
- Add potatoes, salt and pepper and beat with an electric mixer until creamy.
- Pour into a lightly greased 1-quart baking dish.
- Bake at 350 degrees until bubbling around edges, about 20 minutes.
- Cover with ½ cup cheese and bake until cheese melts.

Potato-Broccoli Vinaigrette

6 to 8 servings

1½ pounds fresh broccoli
3 cups cubed new potatoes, cooked
cherry tomatoes, optional
½ cup vegetable oil
¼ cup cider vinegar
2 green onions, sliced
1 clove garlic, minced
1 teaspoon salt
1 teaspoon dried or 1 tablespoon fresh basil
⅛ teaspoon Tabasco

- Cut broccoli into florets and steam until tender-crisp.
- To prepare vinaigrette combine oil, vinegar, onions, garlic, salt, basil and Tabasco in a small bowl.
- Mix well.
- Pour vinaigrette over cooked vegetables and toss.
- Garnish with cherry tomatoes.
- Refrigerate for 1 hour before serving.

Garlic Potatoes With Mushrooms

6 servings

A garlic lover's dish!.

3 pounds medium new potatoes
6 thick slices bacon, cooked crisp and crumbled
2 tablespoons chopped chives
½ pound mushrooms, sliced
salt and freshly ground pepper
½ cup plus 1 tablespoon butter, melted
2 to 3 cloves garlic, pressed

- Preheat oven to 350 degrees.
- Wash and slice potatoes ¼-inch thick.
- Layer potato slices in a shallow 3-quart glass baking dish.
- Sprinkle with bacon and chives.
- Add sliced mushrooms and season with salt and pepper.
- Add pressed garlic to butter and pour over potatoes and mushrooms.
- Cover with foil and bake for 45 minutes.
- Continue baking uncovered until potatoes are tender, about 10 to 15 minutes more.

Potatoes In Dill Cream Sauce
6 servings

2 pounds new potatoes
1 tablespoon butter
½ cup sliced shallots
1 cup sour cream
2 tablespoons heavy cream
2 tablespoons chopped fresh dill
salt and pepper to taste

- Wash potatoes well leaving skins on.
- If some potatoes are large, halve potatoes before cooking.
- Place in a large pan with a small amount of water and bring to a boil.
- Reduce heat and cook until potatoes are tender.
- Remove from heat and cool slightly.
- Remove skins if desired.
- Slice potatoes about ½-inch thick.
- Set aside and keep warm.
- In a skillet, melt butter and sauté shallots until tender.
- Combine sour cream, heavy cream, dill, salt and pepper.
- Add mixture to shallots and warm over low heat.
- Pour sauce over potatoes and gently toss to coat.
- Serve warm.

Corn Pudding
6 servings

2 cups fresh corn kernels (8 to 10 ears) or 2 10-ounce packages frozen corn, thawed
3 tablespoons butter, melted
2 eggs, beaten
2 tablespoons sugar
1 teaspoon salt
1½ cups milk

- Combine corn, butter, eggs, sugar, salt and milk.
- Mix well and pour into a buttered 1½-quart baking dish.
- Bake at 350 degrees uncovered for 30 minutes, or until custard is set.

Southern Style Creamed Corn

6 servings

15 ears sweet white or yellow corn
1/3 cup butter
1/3 cup bacon drippings
salt and pepper to taste

- Cut corn from cob with a very sharp knife by cutting about half the depth of the kernels first and then using the dull side of the knife to scrape out the remaining juice and pulp.
- Put the cut corn into a medium skillet with butter and bacon drippings.
- Add enough water to give the consistency of thin gravy.
- Season with salt and pepper.
- Cook over medium-high heat for 5 minutes, stirring constantly.
- Cover, reduce heat and simmer for 25 to 30 minutes.

Bok Choy With Pine Nuts

6 servings

1½ to 2 pounds bok choy or Swiss chard
1 tablespoon vegetable oil or olive oil
2 cloves garlic
2 tablespoons pine nuts
1/3 cup raisins

- Separate leaves of vegetable and rinse well.
- Bundle leaves together and slice in approximately 1-inch slices.
- Fill a Dutch oven half full of water and bring to a boil.
- Add vegetable and cook until just tender, about 3 minutes.
- Remove from heat and drain well.
- In same Dutch oven, heat oil.
- Add garlic and cook until golden.
- Remove garlic and reduce heat to medium.
- Stir in pine nuts and raisins.
- Cook until lightly browned, stirring to prevent burning of pine nuts.
- Return cooked vegetables to pan and toss.

Tarragon And Parsley Butter ½ cup

Serve with potatoes, cauliflower or broccoli. Also good with chicken, turkey and fish.

½ cup butter
1½ teaspoons chopped tarragon or ¾ teaspoon dried crushed tarragon
1 tablespoon chopped parsley
1 tablespoon lemon juice
sea salt and pepper

- Pound butter with a mortar and pestle or process with metal blade in a food processor until smooth.
- Add tarragon and parsley and continue to process until smooth.
- Add lemon juice, sea salt and pepper.
- Cover and refrigerate overnight before serving.

Basil And Garlic Butter ½ cup

½ cup butter
2 tablespoons chopped basil
1 clove garlic, pressed
salt and freshly ground pepper

- Pound butter until smooth with a mortar and pestle or process with metal blade in a food processor.
- Add basil and garlic and process until smooth.
- Season with salt and pepper.
- Serve over potatoes, green beans, or spread on French bread.

Remember This:

Parsley can always be on hand if you wash 2 to 3 bunches and let dry in a dish drainer or spin in a salad spinner until very dry. Then process in a food processor and freeze in an airtight container.

Mint Butter ½ cup

Serve with lamb, new potatoes, carrots and green peas.

½ cup butter
2 tablespoons chopped fresh mint
1½ teaspoons lemon juice
sea salt and freshly ground pepper

- Pound butter until smooth with a mortar and pestle or process with metal blade in a food processor.
- Add chopped mint and continue to process until smooth.
- Blend in lemon juice, salt and pepper.
- Cover and refrigerate overnight before serving.

Mixed Herb Butter ½ cup

Serve with meat, fish, pasta or broiled tomatoes.

½ cup butter
1½ teaspoons chopped fresh or ¾ teaspoon dried, crushed tarragon
1½ teaspoons fresh or ¾ teaspoon dried chervil
1½ teaspoons fresh or ¾ teaspoon dried dill
1½ teaspoons chopped fresh or ¾ teaspoon dried chives
1½ teaspoons chopped fresh mint
1 tablespoon lemon juice
salt and freshly ground pepper

- Pound butter until smooth with a mortar and pestle or process with metal blade in a food processor.
- Add herbs and continue to process until smooth.
- Add lemon juice, salt and pepper.
- Cover and refrigerate overnight before serving.

Poppyseed Sauce ¼ cup

¼ cup butter, melted
2 teaspoons poppyseeds
1 tablespoon lemon juice
a dash of dried marjoram or thyme
pinch paprika
¼ teaspoon salt

- Mix all ingredients in a small heavy saucepan over low heat.
- Serve over green beans or carrots.

Company Vegetable Sauce ½ cup

This sauce compliments broccoli or spinach.

½ cup butter
¼ cup soft bread crumbs
2 small hard-cooked eggs, finely chopped
1 tablespoon finely chopped parsley
salt and pepper to taste

- Melt butter in a saucepan.
- When butter foams, stir in bread crumbs and cook for several minutes.
- Remove from heat and stir in eggs, parsley, salt and pepper.

Sunflower Sauce ½ cup

This sauce is also delicious on fruit salads.

½ cup melted butter
2 teaspoons honey
¼ teaspoon pepper
2 tablespoons fresh lemon juice
¼ teaspoon freshly grated lemon peel
½ cup sunflower seeds

- Heat all ingredients in a saucepan.
- Pour hot sauce over steamed vegetables.
- Suggested vegetables for this sauce include carrots and sweet potatoes.

Creamy Mustard Sauce 1 cup

As a variation, try this sauce with beef or lamb.

2 tablespoons butter
1 tablespoon flour
¾ cup milk
¼ teaspoon salt, or less
⅛ teaspoon white pepper
1½ tablespoons Dijon mustard
1 egg yolk, beaten
2 teaspoons lemon juice

- Melt butter in a saucepan over low heat.
- Add flour, stirring until smooth.
- Gradually stir in milk, cooking over medium heat until mixture is thickened and bubbly.
- Blend in salt, pepper and mustard.
- Add about ¼ of mixture to beaten egg yolk.
- Stir and add to remaining hot mixture.
- Mix in lemon juice.
- Serve hot over broccoli, cauliflower, carrots and asparagus.

Hearty Baked Beans 8 to 10 servings

1 pound ground chuck
1 tablespoon butter
1 medium onion, chopped
1 green bell pepper, seeded and chopped
¾ cup light brown sugar
2 15-ounce cans pork and beans
6 tablespoons catsup
1 tablespoon chili powder
4 tablespoons barbecue sauce
5 tablespoons Worcestershire sauce
1 teaspoon prepared mustard

- Brown meat in skillet.
- Remove meat from skillet and pour off any drippings.
- Melt butter in same skillet.
- Sauté onions and green bell pepper until tender.
- Combine meat, onions, green bell pepper and remaining ingredients.
- Place mixture in a 9x13-inch baking dish.
- Bake at 350 degrees for 1 hour.

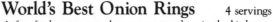

World's Best Onion Rings

4 servings

A fun food to prepare when everyone gathers in the kitchen.

2 large Spanish or Bermuda onions
1½ cups flour
1 teaspoon salt
2 eggs, beaten
2 tablespoons milk
2 cups finely crushed butter flavored crackers
½ teaspoon garlic powder
oil for frying

- Slice onions about ⅜-inch thick and separate into rings.
- Place rings in a large bowl and cover with water.
- Refrigerate overnight or for at least 3 hours.
- Drain onion rings.
- Combine flour and salt in a medium bowl.
- While onion rings are damp, dredge in flour.
- Combine eggs and milk in a medium bowl.
- In a separate bowl, combine cracker crumbs and garlic powder.
- Completely coat dredged onion rings with egg mixture by dipping them a few at a time.
- Cover with cracker crumbs.
- Fry in hot oil at 350 degrees for 2 to 3 minutes.
- Longer frying time will increase crispness if desired.
- Drain well and serve hot.

Remember This:

Add 1 teaspoon of lemon juice or vinegar to a bowl of water to keep peeled potatoes pearly white.

Onions In Chervil Cream Sauce

6 servings

Tasty with beef!

2 pounds boiler onions, peeled
3 tablespoons butter
3 tablespoons flour
2 cups milk, warmed
1 teaspoon dried chervil
salt and pepper to taste

- Place onions in a saucepan and add enough water to almost cover.
- Bring to a boil over high heat.
- Reduce heat to medium, cover and cook for 15 minutes or until just tender.
- Drain and set aside.
- Melt butter in a heavy skillet.
- Add flour and stir for 2 minutes.
- Remove skillet from heat and gradually stir in warmed milk.
- Add salt and pepper.
- Return to medium heat and cook until thickened; stir in chervil.
- Pour sauce over onions and serve.

Vidalia Bake

8 servings

¼ cup butter
7 medium Vidalia onions, sliced (or mild onions)
1 cup cooked rice
1 cup shredded Jarlsberg cheese
⅔ cup evaporated milk or half and half
pepper to taste

- Preheat oven to 350 degrees.
- Melt butter in a large saucepan and sauté onions until soft.
- Remove from heat.
- Blend rice with cheese and milk.
- Stir mixture into cooked onions.
- Transfer mixture to a 2-quart shallow dish and bake for 30 minutes at 350 degrees.

Corn Bread Dressing

10 servings

A delicious, light dressing!

3 cups self-rising cornmeal
1/4 cup flour
1 tablespoon sugar
1 teaspoon salt
pinch of baking soda
3 cups buttermilk
2 eggs, well beaten
1 cup chopped celery
3/4 cup chopped onions
4 tablespoons bacon drippings
1 3/4 cups herb-seasoned stuffing mix
1/2 teaspoon sage
1 10 3/4-ounce can cream of mushroom soup
3 cups chicken broth

- Preheat oven to 450 degrees.
- Combine cornmeal, flour, sugar, salt and soda.
- Add buttermilk and eggs.
- Mix well and stir in celery and onion.
- Heat bacon drippings in a 10-inch cast iron skillet in preheating oven.
- Add 1 tablespoon bacon drippings to batter and mix well.
- Pour batter into very hot skillet.
- Bake at 450 degrees for 20 to 30 minutes or until lightly browned.
- Turn cornbread out onto a plate to cool.
- Crumble cornbread into large mixing bowl and add stuffing mix and sage; set aside.
- Place soup in a medium saucepan and gradually stir in broth.
- Cook over medium heat, stirring occasionally until heated.
- Pour over crumb mixture; stir well.
- Spoon into a greased 13x9x2-inch baking dish and bake at 375 degrees for 35 minutes or until heated thoroughly.

Remember This:

To sour 1 cup fresh milk measure 1 cup milk minus 1 tablespoon. Add 1 tablespoon vinegar and let stand for 5 minutes.

Fruited Rice
8 to 10 servings

Delicious with a special Fall game dinner.

4 cups chicken broth
1 cup wild rice
1 cup long grain white rice
½ cup butter
3 tablespoons minced shallots
1 cup chopped celery
½ cup chopped toasted walnuts
salt to taste
1 cup cranberries, washed and drained
1 cup golden raisins
1 cup chopped fresh parsley
1 cup chopped, peeled red delicious apples

- Preheat oven to 400 degrees.
- Combine broth and rices in a covered baking dish and bake for 1 hour.
- Meanwhile, melt butter in a large skillet and sauté shallots for 1 minute.
- Add celery and sauté for 2 minutes.
- Add fruit and parsley and sauté mixture for 4 minutes.
- Stir in walnuts and salt.
- After rice is cooked, combine with fruit and serve immediately.
- May add 1 cup Festive Fruit Sauce as a substitute for fruit.

Pignoli Rice
6 servings

This becomes a meal with the addition of vegetables and diced meat.

1½ cups long grain rice
½ cup butter
¼ pound dried vermicelli spaghetti, broken into ½-inch pieces
½ cup pignoli nuts (pine nuts)
1 tablespoon chopped fresh parsley
2 cups chicken stock
salt and pepper to taste

- Cook rice according to package directions.
- Melt butter in a large skillet or Dutch oven with lid.
- Add vermicelli and pignoli nuts.
- Sauté over medium heat until brown, 5 to 10 minutes.
- Add chicken stock, parsley, salt and pepper and simmer 5 minutes.
- Add to drained rice and let stand for about 30 minutes.
- Serve warm.

Company Rice 4 servings

A very colorful dish.

1 cup long grain rice, cooked
1 cup frozen baby green peas
1/3 cup slivered almonds
1 tablespoon chopped fresh parsley
1/4 cup butter, melted
6 cherry tomatoes, cut in wedges

- As rice cooks, thaw peas under cold running water and toast almonds.
- In a large bowl, combine cooked rice, peas, almonds, parsley and butter.
- Serve in a clear dish and garnish with cherry tomatoes.

Yacht Club Rice 6 servings

Compliments poultry or veal and requires no gravy.

1 cup long grain rice, cooked
1/4 cup butter
1/2 cup chopped onion
1 packed cup grated carrots
1 cup frozen baby green peas, thawed
1 cup broken dry roasted cashew nuts
1 tablespoon butter

- Melt 1/4 cup butter in a medium skillet.
- Sauté onion for 1 minute.
- Add carrots and peas.
- Sauté vegetables for 2 minutes.
- Remove from heat and keep warm.
- In a small skillet, melt 1 tablespoon butter.
- Sauté cashew nuts until thoroughly heated.
- Just before serving, mix rice, vegetables and nuts.

Better Brown Rice 6 to 8 servings

2 1/4 cups beef broth
1 cup brown rice
1/4 cup dry sherry
2 tablespoons dried parsley
1 tablespoon butter
1/2 teaspoon fines herbes, crushed
1 teaspoon salt, optional

- Bring broth to a boil in a medium heavy saucepan.
- Add remaining ingredients.
- Cover, reduce heat to low and simmer for 45 minutes to 1 hour, until all liquid is absorbed.
- Serve immediately.

Almond Wild Rice

8 to 10 servings

½ cup golden raisins
¼ cup dry sherry
1 cup wild rice
4 cups chicken broth, boiling
6 tablespoons butter
1 cup brown rice
1 cup slivered almonds
½ cup chopped fresh parsley
salt and freshly ground pepper to taste

- Bring raisins and sherry to a boil in a small saucepan.
- Reduce heat and simmer for 5 minutes; set aside.
- Combine wild rice, 2 cups boiling stock and 2 tablespoons butter in a double boiler over simmering water.
- Cook covered for 1¼ hours.
- Place brown rice, remaining boiling stock and 2 tablespoons butter in a heavy medium saucepan.
- Bring to boil, reduce heat to low and cook until all water is absorbed, about 40 minutes.
- Meanwhile, sauté almonds in the remaining 2 tablespoons butter in a small skillet over low heat until lightly toasted.
- Combine wild rice, brown rice, raisins with sherry, almonds and parsley in a large mixing bowl.
- Season to taste with salt and pepper, stirring to combine.
- Transfer to a serving bowl and serve immediately.

Remember This:

Improve the taste of raisins by soaking them overnight in orange juice or sherry. Drain before using. They will be plump and delicious.

Green Rice

6 servings

This makes a great light supper topped with cheese sauce.

2 tablespoons olive oil
2 tablespoons butter
1 cup minced green onions
1 cup minced fresh parsley
1½ cups finely chopped spinach leaves
2 cups long grain rice
3½ cups chicken broth
1½ teaspoons salt
¼ teaspoon white pepper

- Heat oil and butter in a heavy saucepan.
- Stir in onions, parsley and spinach.
- Cover and cook over low heat for 15 minutes.
- Stir in rice.
- Add 2 cups chicken broth, salt and pepper.
- Cover and bring to a boil; reduce heat and simmer for 15 minutes.
- Add remaining broth and continue to simmer covered for 10 more minutes.
- Fluff rice with a fork and serve immediately.

Baked Pineapple

4 servings

1 20-ounce can pineapple chunks in unsweetened juice
½ cup sugar
3 tablespoons flour
1 cup shredded sharp Cheddar cheese
¼ cup butter, melted
½ cup Ritz cracker crumbs

- Preheat oven to 350 degrees.
- Drain pineapple reserving 3 tablespoons juice.
- In a small bowl, mix sugar and flour.
- Slowly stir in reserved 3 tablespoons pineapple juice and mix well.
- In a separate bowl, combine melted butter and cracker crumbs.
- In a greased 1-quart baking dish, layer pineapple, flour mixture, shredded cheese and top with cracker crumbs.
- Bake for 20 to 30 minutes and serve hot.

Florida Oranges Imperial

8 servings

zest of 2 oranges
2 tablespoons sugar
2 tablespoons orange juice
1/4 cup Grand Marnier
6 large seedless oranges
red seedless grapes
red leaf lettuce

- Remove orange zest in long thin strips using a zester.
- Gently mix zest, sugar, orange juice and liqueur.
- Peel oranges, removing all white membrane and cut into 1/8-inch slices.
- Place orange slices and grapes in a shallow dish and top with zest mixture.
- Cover and chill overnight or for at least 1 hour.
- Let stand at room temperature for 15 minutes before serving.
- Serve as a side dish on a bed of lettuce with zest of orange as garnish.
- Spoon sauce over fruit.

Sour Cream Oranges

8 to 10 servings

6 large seedless oranges
1 tablespoon brown sugar
1 cup sour cream
1/2 teaspoon ground cinnamon
2 tablespoons grated orange peel

- Peel and slice oranges crosswise 1/4-inch thick.
- Place on a shallow serving dish and sprinkle with brown sugar.
- Cover with sour cream and sprinkle with cinnamon and orange peel.

Remember This:

A zester should be used to remove the thinnest peel from the orange.

Apricot Supreme

6 servings

Excellent served as a side dish with game or as a dessert with ice cream.

2 17-ounce cans apricot halves, drained
½ cup flaked coconut
¾ cup light brown sugar, divided
2 cups Ritz cracker crumbs, divided
½ cup butter, melted and divided

- Preheat oven to 300 degrees.
- Place apricots, pitted side up, in a 1½-quart shallow glass baking dish.
- Sprinkle flaked coconut over apricots.
- Sprinkle half of brown sugar over apricots.
- Cover with half of cracker crumbs and drizzle with half of butter.
- Repeat layers with remaining sugar, cracker crumbs and butter.
- Bake for approximately 1 hour or until thick and crusty on top.

Hot Fruit Casserole

16 servings

2 29-ounce cans peach slices
1 20-ounce can pineapple chunks
1 17-ounce can apricot halves
1 29-ounce can pear halves
1 16-ounce can pitted dark cherries
1 17-ounce can Kadot figs
juice of ½ lemon
1 large banana
1 13¾-ounce package coconut macaroon cookies, crumbled
⅔ cup banana liqueur
½ cup light brown sugar
¼ cup unsalted butter
¼ cup sliced almonds

- Drain canned fruit.
- Slice banana and toss in lemon juice.
- Layer half of fruit in a 9x13-inch non-metallic dish.
- Add half of crumbled macaroons.
- Layer remaining fruit, then remaining crumbs.
- Stir together banana liqueur and brown sugar.
- Pour mixture over fruit.
- Dot with butter and sprinkle with sliced almonds.
- Bake at 350 degrees for 25 to 30 minutes.
- Serve warm.

Desserts

Desserts

Fresh Florida Orange Cake

16 servings

Cake:
½ cup butter, softened
¼ cup shortening
1½ cups sugar
3 eggs
2¾ cups flour
1½ teaspoons baking soda
¾ teaspoon salt
1½ cups buttermilk
1½ teaspoons orange extract
1 cup chopped dates
½ cup chopped pecans
1 tablespoon grated orange rind
Frosting:
¼ cup plus 2 tablespoons butter, softened
6 cups sifted confectioner's sugar
¼ cup plus 2 tablespoons fresh orange juice
1 teaspoon orange extract
1 teaspoon grated orange rind
red and yellow food coloring, optional
Garnishes:
orange segments
grated orange rind
orange rind strips
mint leaves

- Preheat oven to 350 degrees.
- To prepare cake, cream butter and shortening.
- Gradually add sugar, beating well at medium speed.
- Add eggs, 1 at a time, beating well after each addition.
- Combine flour, soda and salt.
- Add to creamed mixture alternately with buttermilk, beginning and ending with flour mixture.
- Beat at high speed for 3 minutes.
- Stir in next 4 ingredients.
- Pour batter into 3 greased and floured 9-inch round cake pans.
- Bake for 30 minutes, or until wooden toothpick comes out clean.
- Cool in pans for 10 minutes.
- Remove layers from pans and let cool completely.
- To prepare frosting, cream butter.
- Add powered sugar alternately with orange juice.
- Add orange extract and orange rind and beat until smooth.
- Add more juice, if needed to reach desired spreading consistency.
- Add food coloring, if desired.
- Spread orange frosting between layers and on top and sides of cake.
- Garnish frosted cake with orange segments, grated orange rind, orange rind strips and mint leaves.

Coconut Cake With Lemon Filling

16 servings

Cake:
1 cup butter
2 cups sugar
4 eggs
3 cups flour
3 teaspoons baking powder
pinch of salt
1 cup milk
2 teaspoons vanilla extract

Filling:
½ cup butter
½ cup sugar
rind and juice of 2 lemons
2 large eggs

Frosting:
2 cups sugar
1 cup water
3 egg whites
⅛ teaspoon cream of tartar
⅛ teaspoon salt
2 teaspoons vanilla extract
flaked coconut

- Preheat oven to 350 degrees.
- To prepare cake, cream butter and sugar.
- Add eggs, 1 at a time, beating well.
- Sift flour, baking powder and salt 3 times.
- Add flour mixture, alternately with milk, to creamed mixture.
- Add vanilla extract.
- Pour into 2 10-inch greased and floured cake pans.
- Bake for approximately 20 minutes or until cake pulls away from sides of pan.
- Cool for a few minutes, then invert layers onto racks to continue cooling.
- To prepare filling, cook butter, sugar, lemon juice and rind in a double boiler.
- When butter has melted, add well beaten eggs.
- Stir until thickened; set aside.
- To prepare frosting, cook sugar and water until it reaches hard ball stage.
- Beat egg whites until stiff.
- Add sugar syrup slowly in a thin stream, beating constantly.
- Add cream of tartar, salt and vanilla extract.
- Cover bottom layer with filling.
- Top with remaining layer and ice cake.
- Sprinkle top and sides with flaked coconut.

Orange Vacherin

10 to 12 servings

An impressive dessert!

5 large egg whites, room temperature
1 ½ cups sugar
4 cups well-chilled heavy cream
2 tablespoons orange liqueur
1 ½ tablespoons freshly grated orange rind
fresh orange slices and mint leaves

- Butter a 16-inch long piece of parchment paper.
- Press buttered side down onto a large baking sheet, then turn parchment over.
- Preheat oven to 200 degrees.
- In a large bowl, with an electric mixer, beat egg whites to form stiff peaks.
- Add 1¼ cups sugar very quickly and beat at high speed for 15 seconds.
- Transfer beaten egg whites to a pastry bag with ¾-inch tip and pipe outline of 2 rectangles, 15x4½-inches each, onto parchment paper.
- Fill insides of rectangles with meringue.
- Pipe remainder into 2 or 3 ovals next to rectangles.
- Smooth tops of rectangles with a spatula.
- Bake meringues for 3 to 4 hours, or until hard or brittle.
- Let meringues cool and peel off paper.
- Trim meringue rectangles carefully with small knife to smooth edges.
- Cut a piece of cardboard the size of the rectangle and cover with foil.
- In a large bowl with mixer, combine cream with remaining ¼ cup sugar, orange liqueur and rind and beat until it just holds stiff peaks.
- Place 1 rectangle, smooth side down, on cardboard.
- Spread 1-inch thick layer of orange cream.

Continued

Orange Vacherin (continued)

- Crumble meringue ovals and trimmings over orange cream.
- Put remaining rectangle, smooth side up, on top of crumbled meringue.
- Spread a thin layer of orange cream on top and sides of cake.
- Transfer remaining orange cream to a pastry bag with star tip.
- Pipe 3 rows along length of cake and pipe rosettes at base of cake.
- Freeze cake, uncovered, for 5 to 6 hours.
- Transfer to refrigerator for 30 minutes before serving.
- Garnish with thinly sliced fresh orange and mint leaves.

Ricotta Torte 6 servings

1 15-ounce container ricotta cheese
½ cup sugar
1½ teaspoons vanilla extract
4 1-ounce squares semisweet chocolate, chopped (optional)
1 15-ounce loaf pound cake
6 tablespoons orange liqueur
2 tablespoons cocoa powder
½ cup sifted confectioner's sugar
1 tablespoon butter or margarine, melted
boiling water
2 tablespoons chopped pecans or walnuts

- Combine cheese, sugar and vanilla extract.
- Add chopped chocolate to mixture, if desired.
- Slice cake horizontally into 3 layers.
- Drizzle 2 tablespoons liqueur on 1 side of each layer.
- Divide cheese mixture into 2 equal parts.
- Spread half the cheese mixture on bottom layer of the soaked side of cake.
- Stack second layer on top and spread with remaining cheese mixture.
- Top with third layer.
- Mix cocoa and confectioner's sugar; stir in butter.
- Add enough boiling water to achieve a glaze consistency.
- Pour over torte and sprinkle with nuts.
- Chill for at least 30 minutes.

Chocolate Génoise

16 servings

2 cups sugar
4 heaping tablespoons cocoa
½ cup butter
2 eggs, separated
2 egg yolks
1½ cups milk
2 cups flour
2 heaping teaspoons baking powder
¾ teaspoon salt
2 teaspoons vanilla extract

- Preheat oven to 375 degrees.
- In a mixer, cream sugar, cocoa and butter.
- Stir together 4 egg yolks and milk; set aside.
- Sift together flour, baking powder and salt.
- Add liquid and dry ingredients alternately to creamed mixture; beat well after each addition.
- Add vanilla and fold in stiffly beaten egg whites.
- Pour batter into 2 greased and floured 11-inch cake pans.
- Bake for 20 minutes or until cake comes away from sides of pans.
- Cool on a wire rack in pans for 5 minutes.
- Remove from pans and let cool completely before icing with Special Chocolate Frosting.

Special Chocolate Frosting

Icing for 1 2-layer cake

1½ pounds 4X confectioner's sugar
6 heaping teaspoons cocoa
¼ cup butter
4 tablespoons hot coffee
2 teaspoons vanilla extract

- Sift together confectioner's sugar and cocoa.
- Cut butter into 6 pieces and place in center of sugar mixture.
- Pour hot coffee over butter and mix all together.
- Add additional coffee if necessary to achieve a smooth consistency.
- Add vanilla and mix well.
- Spread icing over completely cooled cake.

Desserts

Banana Layer Cake
16 servings

2¼ cups sifted cake flour
2½ teaspoons baking powder
½ teaspoon baking soda
½ teaspoon salt
½ cup margarine
1 cup sugar
2 eggs
1 teaspoon vanilla extract
1 cup mashed, ripe bananas
¼ cup sour milk or buttermilk
2 cups heavy cream, whipped and sweetened
sliced bananas

- Preheat oven to 350 degrees.
- Sift flour, baking powder, soda and salt together.
- Cream margarine with sugar until fluffy.
- Add eggs, 1 at a time, beating thoroughly after each addition.
- Stir in vanilla extract.
- Combine bananas and milk; set aside.
- Add dry ingredients and milk mixture alternately in equal amounts, beating thoroughly after each addition.
- Pour into 2 greased and floured 9-inch cake pans.
- Bake at 350 degrees for 25 to 30 minutes.
- Spread layers, tops and sides with sweetened whipped cream, and garnish with sliced bananas.
- A seven-minute icing may be substituted.

Cream Cheese Pound Cake
12 to 14 servings

1½ cups butter
1 8-ounce package cream cheese, softened
3 cups sugar
3 cups cake flour, sifted
6 large eggs, room temperature

- Preheat oven to 300 degrees.
- Cream butter and cream cheese together.
- Add sugar and beat until light.
- Add flour and eggs alternately, beating after each addition.
- Pour batter into a greased and floured 10-inch tube pan.
- Bake for 1½ hours.
- Cool on a wire rack for 20 minutes before removing from pan.

Famous Cheesecake

12 to 16 servings

Everyone you serve will request this recipe.

Crust:
1 cup sifted flour
¼ cup sugar
1 teaspoon grated lemon rind
½ cup butter
1 egg yolk
¼ teaspoon vanilla extract

Filling:
5 8-ounce packages cream cheese, softened
¼ teaspoon vanilla extract
¾ teaspoon grated lemon rind
1¾ cups sugar
3 tablespoons flour
¼ teaspoon salt
5 eggs
2 egg yolks
¼ cup heavy cream

Strawberry Glaze:
2 to 3 cups fresh strawberries, hulled
1 cup water
1½ tablespoons cornstarch
½ to ¾ cup sugar

- Preheat oven to 400 degrees.
- To prepare crust, combine flour, sugar and lemon rind.
- Blend in butter until the mixture is crumbly.
- Add egg yolk and vanilla extract.
- Mix thoroughly.
- Pat ⅓ dough on the bottom of a 9-inch tube pan with a removable bottom.
- Bake for approximately 6 minutes, or until golden.
- Cool.
- Preheat oven to 500 degrees.
- Butter sides of pan.
- Pat remainder of dough evenly on the sides to a height of 2 inches.
- To prepare filling, beat softened cream cheese until fluffy.
- Add vanilla extract and rind.
- Mix sugar, flour and salt, and gradually blend into cheese.
- Add eggs and yolks, 1 at a time, beating well after each addition.
- Gently stir in cream and turn into crust-lined pan.
- Bake for 5 to 8 minutes, or until top edge of crust is golden.
- Reduce oven heat to 200 degrees and bake 1 hour longer.
- Remove from oven and cool in pan about 3 hours.

Continued

Famous Cheesecake (continued)

- To prepare strawberry glaze, crush 1 cup strawberries.
- Add water and cook for 2 minutes; sieve.
- Mix cornstarch with sugar and stir into hot berry mixture.
- Bring to a boil, stirring constantly.
- Cook and stir until thick and clear.
- Add a few drops of food coloring, if needed.
- Cool to room temperature.
- Place remaining strawberries on top of cooled cheesecake.
- Pour glaze over strawberries and chill for about 2 hours.

Chocolate Pound Cake

16 servings

1½ cups butter, softened
3 cups sugar
5 eggs
3 cups flour
½ cup cocoa
1 teaspoon baking soda
⅛ teaspoon salt
1 8-ounce carton sour cream
1 cup boiling water
3 teaspoons vanilla extract

- Preheat oven to 325 degrees.
- Cream butter and gradually add sugar, beating well.
- Add eggs, 1 at a time.
- Combine flour, cocoa, baking soda and salt.
- Add to creamed mixture, alternating with sour cream, beginning and ending with flour mixture.
- Mix well after each addition.
- Add boiling water and mix well.
- Stir in vanilla extract.
- Pour into a greased and floured 10-inch tube pan.
- Bake for 1 hour and 20 minutes, or until done.
- Cool cake in pan for 15 minutes.
- Remove from pan and cool completely.

Chocolate Truffle Cake

6 to 8 servings

16-ounces semisweet chocolate
½ cup unsalted butter
1½ teaspoons flour
1½ teaspoons granulated sugar
1 teaspoon hot water
4 eggs, separated
1 cup whipping cream
shredded chocolate

- Preheat oven to 450 degrees.
- Grease an 8-inch springform pan.
- In a double boiler, melt chocolate and butter.
- Add flour, sugar and water, mixing well.
- Add egg yolks, 1 at a time, beating well after each addition.
- Beat egg whites until stiff, but not dry.
- Remove chocolate mixture from heat; fold in egg whites.
- Pour batter into a springform pan, bake for only 15 minutes.
- Cool on a rack; cake will sink in center.
- Refrigerate or freeze in or out of cake pan to keep longer.
- Top with sweetened whipped cream.
- May be garnished with shredded chocolate.

Remember This:

Keep a powder puff in a flour canister for dusting greased cake pans.

Valentine Torte

10 servings

A delicious way to say, "I love you"!

Cake:
- *2 eggs, separated*
- *½ cup sugar*
- *1¼ cups flour*
- *1 cup sugar*
- *½ cup unsweetened cocoa*
- *¾ teaspoon baking soda*
- *½ teaspoon salt*
- *½ cup vegetable oil*
- *1 cup buttermilk*
- *1 21-ounce can cherry pie filling*

Filling:
- *1 cup heavy cream, whipped*
- *2 tablespoons sugar*
- *1 teaspoon vanilla extract*

Topping:
- *½ cup sugar*
- *¼ cup unsweetened cocoa*
- *1 cup heavy cream*
- *1 teaspoon vanilla extract*

- Preheat oven to 350 degrees.
- To prepare cake, beat egg whites until foamy.
- Gradually beat in ½ cup sugar until stiff peaks form; set aside.
- In an electric mixer, combine flour, 1 cup sugar, cocoa, baking soda and salt.
- Stir to combine ingredients.
- Add oil, buttermilk and egg yolks, beating until smooth.
- Gently fold in egg whites.
- Grease and flour 2 heart-shaped cake pans.
- Pour 1⅔ cups batter into each pan and reserve remaining batter in refrigerator.
- Bake cakes for 18 to 20 minutes and cool for 5 minutes.
- Remove cakes from pan and invert on wire racks.
- Bake remaining layer using reserved batter and cool completely.
- To prepare filling, whip cream with sugar and vanilla extract until stiff peaks form.
- Place 1 cake layer on a serving plate.
- Pipe or spoon cream filling around layer, about ½-inch thick covering 1-inch from edge of cake.
- Spread half of cherry filling in center and top with second layer.
- Spread with half of remaining cream filling and top with third layer.

Continued

Valentine Torte (continued)

- Spoon remaining cherry filling over cake, leaving a 1-inch edge.
- To prepare topping, combine sugar and unsweetened cocoa in a small mixing bowl.
- Add heavy cream and vanilla extract; beat at low speed to combine.
- Increase speed to medium and beat until stiff peaks form.
- Frost sides of cake with whipped cream.
- Pipe top edge with remaining cream filling.
- Chill cake completely in refrigerator.

Grandmother's Favorite Pound Cake 16 servings

3 cups sugar
1 cup butter, softened
1 teaspoon vanilla extract
1 teaspoon lemon extract
1 teaspoon almond extract
1 cup whipping cream
6 eggs
3 cups flour, sifted

- Preheat oven to 350 degrees.
- Cream sugar and butter.
- Add vanilla extract, lemon and almond extract.
- Add eggs, cream and flour alternately, ending with flour, until all eggs, flour and cream are combined.
- Bake in a greased and floured 10-inch tube pan for 1½ hours.
- Let cool in pan on a wire rack for 15 minutes.
- Turn out onto rack to continue cooling.

Divine Chocolate Dessert

10 to 12 servings

A wonderful combination of chocolate and nuts!

Graham Cracker Crust:
2 cups graham cracker crumbs
½ cup ground almonds
½ cup ground pecans
¼ cup sugar
¾ cup butter, melted
Cake:
4 1-ounce squares unsweetened chocolate
1 cup butter or margarine
1½ cups sugar
4 eggs, beaten
2 teaspoons vanilla extract
1 cup flour
¼ teaspoon salt
1 cup chopped pecans
whipped cream
finely chopped pecans

- To prepare crust, combine all ingredients, mixing well.
- Press into bottom and side of a 9-inch springform pan.
- Bake at 350 degrees for 8 to 10 minutes; let cool.
- To prepare cake, combine chocolate and butter in a heavy saucepan.
- Cook over low heat until melted, stirring constantly.
- Add sugar, mixing well.
- Remove from heat and cool.
- Stir in eggs and vanilla extract.
- Combine flour and salt and add to chocolate mixture.
- Stir in 1 cup pecans and pour into prepared graham cracker crust.
- Bake at 325 degrees for 45 to 50 minutes.
- Cool and chill for 8 hours.
- Remove from pan and cover with whipped cream topping.
- Sprinkle with finely chopped pecans.

Remember This:

For chocolate cakes, dust pan with cocoa instead of flour for a more attractive and tastier concoction.

Fresh Lemon Charlotte Russe

8 servings

A light, zesty ending for any meal.

4 eggs, separated
½ cup lemon juice
⅛ teaspoon salt
1 envelope unflavored gelatin
1½ cups sugar, divided
3 tablespoons butter or margarine
1½ teaspoons grated lemon rind
1 teaspoon vanilla extract
12 ladyfingers, split lengthwise
1 cup heavy cream, whipped
sweetened whipped cream for garnish

- Combine egg yolks, lemon juice and salt in top of a double boiler; mix well.
- Stir in gelatin and 1 cup sugar.
- Cook over simmering water until thickened, stirring constantly.
- Add butter, lemon rind and vanilla stirring until butter melts.
- Chill mixture until partially thickened.
- Arrange ladyfingers around bottom and sides of a 9½-inch springform pan; set aside.
- Beat egg whites until soft peaks form.
- Gradually add remaining sugar and continue beating until stiff peaks form.
- Fold whipped cream and gelatin mixture into egg whites.
- Spoon into prepared pan; cover and chill for 4 to 5 hours or until firm.
- Garnish with sweetened whipped cream if desired.

Remember This:

Keep buttermilk on hand by freezing in ice trays. Pop out and bag for later use.

Crème à l'Orange

5 to 7 servings

2 cups heavy cream
7 egg yolks
4 tablespoons sugar
2 tablespoons Cointreau or orange flavored liqueur
grated rind of 1 orange
1 cup dark brown sugar

- Rinse a heavy saucepan with cold water and leave wet.
- Pour in cream and heat to just below simmering over low heat.
- In a mixing bowl, beat egg yolks and sugar together until thick and pale colored.
- Slowly pour hot cream into yolk and sugar mixture, stirring slowly to form custard mixture.
- Blend in liqueur and orange rind.
- Rinse saucepan and leave wet.
- Pour in custard and cook over low heat, stirring continuously with a wooden spoon.
- Continue stirring until thickened; custard should leave a trail when spoon is lifted.
- Do not boil.
- Pour custard into ramekins and allow to cool.
- Refrigerate for 5 to 6 hours.
- One hour before serving, preheat broiler and place ¼-inch layer of brown sugar over custard.
- Place ramekins in baking pan filled with ice cubes and place under broiler until sugar melts and caramelizes.
- Remove from broiler and cool to room temperature.

Raspberry Cream Tart

10 servings

A delicate custard crowned with raspberries.

Pastry:
1½ cups flour
½ cup butter, softened
⅓ cup sugar
1 egg white

Custard Filling:
¼ cup sugar
3 tablespoons flour
1 envelope unflavored gelatin
¼ teaspoon salt
2 eggs
1 egg yolk
1½ cups milk
2 tablespoons almond liqueur or ½ teaspoon almond extract
½ cup heavy cream
1 pint fresh raspberries

- Tart should be made at least 3 hours before serving.
- Preheat oven to 350 degrees.
- To prepare pastry, combine flour, butter and sugar.
- Knead until blended.
- Pat into bottom and sides of a 10-inch tart pan with removable bottom.
- Bake for 20 minutes or until pastry is golden.
- Beat egg white and brush onto hot pastry shell.
- Cool on wire rack and remove side from pan.
- To prepare custard filling, combine sugar, flour, gelatin and salt in a heavy 2-quart saucepan; stir.
- In a medium bowl, beat eggs, egg yolk and milk with a fork; stir into sugar mixture.
- Cook over medium-low heat, stirring for about 15 minutes until gelatin dissolves completely and custard thickens to coat a spoon.
- Do not boil; remove from heat and stir in almond flavored liqueur.
- Refrigerate until mixture mounds when dropped from a spoon.
- In an electric mixer, beat heavy cream at medium speed until soft peaks form.
- Fold whipped cream into custard and spoon mixture into cooled shell.
- Refrigerate for 1 hour or until custard is set.
- Arrange raspberries on custard.

Fresh Georgia Peach Tart

6 servings

Simple to prepare. Impressive to serve.

3 large or 5 small firm, ripe peaches
1 9-inch pie pastry, unbaked
1 egg, separated
juice of ½ lemon
¼ cup granulated sugar
¼ cup light brown sugar
1 teaspoon cinnamon
pinch of freshly grated nutmeg
pinch of salt
2 tablespoons unsalted butter
¼ cup heavy cream

- Preheat oven to 350 degrees.
- Blanch peaches in a large saucepan of boiling water, about 30 seconds.
- Remove and slip off skins; cut peaches in half and remove pits.
- Place pie pastry in a 10-inch tart pan and brush crust with unbeaten egg white.
- Place peach halves, pit side down, on pastry.
- Peach halves should not overlap.
- Brush peaches with lemon juice.
- Combine sugars, spices and salt and sprinkle over peaches; dot with butter.
- Bake for 25 minutes.
- Heat cream to lukewarm and whisk into egg yolk.
- Pour gently over fruit and return tart to oven for 15 minutes.

Remember This:

Remove skin and pits from freshly harvested peaches, toss in lemon juice and freeze for year-round enjoyment.

Chocolate Soufflé à l'Orange

5 servings

4 1-ounce squares semisweet chocolate
3 eggs, separated
1½ teaspoons vanilla extract
½ teaspoon almond extract
1 tablespoon orange liqueur
½ teaspoon cream of tartar
½ cup sugar
1 cup heavy whipping cream

- Melt chocolate and set aside to cool slightly.
- Beat egg yolks lightly.
- Stir in flavorings and chocolate.
- Beat egg whites with cream of tartar at high speed until foamy.
- Add sugar, 1 tablespoon at a time, beating until stiff peaks form and sugar dissolves.
- Fold in about ¼ of beaten egg whites to chocolate mixture.
- Fold in remaining egg whites.
- Beat cream at medium speed, until soft peaks form.
- Fold into chocolate mixture.
- Fill individual dessert goblets or mousse cups.
- Cover and chill for several hours.

Fresh Blueberry Cream Pie

6 to 8 servings

1 cup sour cream
2 tablespoons flour
¾ cup sugar
1 teaspoon vanilla extract
¼ teaspoon salt
1 egg, beaten
2½ cups fresh blueberries
1 9-inch pie pastry, unbaked
3 tablespoons flour
3 tablespoons butter, softened
3 tablespoons chopped pecans or walnuts

- Preheat oven to 400 degrees.
- Combine first 6 ingredients in an electric mixer.
- Beat for 5 minutes at medium speed or until smooth.
- Fold in blueberries.
- Pour filling into pastry shell.
- Bake for 25 minutes.
- Combine remaining ingredients, stirring well.
- Sprinkle over pie.
- Bake for 10 additional minutes.
- Chill before serving.

Desserts

French Strawberry Pie

6 to 8 servings

1 3-ounce package cream cheese
3 tablespoons whipping cream
1 9-inch pie pastry, baked
1 quart strawberries
1 cup sugar
¾ cup whipping cream
2 tablespoons cornstarch
3 drops lime juice
whipped cream

- Blend cream cheese and 3 tablespoons whipping cream until soft and smooth.
- Spread over cooled pie shell.
- Wash and hull strawberries.
- Select and set aside half of the best berries; if large, slice in half.
- Add sugar to remaining strawberries and let stand until juicy.
- Mash through sieve.
- Mix strawberry purée with cornstarch and add lime juice.
- Cook mixture over medium heat until thick and transparent, stirring constantly.
- Cool and pour half of sauce over cream cheese.
- Arrange reserved berries in pie and pour sauce over all; chill.
- Serve with whipped cream.

Peach Almond Pie

6 to 8 servings

1 cup sugar
2 tablespoons unsalted butter, melted and cooled
1 tablespoon cornstarch
1 tablespoon flour
2 eggs, beaten
1 teaspoon almond extract
4 cups peeled and sliced fresh peaches
1 9-inch pie pastry, unbaked
freshly grated nutmeg

- Preheat oven to 450 degrees.
- Combine sugar, butter, cornstarch, flour, eggs and almond extract.
- Set mixture aside.
- Fill pie pastry with sliced peaches and pour sugar mixture over all.
- Grate nutmeg over pie.
- Bake for 10 minutes.
- Reduce heat to 350 degrees.
- Bake for 35 to 40 minutes or until custard is set.
- Serve warm or cool the same day as baked.

French Silk Pie

10 to 12 servings

Annella's famous pie!

Crust:
¾ cup butter
¾ cup brown sugar
1½ cups flour
½ cup pecans, chopped

Filling:
3 ounces unsweetened chocolate
1 cup butter, softened
1½ cups sugar
2 teaspoons vanilla extract
4 eggs
pinch of salt
lightly toasted slivered almonds for garnish

- To prepare crust, melt butter in a 9x13-inch pan.
- Add remaining crust ingredients and bake at 350 degrees.
- Stir every 5 minutes for 20 minutes until dry and crumbly.
- Remove from oven and gently spread mixture evenly over pan.
- After crust has cooled, chill in refrigerator.
- To prepare filling, melt chocolate squares over low heat.
- Cream butter and sugar well, then add vanilla extract and chocolate.
- Add 2 eggs and beat for 3 minutes.
- Add remaining eggs and salt; beat for an additional 3 minutes.
- Pour over chilled crust and refrigerate.
- Sprinkle with almonds and serve.

Remember This:

Try whipping 1 cup heavy cream with 1 tablespoon instant Capuccino and a sprinkle of sugar for an interesting topping.

Plantation Pecan Pie 8 servings

3 large eggs, lightly beaten
1 cup light corn syrup
1 cup firmly packed light brown sugar
1/3 cup butter, melted
1/8 teaspoon salt
1 teaspoon vanilla extract
1 cup pecans, halves or broken pieces
1 9-inch pie pastry, unbaked

- Preheat oven to 350 degrees.
- Stir together eggs, corn syrup, brown sugar, melted butter, salt and vanilla extract until well blended.
- Arrange pecans in pie pastry.
- Pour egg-sugar mixture into pie pastry; pecans will float to the top.
- Bake for 55 to 60 minutes or until crust is lightly browned and filling is puffy.
- Let pie cool to room temperature before cutting.

Frozen Chocolate Peanut Pie 8 servings

Peanut Crust:
1 cup chocolate wafer crumbs
1/3 cup finely chopped cocktail peanuts
1/3 cup melted butter
2 teapoons sugar
Filling:
1 3-ounce package fudge pudding and pie filling
1 3/4 cups milk
1/2 cup chunky peanut butter
1 teaspoon vanilla extract
1 cup whipping cream
1/4 cup sugar
1/2 cup crushed peanut brittle

- To prepare crust, mix ingredients together and press into 9-inch pie pan.
- Bake at 350 degrees for 5 to 8 minutes; cool.
- To prepare filling, combine pudding mix and milk in a small saucepan.
- Cook over medium heat, stirring constantly until mixture boils.
- Remove from heat, stir in peanut butter and vanilla extract.
- Lay wax paper on surface of pudding.
- Chill for 30 to 40 minutes; but do not set.
- Beat cream until soft peaks form.
- Gradually beat in sugar.
- Fold into cooled pudding and spoon into crust.
- Cover and freeze.
- To serve, let thaw for 40 minutes.
- Top with crushed peanut brittle.

Desserts

Sweet Potato Pie
6 to 8 servings

1 large sweet potato
1 cup sugar
3 eggs beaten
pinch of salt
1 teaspoon vanilla extract
½ teaspoon ground nutmeg
½ cup butter, melted
½ cup milk
½ cup small marshmallows
1 9-inch pie pastry, unbaked

- Preheat oven to 350 degrees.
- Peel and slice sweet potato.
- Cook sweet potato in a small amount of water until tender; drain and mash to measure 1 cup.
- Beat together sugar and eggs.
- Add sweet potato, salt, vanilla, nutmeg and melted butter; mix well and stir in milk.
- Sprinkle bottom of pie pastry with marshmallows.
- Pour potato mixture into pastry and bake for 1 hour.
- Marshmallows will rise to surface to create a topping.

Melting Moments
2 dozen

A delicate, light cookie.

Cookies:
1 cup butter
⅓ cup confectioner's sugar
¾ cup cornstarch
1 cup flour
Frosting:
3 ounces cream cheese
1 cup confectioner's sugar
1 teaspoon vanilla extract

- To make cookies, preheat oven to 350 degrees.
- Cream butter and sugar.
- Add flour and cornstarch; mix well.
- Cover and chill thoroughly.
- Form into 1-inch balls and place on an ungreased cookie sheet.
- Make an indentation with thumb in the middle of each ball.
- Bake for 10 to 12 minutes.
- Remove from cookie sheet and cool.
- To make frosting, cream sugar and cream cheese.
- Add vanilla extract.
- Place a spoonful of frosting in indentation of each cookie.

Ambrosia Cookies

4 dozen

1 cup butter
1 cup brown sugar
1 cup granulated sugar
2 eggs
1 teaspoon vanilla extract
2 cups flour
1 teaspoon baking powder
½ teaspoon baking soda
½ teaspoon salt
1 cup shredded coconut
1 cup chopped pecans
1 cup raisins
1 cup chopped dates
1 cup uncooked rolled oats

- Preheat oven to 350 degrees.
- Blend butter and sugars.
- Add eggs and vanilla extract.
- Mix together flour, baking powder, baking soda and salt.
- Add coconut, nuts, raisins, dates and oats.
- Mix all ingredients together.
- Drop dough by teaspoon onto greased cookie sheets.
- Bake for 10 minutes.

Almond Crisps

3 dozen

⅔ cup shortening
1⅔ cups sugar
2 eggs
1 teaspoon almond extract
1 teaspoon vanilla extract
2½ cups flour
2 teaspoons baking powder
½ teaspoon baking soda
¼ teaspoon salt
1 egg white, slightly beaten
¼ cup sliced almonds

- Preheat oven to 375 degrees.
- Cream shortening, gradually add sugar; beat well.
- Beat in eggs and extracts.
- Combine flour, baking powder, soda and salt.
- Stir into creamed mixture.
- Shape dough into 1½-inch balls and flatten slightly.
- Brush with beaten egg white.
- Place 3 sliced almonds in center of each cookie.
- Bake for 15 minutes or until lightly browned.
- Cool on wire racks.

Gingerbread Men

3 dozen 3-inch cookies

Cookie Dough:
½ cup butter or margarine, softened
½ cup firmly packed brown sugar
½ cup molasses
1 egg
3½ cups flour
1 teaspoon baking powder
½ teaspoon baking soda
½ teaspoon salt
1 teaspoon ground cinnamon
½ teaspoon ground ginger
¼ teaspoon ground nutmeg
¼ teaspoon ground cloves
½ cup buttermilk
raisins
Royal Icing:
3 large egg whites, room temperature
½ teaspoon cream of tartar
1 16-ounce package confectioner's sugar, sifted
paste food coloring

- To make dough, cream butter; add sugar and beat until light and fluffy.
- Add molasses and egg, mixing well.
- Combine dry ingredients.
- Add to creamed mixture alternately with buttermilk, beginning and ending with dry ingredients.
- Shape dough into a ball.
- Cover and chill for at least 2 hours.
- Preheat oven to 375 degrees.
- On a lightly floured surface, roll dough to a ¼-inch thickness.
- Cut into desired shapes.
- Place on a lightly greased cookie sheet and bake for 10 minutes.
- Remove from pan and cool on wire racks.
- Decorate with Royal Icing.
- To make icing, combine egg whites and cream of tartar in a large mixing bowl.
- Beat with electric mixer at medium speed until frothy.
- Gradually add confectioner's sugar, mixing well.
- Beat for 5 to 7 minutes.
- Color portions of icing with paste food coloring, if desired.
- Prepare decorating bags and decorate cookies.
- Icing dries very quickly, so keep unused portion covered with damp towels.
- Icing hardens as it dries.

Desserts

Sugar Cookies — 2 dozen cookies

Cookie Dough:
½ cup butter, softened
1 cup sugar
1 egg
2 tablespoons milk
½ teaspoon vanilla
2 cups flour
½ teaspoon salt
2 teaspoons baking powder
Icing:
⅓ cup butter, softened
4 cups confectioner's sugar, sifted
1½ teaspoons vanilla
2 tablespoons heavy cream or milk

- Preheat oven to 375 degrees.
- To make dough, cream butter and sugar.
- Add egg, milk and vanilla; beat well.
- Sift together dry ingredients and add to creamed mixture; mix well.
- Roll into a ball; cover with plastic wrap and refrigerate for 4 hours.
- On a lightly floured surface, roll dough to a ¼-inch thickness.
- Cut cookies in desired shapes with cookie cutters.
- Bake for 8 minutes on ungreased cookie sheets.
- Cool on a wire rack.
- To make icing, combine icing ingredients and decorate cookies.

Lemon Custard Bars — 2 dozen bars

¼ cup confectioner's sugar
⅛ teaspoon salt
1 cup flour
½ cup butter, softened
1 cup granulated sugar
½ teaspoon baking powder
⅛ teaspoon salt
2 eggs
2 tablespoons lemon juice
grated rind of 1 lemon
confectioner's sugar

- Preheat oven to 350 degrees.
- Combine confectioner's sugar, salt, flour and butter.
- Press into a 9-inch square cake pan.
- Bake for 15 minutes.
- Mix remaining ingredients in a mixer and pour over cooked crust.
- Bake for 20 minutes longer.
- Cool and cut into bars.
- Sprinkle with confectioner's sugar.

Madeleines

30 cookies

These cake-like cookies make perfect accompaniments to fresh fruit desserts.

- *½ cup butter*
- *4 eggs*
- *⅛ teaspoon salt*
- *⅔ cup sugar*
- *1¼ teaspoons almond extract*
- *1 cup sifted flour*
- *confectioner's sugar*

- Preheat oven to 375 degrees.
- Butter and flour madeleine pans.
- Melt butter and set aside to cool.
- Beat eggs, salt and sugar until thick, about 8 minutes.
- Add almond extract.
- Rapidly but gently fold in flour.
- Fold in cooled butter using the same technique making certain butter does not settle to the bottom.
- Quickly spoon mixture into prepared pans and bake until lightly browned, about 10 minutes.
- Remove from pans and dust with confectioner's sugar.
- Cool on wire racks.

Very Best Blonde Brownie

2 dozen bars

This brownie will make you famous!

- *¾ cup margarine, melted*
- *1 pound brown sugar*
- *3 eggs, beaten*
- *2¾ cups flour*
- *2½ teaspoons baking powder*
- *½ teaspoon salt*
- *1 12-ounce package semisweet chocolate chips*
- *1 teaspoon vanilla extract*

- Preheat oven to 350 degrees.
- In a large bowl, pour melted margarine over sugar and mix well.
- Add eggs and stir.
- Sift together flour, baking powder and salt.
- Add dry ingredients to sugar mixture and stir to combine.
- Stir in chocolate chips and vanilla.
- Pour into a 9x13-inch greased baking pan and bake for 30 minutes.
- Cool completely in pan and cut into bars.

B.T.S. Brownies

12 servings

1 14-ounce bag caramels
2/3 cup evaporated milk, divided
1 18-ounce package German Chocolate cake mix
3/4 cup butter, softened
1 cup chopped nuts
1 6-ounce package semisweet chocolate chips

- Preheat oven to 350 degrees.
- Combine caramels and 1/3 cup evaporated milk in a double boiler.
- Heat, stirring constantly, until caramels melt completely.
- Remove from heat and set aside.
- Combine cake mix, 1/3 cup evaporated milk and butter.
- Beat with mixer until batter holds together.
- Stir in nuts.
- Press half of cake mixture into a well greased 9x13-inch pan and bake for 6 minutes.
- Sprinkle chocolate chips over crust.
- Pour caramel mixture over chips evenly.
- Crumble remaining cake mixture on top.
- Bake for 17 to 20 minutes more.
- Cool; chill for 30 minutes, and cut into squares.

Coconut Nut Bars

24 bars

Crust:
1/2 cup butter
1 cup flour
1 tablespoon brown sugar
Topping:
2 eggs
1 1/2 cups brown sugar
1 cup chopped pecans
1 cup coconut
1 1/2 teaspoons vanilla extract
1 teaspoon baking powder

- Preheat oven to 300 degrees.
- Blend butter, flour and brown sugar together with a fork or pastry blender.
- Spread thinly in 9x12-inch baking dish.
- Bake for 20 minutes.
- To prepare topping, combine all remaining ingredients.
- Spread over crust.
- Bake for 30 minutes.
- Cool and cut into squares.

Desserts

Chocolate Supreme

16 servings

Sinfully delicious!

1 cup unsalted butter
3 ounces unsweetened chocolate, coarsely chopped
½ cup plus 1 tablespoon flour, sifted
½ teaspoon baking soda
2 eggs, room temperature
¼ teaspoon salt
1 cup sugar
2 tablespoons orange liqueur
1 teaspoon vanilla extract
1 6-ounce package semisweet chocolate chips
1 cup chopped walnuts or pecans
confectioner's sugar

- Preheat oven to 350 degrees.
- Grease an 8-inch square baking pan.
- Melt butter and unsweetened chocolate in a double boiler over simmering water.
- Stir until smooth and remove from heat.
- Sift flour and baking soda together.
- In an electric mixer, beat eggs and salt until lemon colored.
- Gradually add sugar and beat until pale yellow ribbons form when beaters are lifted.
- Blend in chocolate mixture, then liqueur and vanilla extract.
- Stir in flour mixture.
- Fold in chocolate chips and nuts and pour into prepared pan.
- Bake for approximately 22 minutes or until top is firm, but center is soft.
- Sprinkle with confectioner's sugar.
- Place on a wire rack to completely cool before cutting.

French Chocolate Sauce

1 cup

2 1-ounce squares unsweetened chocolate
6 tablespoons light cream
½ cup sugar
dash of salt
3 tablespoons butter
1 teaspoon vanilla extract

- Melt chocolate in cream over low heat.
- Add sugar and salt; stir well.
- Remove from heat; add butter and vanilla.
- Stir constantly until cool.
- Pour over slices of cake.

Chocolate Mint Bars

10 bars

½ cup butter
2 1-ounce squares unsweetened chocolate
2 eggs, beaten
1 cup granulated sugar
½ teaspoon salt
½ teaspoon peppermint extract
½ cup flour
Frosting:
1 cup confectioner's sugar
2 heaping tablespoons butter
1 tablespoon cream
1 tablespoon peppermint extract
3 drops green food coloring
Drizzle Layer:
1 1-ounce square semisweet chocolate
2 tablespoons butter

- Preheat oven to 350 degrees.
- To prepare base, melt butter and chocolate over low heat.
- Remove from heat and add eggs, beating well.
- Stir in sugar, peppermint, flour and salt; beat well.
- Pour into a greased 9x9-inch pan.
- Bake for 20 minutes; cool.
- To prepare frosting, beat sugar and butter until smooth.
- Add remaining ingredients and mix well.
- Spread over cooled peppermint bars and allow to set.
- To prepare drizzle layer, melt chocolate and butter together, cool and drizzle in a decorative pattern over frosting.
- Allow to set before cutting into squares.

Sweet Treats 24 bars

Tastes just like miniature pecan pies!

½ cup butter
1½ cups brown sugar, packed
1 cup flour
2 eggs
2 tablespoons vanilla extract
¾ cup chopped pecans
confectioner's sugar

- Preheat oven to 350 degrees.
- Cream butter and ½ cup brown sugar.
- Mix in flour.
- Press in bottom of a greased 8x8-inch pan.
- Bake for 20 minutes; cool.
- Beat eggs and remaining sugar until smooth.
- Add vanilla extract and nuts and spread over crust.
- Bake for 20 minutes more.
- Sprinkle with sifted confectioner's sugar.
- Cut into 1-inch squares.

Lemon Sponge 8 servings

A delightful combination of cake and custard.

1 cup sugar
4 tablespoons butter
4 tablespoons flour
pinch of salt
juice of 2 lemons, at least 5 tablespoons
rind of 1 lemon
3 eggs, separated
1½ cups milk

- Preheat oven to 350 degrees.
- Cream sugar and butter.
- Add flour, salt, lemon juice and rind.
- Stir in beaten egg yolks and milk.
- Beat egg whites until stiff peaks form and fold into batter.
- Pour into 8 custard cups.
- Place cups in a pan and add water to a depth of 1 inch.
- Bake 45 minutes or until lightly browned.
- Each cup will contain custard at bottom and sponge cake on top.

Desserts

Florida Fresh Fruit Cobbler

6 to 8 servings

4 cups fruit, blackberries or blueberries, sliced peaches or pears, or a combination
2 cups sugar, divided
1 cup flour
1 teaspoon baking powder
½ teaspoon ground cinnamon
¼ teaspoon ground mace
¼ teaspoon salt
1 cup milk
½ teaspoon vanilla extract
½ cup butter, melted and cooled
ice cream or heavy cream

- Preheat oven to 350 degrees.
- In a bowl, toss fruit with 1 cup sugar and let stand for 30 minutes.
- Sift together remaining sugar, flour, baking powder, cinnamon, mace and salt.
- Add milk and vanilla; stir until combined.
- Pour melted butter into a 10-inch square and 2-inch deep baking pan, and add batter, stirring to combine.
- Spoon fruit mixture over batter.
- Bake for 30 minutes.
- Increase heat to 400 degrees and bake for 10 to 15 minutes longer.
- Let cobbler cool for 20 minutes before serving.
- Serve with ice cream or heavy cream.

Strawberries Fantastic!

6 servings

1 quart large ripe strawberries, hulled
½ cup confectioner's sugar
2 ounces Cointreau
½ cup sugar
2 10-ounce packages frozen raspberries, thawed
2 ounces crème de cassis

- Arrange single layer of strawberries in large flat glass container.
- Dust with confectioner's sugar and drizzle with Cointreau.
- Combine thawed raspberries and sugar in a blender and blend briefly.
- Strain mixture through a fine sieve and add crème de cassis.
- Pour over strawberries, cover, and let stand at room temperature for a few hours.
- Do not chill.
- Serve in champagne glasses with Melting Moments cookies.

Desserts

Summer Fruit Compote

6 servings

2 peaches, sliced
1 cup blueberries
1 cup melon balls
1 cup strawberries, hulled
1 cup seedless grapes
3 tablespoons orange-flavored liqueur or orange juice
2/3 cup sour cream
3 tablespoons packed brown sugar
carambola, sliced

- Toss fruit with liqueur or juice.
- Mix sour cream and brown sugar.
- Serve fruit mixture with a dollop of sour cream dressing.
- Garnish with slices of carambola fruit.

Baked Apples With Custard Sauce

8 servings

Custard Sauce:
4 eggs, slightly beaten
3/4 cup sugar
dash of salt
3 cups milk
3/4 teaspoon vanilla extract
Baked Apples:
8 large red baking apples
2 to 3 tablespoons sugar
1 teaspoon ground cinnamon
raisins

- To prepare sauce, combine eggs, sugar and salt in a double boiler.
- Stir in milk.
- Place over gently boiling water and cook, stirring until mixture coats a metal spoon.
- Remove from heat and stir in vanilla; chill.
- To prepare baked apples, core apples being careful not to cut all the way through.
- Peel apples once around stem end.
- Combine sugar and cinnamon and spoon 1/2 teaspoon of mixture into each apple cavity.
- Add raisins to fill.
- Place in an uncovered baking dish and bake at 350 degrees until tender.
- Serve hot with custard sauce spooned over apples.

English Fruit Trifle

12 to 14 servings

A divine dessert, well worth the time and effort to prepare.

Custard Sauce:

1 1/2 tablespoons cornstarch
2 cups light cream, divided
4 large egg yolks, beaten
1/2 cup sugar
1 teaspoon vanilla extract
24 ladyfingers, filled with 1/2 cup strawberry or seedless raspberry jam
1/4 to 1/2 cup dry sherry
3 tablespoons brandy
24 coconut macaroons, coarsely crumbled (about 4 cups)
4 cups of a variety of diced, sliced, or halved seasonal fresh fruit such as kiwi, peaches, blueberries, strawberries, raspberries, pineapple, nectarines and bananas
2 cups heavy cream, whipped
1/2 cup toasted, slivered almonds

- Dissolve cornstarch in 1/4 cup light cream.
- Combine beaten egg yolks with cornstarch.
- In a heavy saucepan, heat remaining light cream, being careful not to boil.
- Add sugar; stir to dissolve.
- Pour 1 cup hot cream mixture into egg yolks, stirring constantly.
- Return egg mixture to saucepan.
- Continue to cook over medium heat, stirring constantly, until sauce thickens and coats a metal spoon, about 5 to 10 minutes.
- Remove from heat and blend in vanilla.
- Transfer sauce to a bowl, cover with plastic wrap and let cool to room temperature.
- To assemble trifle, place half the ladyfingers spread with jam in a crystal or decorative 8-inch wide 4-inch deep serving bowl.
- Sprinkle with half of sherry and half of brandy.
- Cover with a layer of half the macaroons.
- Let stand for 30 minutes; top with 2 cups fruit.
- Cover with half of the custard sauce.
- Repeat layers of remaining ladyfingers, sherry, brandy, macaroons, and fruit.
- Pour remaining custard sauce over trifle and cover with plastic wrap.
- Refrigerate until thoroughly chilled, about 1 to 2 hours.
- Just before serving, top with whipped cream and almonds.

Chocolate Dipped Strawberries

4 to 6 servings

1 pint perfect strawberries, room temperature
1 6-ounce package semisweet chocolate chips
2 teaspoons vegetable shortening

- Leaving the hulls on, remove any dirt from berries with a pastry brush or paper towel.
- If rinsing is necessary, do so the day before because berries must be dry to dip in chocolate mixture.
- Line bottom of a baking sheet with foil and place in freezer.
- Melt chocolate chips in a measuring cup set in a small pan of hot water.
- Stir in shortening until smooth.
- Remove baking sheet from freezer.
- Hold berry by stem and dip 1 at a time into chocolate to cover about two-thirds of berry.
- Shake gently to remove excess chocolate.
- Place berry on baking sheet.
- Repeat with remaining berries.
- Let berries stand at room temperature for 1 hour or up to 24 hours before serving.
- Do not refrigerate.

Crème Fraîche

2 cups

1 cup heavy cream
1 cup sour cream

- Whisk creams together in a bowl.
- Cover loosely with plastic wrap and let stand in a warm place in kitchen overnight or until thickened.
- Cover and refrigerate for a few hours.
- The tart flavor will continue to develop.
- Serve over fruit.
- May be stored in refrigerator for up to 4 weeks.

Pineapple Torte

12 servings

Chocolate Wafer Crust:
2¼ cups chocolate wafer crumbs
½ cup butter, melted
Filling:
8 ounces cream cheese, softened
1¼ cups sugar
½ teaspoon grated lemon rind
1 15-ounce can crushed pineapple
1 8-ounce can pineapple tidbits
2 envelopes unflavored gelatin
2¼ cups heavy cream, whipped
pineapple tidbits, shaved chocolate or mint leaves for garnish

- Mix crust ingredients together and press into bottom of a 9-inch springform pan.
- Blend cream cheese with sugar and lemon rind.
- Drain juice from crushed pineapple and tidbits into saucepan.
- Sprinkle gelatin over juice.
- Place over low heat and stir until gelatin is dissolved.
- Add crushed pineapple to cream cheese mixture.
- Stir gelatin-juice into cream cheese mixture.
- Fold in whipped cream thoroughly and pour over crust.
- Chill for at least 5 hours or overnight.
- Garnish with pineapple tidbits, shaved chocolate or fresh mint.

Remember This:

Use Crème Fraîche in sauces to add richness. Crème will not separate when heated.

Lemon Curd 2 cups

1 cup fresh lemon juice, 4 to 6 lemons
¼ cup finely shredded lemon rind
1¼ cups sugar
6 tablespoons butter
3 eggs, lightly beaten

- In a medium saucepan, combine lemon juice, lemon rind and sugar.
- Bring to a boil and simmer for 5 minutes.
- Add butter and stir until melted.
- Remove from heat and cool to room temperature.
- Beat eggs into lemon-sugar mixture until well blended and cook over low heat.
- Bring to just below the simmering point and cook, stirring constantly for 7 to 10 minutes or until mixture coats spoon.
- Remove from heat and pour into a sterilized pint jar.
- Cool, cover and refrigerate.
- Serve with Scottish Shortbread.

Scottish Shortbread 8 to 10 servings

1¼ cups flour
3 tablespoons cornstarch
⅓ cup sugar
½ cup butter

- Preheat oven to 325 degrees.
- Mix all ingredients in a food processor until cornmeal consistency.
- Pat mixture into an ungreased springform pan.
- Bake for 40 minutes.
- Serve with Lemon Curd.

Dark Chocolate Sauce

1½ cups

½ cup whipping cream
3 tablespoons unsalted butter, cut into pieces
⅓ cup sugar
⅓ cup firmly packed dark brown sugar
½ cup sifted unsweetened cocoa powder
pinch of salt
1 teaspoon vanilla extract
¼ cup strong coffee

- Bring cream and butter to a boil over medium heat.
- Stir until butter melts.
- Add white and brown sugar and stir until dissolved.
- Reduce heat to low.
- Add cocoa and salt and stir until smooth.
- Remove from heat and stir in vanilla and coffee.
- Serve warm over ice cream or cake.

Raspberry Sauce

2⅓ cups

2 tablespoons cornstarch
¼ cup sugar
1 cup water
1 10-ounce package frozen raspberries, thawed and undrained
⅓ cup sherry

- Combine cornstarch and sugar in a saucepan.
- Stir in water.
- Cook, stirring constantly, until thick and clear.
- Stir in raspberries; cool and add sherry.
- Cover and chill for 1 to 2 hours.
- Serve over pound cake or ice cream.

Remember This:

Avoid doubling candy recipes. It is better to make a second batch.

Orange Ice
6 servings

4 oranges
1 grapefruit
1 lime
1 lemon
¼ cup sugar
vanilla ice cream

- Squeeze juice from fruits and add sugar.
- Freeze for 2 hours, or until mushy ice, but not frozen hard.
- Spoon over individual servings of vanilla ice cream and serve.

Lemon Ice Cream
10 to 12 servings

4 lemons
2 cups sugar
5 cups half and half

- Grate rinds and juice lemons.
- Mix sugar and lemon juice.
- Let stand long enough for sugar to dissolve.
- Add milk and lemon rind.
- Let chill overnight before making ice cream.
- Pour into ice cream freezer container and freeze according to manufacturer's directions.

Remember This:

Lemons heated in a microwave for 20 seconds release more juice when squeezed.

Strawberry Frost

10 servings

A summer dessert that reminds you of Italian Ice.

3 pints ripe strawberries, hulled
2 cups sugar
1½ cups orange juice
½ cup lemon juice
¼ cup Grand Marnier

- Place half of all ingredients except Grand Marnier in a blender or food processor.
- Blend well until sugar dissolves.
- Repeat with remaining half of ingredients.
- Pour mixture into a shallow 3-quart dish and stir in Grand Marnier.
- Freeze until partially frozen.
- Put into a mixing bowl and beat until smooth.
- Return mixture to pan, cover and refreeze.
- Remove from freezer 10 minutes before serving.

Summer Delight

12 servings

This refreshing snack is great for the beach or pool parties.

1 16-ounce can sliced peaches, undrained
1 15-ounce can apricots, undrained
1 10-ounce package frozen strawberries, thawed
2 medium bananas, sliced
1 cup pineapple juice
1 6-ounce can orange juice concentrate, thawed
¼ cup lemon juice

- In a large mixing bowl, combine peaches, apricots, strawberries, bananas, pineapple, orange and lemon juice.
- Mix well and pour into 5½-ounce paper cups.
- Cover cups with foil and place on a tray; freeze.
- When ready to eat, remove from freezer and peel the paper cup off as you eat.

Homemade Strawberry Ice Cream

1 gallon

A rich, velvety ice cream that features Florida strawberries.

4 large eggs
2¼ cups sugar
4 cups milk
3 pints heavy cream
1 tablespoon vanilla extract
1½ cups strawberry purée, about 1½ pints fresh berries
approximately 4½ cups rock salt
2 10-pound bags crushed ice

- Beat eggs with an electric mixer.
- Gradually add sugar, ¼ cup at a time, beating after each addition.
- Continue to beat until mixture is very stiff.
- Add remaining ingredients and stir well.
- Pour into gallon container of an electric ice cream freezer and freeze using rock salt and ice as directed by ice cream freezer manufacturer.
- When process is complete, lift out dasher and replace cover.
- Drain off as much brine (salt water) as possible leaving container in freezer.
- Pack sides and top with 3 parts ice and 1 part rock salt.
- Wrap top with thick towels and allow ice cream to harden for 2 hours.

Triple Chocolate Peanut Clusters

3 pounds

Simple, but elegant!

2 pounds white chocolate
1 12-ounce package semisweet chocolate chips
1 12-ounce package milk chocolate chips
1 24-ounce jar unsalted dry roasted peanuts

- Melt all chocolate in an electric skillet on lowest setting, or in double boiler, stirring until melted.
- Cool for 5 minutes and stir in peanuts.
- Drop onto wax paper by tablespoons.
- Let cool completely.
- Wrap and keep in refrigerator until ready to serve.

Desserts

Best Ever Peanut Brittle   2 pounds

Children enjoy breaking and packaging brittle for holiday gifts.

2 cups sugar
1 cup white corn syrup
1 cup hot water
3 cups peanuts with skins
1 tablespoon baking soda, sifted to remove any lumps

- Grease a 13½x16-inch cookie sheet; set aside.
- Combine sugar, corn syrup and hot water in a 4-quart heavy-bottomed saucepan.
- Cook over high heat until syrup comes to a soft ball stage, 235 degrees on a candy thermometer.
- Add peanuts and cook to hard crack stage, 300 degrees, stirring constantly to prevent burning.
- Remove from heat and quickly add baking soda.
- Stir just to combine soda; candy will bubble.
- Pour immediately onto prepared cookie sheets.
- Do not spread.
- Allow to cool and break into pieces.

English Toffee   12 pieces

¾ cup brown sugar
½ cup butter
1 cup chopped pecans, divided
¾ cup semisweet chocolate chips

- Melt butter and sugar; bring to a boil.
- Continue to boil for 7 minutes at medium heat.
- Butter a 9x9-inch pan.
- Spread ½ cup pecans in bottom of pan.
- Pour butter-sugar mixture over nuts.
- Sprinkle chocolate chips and remaining pecans over mixture.
- Cut into bars before candy hardens.

Desserts

Brown Sugar Nut Crust
1 9-inch pie crust

1¼ cups flour
½ cup margarine
½ cup light brown sugar
½ cup pecans, chopped fine

- Preheat oven to 400 degrees.
- Place all ingredients into pie pan and stir to combine.
- Bake and stir every 5 minutes for 15 minutes, until dry and crumbly.
- Remove from oven and gently press crust down.
- Cool completely.

Meringue Shell
2 9-inch pie crusts

4 egg whites, room temperature
¼ teaspoon cream of tartar
1 cup granulated sugar
½ teaspoon vanilla extract
⅛ teaspoon salt

- Preheat oven to 300 degrees.
- Beat egg whites with cream of tartar until stiff and dry.
- Gradually add sugar, beating well.
- Add vanilla and salt; mix well.
- Spoon into well greased 9-inch pie pans, forming a rim around edges.
- Bake 45 minutes or until very lightly browned.
- Cool before adding a pie filling.

Coconut Almond Pie Crust
1 9-inch pie crust

1 cup blanched almonds
1 cup moist-style flaked coconut
¼ cup sugar
¼ cup butter

- Preheat oven to 375 degrees.
- Grind almonds medium fine and mix with coconut.
- Add butter and sugar; mix well.
- Press evenly into bottom and sides of pie pan.
- Bake for 10 to 12 minutes or until light golden brown.

Nut Crust
1 9-inch pie crust

2 cups pecans
½ cup granulated sugar
3 tablespoons unsalted butter, melted

- Chop nuts fine in a food processor.
- Combine nuts with sugar and melted butter.
- Press mixture evenly onto bottom and sides of pie pan.
- Chill pie shell for 20 minutes and place on a baking sheet.
- Bake at 350 degrees for 12 to 15 minutes or until lightly browned.
- Cool on a wire rack.

Pastry Pie Crust
3 9-inch pie crusts

2½ cups sifted flour
1 teaspoon salt
3/4 cup shortening
5 tablespoons cold water or enough to moisten dough

- Preheat oven to 400 degrees.
- Combine flour and salt.
- Add shortening and cut in with a pastry blender until mixture is very fine.
- Add water, a little at a time, until mixture is moist.
- Press into a ball.
- Divide dough and roll out pastry on a lightly floured surface.
- Turn onto a pie plate and trim to a 1-inch overhang.
- Flute edges.
- Prick pastry all over with a fork.
- Bake for 12 to 15 minutes.

Cinnamon Vanilla Sugar
3 cups

Wonderful for cinnamon toast, muffins or on top of sweet breads.

3 cups extra fine sugar
½ vanilla bean, split
1 tablespoon ground cinnamon

- Mix all ingredients together.
- Store in an airtight container.
- Keeps indefinitely.

The Junior League of Tallahassee wishes to acknowledge those who have generously supported the creation of *Thymes Remembered* and provided valuable expertise.

Ann Coleman
Annella's
Appetite Delight
Bass and Bass Ltd. Interior Design
Bedfellows
Carol Moore
Carriage Gate Gifts
Carroll Walker
Christensen's Antiques
Culpepper Construction
Cuneo Creative Group
Garden Flowers
Hallway Antiques
Haystack
Heart to Hand
Homes & Land Publishing Corporation
Jackie Harvey
John and Jane Aurell
Kerr and Downs Research
Kathy Ferrell
Lafayette Vineyards LTD
Liz Abberger
Maas Brothers
Maclay Gardens
Mavis Fletcher
Messer, Vickers, Caparello, French and Madsen Attorneys
Moon Jewelry Company
My Favorite Things
Nora McDaniel
Pam Shields
Pedler's Antique Mall
Persnickety
Ron Schombuger
Sawgrass
Seven Hills Interiors
Someone's in the Kitchen
Tallahassee Nurseries
The Carriage Shop
The Mill Bakery and Eatery
The Raspberry Mousse
Tony Hunter
Unijax

Contributors and Testers

The Junior League of Tallahassee thanks its members, families and friends who contributed and tested recipes. It is our sincere hope that no one has been mistakenly omitted.

Elizabeth Small Abberger
Michele Ackerman
Brenda Reese Adeeb
Earline Welch Adkison
Patty Aiello
Debbie Roberts Akins
Alice Alford
Connie McCall Alford
Kay Allen
Leslie Frye Allen
Stephanie Bechtel Andrews
Kay Harrison Ansley
Leigh Ansley
Agnes P. Armstrong
Lynn Foster Arrington
Katherine Ashmore
John and Jane Aurell
Lucy Mitchell Baer
Lyn Baggett
Cornelia Bailey
Nanette Barber
Mary Lee Barineau
Helen Barker
Jim Bascom
Ruth Bass
Irma Bass-Paul
Walli Harper Beall
Martha Lines Beasley
Evelyn G. Beazley
J. Stanton Beazley
Betty J. Beck
Cheryl Beck
Bettie Moor Bedell
Mamie Posey Belcher
Aggie Holley Bell
Margaret Gwynn Bennett
Jonie Donaldson Bettinger
Mike Bettinger
Betty Jane Owens Betts
Libby Bigham
Susan Bigsby
Frances B. Blackburn
Col. John Blackwell
Jean Blackwell
Becky Blanton
Sheila Shea Boggs
Melanie Boone
Janet Borneman
Valorie Boyd
Sue Brady
Joyce Jones Bramblett
Sherry Brand
Pamela Brannon
Nancy Breslin
Jane Tomlinson Brightbill
Wendy Briley
Carol Palmer Brock
Jamie Withers Brown
Joe Brown
Joyce Brubaker
Pat Brueckheimer
Marianne Bryant
Nancy B. Bryant
Mary Douglas H. Buchanan
Tom Buchanan
Nelle Carter Bunn
Susan Reimel Bunn
Judy O'Neill Burgert
Jayne P. Burgess
Peggy Farrell Butler
Ann Bannerman Camp
Kitty Ball Camp
Gina Campbell
Hilda M. Carney
Maryanne Brown Carothers
Nancyanne Carothers
Kay Kinney Carraway
Sandi Carter
Charlotte W. Casey
Donna Anderson Cassedy
Susan R. Cassedy
Betsy W. Champion
Delyne Moore Chapman
Dianne Cheek
Jane Hudson Chichetti
Richard J. Chichetti
Mary Noel Childers
Vickie Sue Childers
Michal Ann Wooste Cierpik
Margaret Anne F. Clark
Virginia Stitt Clements
Gary Click
Marsha MacDonald Click
Cheryl Cliett
Elizabeth Lee Clifford
Suzanne Cognetta
Barbara Robinson Cooksey
Mary Cooper
Carla Ferrell Cowles
Kathy Cowles
Ginger Lee Cox
Shirley Van Kirk Coyle
Ellen Haselwood Crabtree
Nancy Crane
Camilla DeNisco Croy
Barbara Council Culbreath
Virginia Michie Culpepper
Van Culverhouse
Elizabeth Cunningham
Mary Curtis
Mildred Dadisman
Diana Podrecca Daniels
Louise Mettler Davenport
Lysbeth Kelly Davidson
Ann Graham Davis
Jean Davis
Judy Davis
Ann Deal
Teresa L. Dean
Betty Dearing
Penelope Maxwell Dehler
Debbie Dekle
Beth Moor Desloge
Chris Dobbins
Iris Donaldson
Caryl Donnellan
Fran Dorsey
Fanny Jo Drake
Margaret Lynn Duggar
Deborah Dugger
Shirley Williams Dunbar
Jan Dickens Dunlap
Frances S. Durham
Phyllis Langford English
Ginger Butts Farrell
June McPhaul Farrell
Catherine Scoggin Ferrell
Jackie Ferrell
Kathy Ferrell
Patricia Ferrell
Janet Segal Fixel
Jean Gard Fletcher
Mavis Clark Fletcher
Jeanne Clark Flowers
Debbie Fonvielle
Noreen Gardner
Cathy Garrett
Harold Gibbs
Robin Gibson
Alinda Lindgren Goodwin
Nell Woodham Green
Reba Green
Leota Gregory
Margaret Black Groves
Katrina Guensch
Lecta L. Guensch
Lorrie Guttman
Noanne Gwynn
Susan Parkhurst Gwynn
Diana M. Hadi
Nancy Hahn
Carolyn G. Haley
Margaret O'Connor Hall
Dianne George Haney
Nancy Ausley Hannon
Ann Page Hanson
Dorothy A. Hanson
Wanda Hanson
Susan Harkness
Lenora Hughes Harman
Gail Palmer Harris
Arden Armstrong Harrison

Mildred Klarer Harrison
Carol Hart
Dinah Hart
Sharon Desvousges Hartman
Mary Anne Cannon Hartwell
Jacqueline Jackso Harvey
Sarah Teresa Haskell
Dot M. Hayward
Linda Hall Heller
Deidre Wood Hemphill
Ruth Boyd Henderson
Khara High
Gini Hosford Hill
Julie Hill
Mart Pierson Hill
Mollie Hunter Hill
Marylou Hinkle
Dot Hinson
Lucy Ho
Sissy Hofmeister
Janice Hogenmuller
Nancy B. Hope
Judy Jones Hopkins
Vicki Manuel Hopkins
Rachel Plant Hubbs
Sue Ann Humphress
Mrs. John E. Hunt
Tony Hunter
Debbie Haskell Hurley
Jean Wimmer Isenberg
Ellen Foley Jablon
Cheryl D. Joanos
Gwen Parrott Johnson
Jann Johnson
Marsey Johnson
Mary Crit Johnson
Laurie Jones
Cheryl Jordan
Deborah Jordan
Barbara Keliehor
Brooke S. Kennerly
Sharon Grantham Kepper
Mary Jane King
Patricia Gautier Kitchen
Jan Kleman
Linda Webb Knox
Joanne Kotz
Priscilla L. Kuersteiner
Betty Kummer
Isabel Lamb
Mary Alma Roberts Lang
Michelle Rene Langston
Marnie Law
Anne Ausley Lee
Betty Rowell Lee
Laura Hopkins Lee
Paula Ayers Lee
Tricia Lee
Inez Lee-Booth
Rebecca Smith Liner
Laura Hopkins Long
Nell Siceloff Long
Beth Melton Lorca
Julianne Smith Lovett
Fran Ferrell Lyles
Maryann P. Lyles
Linda S. Mabry
Phoebe Dann Mackie
Barbara Lennon Madigan
Marylou Green Madigan
Janis Perkins Mahaffey
Mary Katherine Mannheimer
Janice Marsh
Alison Row Mattice
Kathy Mayne
Tavia McCuean
Laura McCuen
Trude McCarty
Rae Miller McClure
Antoinette McHale McCoy
Laura Cummings McCue
Imogene Elrod McCully
Patti Ann McCully
Nora McDaniel
Robert M. McDavid
Beth Arnold McGehee
Lynn Scott McKenzie
Laura McLeod-Keene
Mary Ann McMullen
Billie Bailey McNab
Patti Stallings Megahee
Ann Melton
Dorothy Seiber Melton
Chip Melton
Sheila Sharkey Melton
Cyndi Evans Mendelson
Elizabeth Sutton Messer
Eleanor Travers Mettler
Delia Appleyard Mickler
Cheryl Bosenberg Miles
A. S. "Shorty" Milian
Judy Miller
Kathy Perkins Miller
Sarah Henderson Moor
Carol Moore
Mary Pat Varn Moore
Sarah Moore
Shelley Emerson Moorefield
Pickens Talley Morgan
Sandra Moore Mowell
Lisa Council Munroe
Lynn Phillips Munroe
Vickie Murphy
Christie Tyler Newell
Chrystie Newell
Carolyde Philips O'Bryan
Sharon Oberlin
Anne Dalton Olson
Jane Straubinger Olson
Marilyn Overton
Dot Jean Glass Owen
Lynn Thomas Palmer
Margaret Palmer
Julie Palmer Pararo
Louise Phillips Patterson
Mr. T. J. Peacock
Anne Rouse Peede
Calynne Andrews Peeples
Katherine Perkins
Virginia Barber Perkins
Nancy J. Petrandis
Ley Pichard
Judy Conn Pickrell
Kaki Turner Pope
JoAnn Wright Prescott
Ellen B. Prest
Anne Jolley Proctor
Susan Tully Proctor
Jane Pruitt
Marti Puri
Alice S. Ragsdale
Shirley Raines
Judy C. Rainey
John S. Rawls
Ellen Resch
Janice Harvey Rhodes
Nan Richerson
Sandy Bloodworth Riddle
Anna Johnson Riedel
Carolyn Love Riedel
Charlotte Rigsby
Stuart Riordan
Jean McMillan Rivers
Sallie Sturgis Robinson
Laura Kilby Rogers
Mary Margaret Rogers
Judy Rubin
Dianne Peacock Ruff
Cheryl Rye
Nancy Salokar
Carrie Kate Sandy
Mary Ann Scawthorn
Shelby S. Schnebly
Sidney Roesch Schneider
Nella Schomburger
Micky S. Searcy
Patti Fain Searcy
Jamesine Brown Sears
Jackie Sharkey
Ginny Miller Sharpe
Betty Jo Sheill
Polly Shelley
Kim Standland Skelding
Betty Ann Skelton
Karen Lee Watson Skilling
Elaine Smith
Fraser Munroe Smith
Leslie Waddell Smith
Patty Hill Smith
Virginia Wilson Smith
Edith Munson Solomon
Mary Solomon
Carolyn Spooner
Clark Stewart
Diane Stewart
LuAnn Farmer Stiles
June Clark Stivers
Cindy McLean Strom
Martha H. Stubbs
Adelaide Munroe Suber
Anita Sullivan
Madelon Elliott Sweat
Ma'Su Beneke Sweeney
Betty Smith Taylor
Beth Tedio
Mrs. Glenn Terrell
Cecilia Thomas
Linda S. Thomas
Susan Thomas
Cindy Fletcher Thompson
Janice C. Thompson
Kathie Thornberry
Susan Grimm Thurmond
Ann Todd
Dorothy Ann Todd
Tenley L. Toole
Hillis C. Tribble
Beth Trotman
Elaine Tully
Rosetta Tully
Susan Turner
Susan Gifford Van Leuven
Cherly Miller Van Ostrand
Annie S. Gwynn Vereen
Pierre Vivier
Sheryl Burgess Wagner
Newell C. Walls
Marsha Wright Walper
Susan Walton
Sylvia Warner
Shelly Watkins
Mary Watson
Gayle Webb
Ann S. Weir
Mrs. Lou Wesley
Marre White
Mahaska Whitley
Martha Gene Wigginton
Patricia Wilhoit
Joanne Owsley Williams
Kay Lynne Williams
Leslie Schmidt Williams
Priscilla Patters Williams
Tina F. Williams
Wendy Williams
Barbie W. Williamson
Dot Williamson
Eunice N. Williamson
Christine Pirrung Willis
Helen Ausley Willis
Tricia Forehand Willis
Liz Willyoung
Ann Becker Wilson
Arlene Berstrom Wingate
Judy Winn
Cynthia Curtiss Wise
Beth Anderson Witherspoon
Jolen Wolf
Jeanie Lamb Wood
Patricia C. Wood
Dena Oetjen Woodburn
Candace Woodward
Ann Wright
Beverly Wright
Barbara Timmons Yon
Nell Couch Young
Peggy Cooper Young

Notes

Index

Index

Index

Index

Index

Index

Index

Index

Thymes Remembered

A lifetime of treasured recipes.

Profits from the sale of THYMES REMEMBERED will be used to support community projects and programs of the Junior League of Tallahassee, Inc.

Please send copies to:

Name______________________________
(print)

Address______________________________

City/State/Zip__________________________

Telephone (   ) ________________________

Phone orders accepted. Gift order form on back.

Quantity	Price	Tax (FL residents only)	TOTAL
______	$16.95	$1.02	______

plus $2.00 each for shipping and handling ______

TOTAL ENCLOSED: ______

Please make checks payable to:

JUNIOR LEAGUE OF TALLAHASSEE, INC.

Please do NOT send cash.
Sorry, no COD's.

Send to:

THYMES REMEMBERED
The Junior League of Tallahassee, Inc.
259-B John Knox Road
Tallahassee, Florida 32303
(904) 385-5305

Please charge to my VISA______
or Master Card______

Card Number____________________

Expiration Date__________________

Cardholder's Signature______________

Thymes Remembered

A lifetime of treasured recipes.

Profits from the sale of THYMES REMEMBERED will be used to support community projects and programs of the Junior League of Tallahassee, Inc.

Please send copies to:

Name______________________________
(print)

Address______________________________

City/State/Zip__________________________

Telephone (   ) ________________________

Phone orders accepted. Gift order form on back.

Quantity	Price	Tax (FL residents only)	TOTAL
______	$16.95	$1.02	______

plus $2.00 each for shipping and handling ______

TOTAL ENCLOSED: ______

Please make checks payable to:

JUNIOR LEAGUE OF TALLAHASSEE, INC.

Please do NOT send cash.
Sorry, no COD's.

Send to:

THYMES REMEMBERED
The Junior League of Tallahassee, Inc.
259-B John Knox Road
Tallahassee, Florida 32303
(904) 385-5305

Please charge to my VISA______
or Master Card______

Card Number____________________

Expiration Date__________________

Cardholder's Signature______________

Thymes Remembered

A lifetime of treasured recipes.

Ship_________ gift copies to:

Name____
(PRINT)

Address____

City/State/Zip______________________________________

Gift Card Message:

____

Thymes Remembered

A lifetime of treasured recipes.

Ship_________ gift copies to:

Name____
(PRINT)

Address____

City/State/Zip______________________________________

Gift Card Message:

____